M

Dungeons and Dreamers
The Rise of Computer Game Culture
from Geek to Chic

Brad King and
John Borland

McGraw-Hill/Osborne

New York Chicago San Francisco
Lisbon London Madrid Mexico City
Milan New Delhi San Juan
Seoul Singapore Sydney Toronto

The *McGraw·Hill* Companies

McGraw-Hill/Osborne
2100 Powell Street, 10th Floor
Emeryville, California 94608
U.S.A.

To arrange bulk purchase discounts for sales promotions, premiums, or fund-raisers, please contact **McGraw-Hill**/Osborne at the above address. For information on translations or book distributors outside the U.S.A., please see the International Contact information page immediately following the index of this book.

Dungeons and Dreamers:
The Rise of Computer Game Culture from Geek to Chic

1234567890 DOC DOC 019876543

ISBN 0-07-222888-1

Publisher	Brandon A. Nordin
Vice President & Associate Publisher	Scott Rogers
Editorial Director	Roger Stewart
Project Editor	Madhu Prasher
Acquisitions Coordinator	Tana Allen
Technical Editor	Steve Kent
Copy Editor	Lisa Theobald
Proofreader	Paul Tyler
Composition	Elizabeth Jang, Lucie Ericksen
Illustrator	Lyssa Wald
Series Design	Jean Butterfield
Cover Design	Tree Hines

This book was composed with Corel VENTURA™ Publisher.

For mom, dad, Cheri, and Kendra.
All my love.
—BK

To my parents and my brother.
—JB

About the Authors

Brad King (Austin, TX) is currently living the life of a freelance writer in Austin, Texas, where he pens stories about technology and culture. In between gigs, he'll be teaching a class on new media journalism at the University of Texas. Brad was the digital entertainment reporter for *Wired News* for three years, where he covered the video game, movie, and music industries. An expert on digital entertainment issues, Brad has delivered talks on emerging, new media trends in London, San Francisco, and New York and regularly appears on national television and radio programs. Throughout his nine-year career, his work has appeared in *The Hollywood Reporter*, *Hits* magazine, *Business 2.0*, Variety's *eV*, and *MP3* magazine. Long before he became a journalist, Brad was a gamer, playing Lemonade Stand and M.U.L.E. on a Commodore Pet in 1985. For two years, Brad spent every Saturday morning at his math teacher's house, programming sports simulations in BASIC and saving them on cassette tapes. Brad has a master's degree in journalism from the University of California at Berkeley.

John Borland (San Francisco, CA) is a senior writer at CNET Networks.com, where he covers digital entertainment, including music, movies, and video games. John routinely appears on television and radio programs as an invited technology expert, including ABC World News, NPR's "Talk of the Nation," and BBC Radio. Throughout his 10-year career, John's work has appeared in *Fortune* magazine, the *New York Post*, the *San Francisco Examiner*, and *The New York Times* Online. John's work has won industry awards from the national Society of Professional Journalists, the Online News Association, the Society of Professional Journalists Northern California Chapter, and the Western Publications Association. In 2001 he was named in Technology Marketing's list of most influential online journalists. John has a master's degree in journalism from the University of California at Berkeley.

CONTENTS

ACKNOWLEDGMENTS

This book has been the single best experience of my life. One of the most brilliant parts of being a journalist is the people you come across. Richard Garriott is one of those people. He has been more than generous with his time, and we certainly couldn't have written this book without him.

I'd like to thank my friend John Borland who provided countless hours of stimulating conversation and laughter, and he confined his yelling to instant messaging, which I appreciate.

The McGraw-Hill/Osborne Media team has been outstanding. Our editor, Roger Stewart, has been patient and kind in the face of an endless series of missed deadlines, half-finished chapters, and smart-ass emails. Those mostly came from John. Bettina Faltermeier, Madhu Prasher, and Lisa Theobald have been invaluable in promoting, shaping, and editing the book.

My Austin crew never once hassled me when I'd disappear for weeks on end, locked in my bedroom, writing. Andy Wilson provided emotional support when I was down, and he always made me laugh when I needed it. Andy Erdmann offered countless hours of welcome relief at the PlayStation 2. Jimmy and Dana McArthur, Avery Simmons, Bill Jerram, Jason and Andrea Roe, Austin and Becky Walker, and Chris Keistler weathered a multitude of mood swings.

x   Acknowledgments

The Cincinnati crew never failed to answer the phone when I freaked out. Jimmy Maple, Greg Taylor, and Matt Colwell are the greatest collection of baseball players ever. And Kevin Fox is the finest musician.

I've been blessed throughout my life to find a community of writers who have taken an interest in me. A big shout out to Mary Jean Corbett, Jason Barbacovi, Amy Firis, Jeff O'Brien, Eric Hellweg, Julie Case, Jeff Howe, Tamara Conniff, Paul Grabowicz, Bill Drummond, John Fox, David Simutis, and David Pescovitz.

This book would certainly not have been written without the help of many kind servers at bars, coffeehouses, and restaurants. Special kudos to the Mallard (Berkeley), Squat & Gobble (San Francisco), Trudy's North Star (Austin), Trudy's Tex Star (Austin), The Spiderhouse (Austin), and Kaldi's (Cincinnati). I spent far too many hours drinking coffee, poring over text, and using their electricity, and never once did I hear a complaint. Tip those servers 20 percent.

Special kudos to the band Plow On Boy. The manuscript was written and edited with their wonderful sounds playing. They broke up far too soon. Extra special thanks to my Palm i705—with wireless Internet connectivity and a mobile keyboard, I was able to transcribe interviews as I went.

Thanks to the family. They are truly one of those dysfunctional groups that you read about, and I wouldn't trade any of them. John and Carol King, my parents, have given me a safety net wider than any child could ever ask for. My sister, Cheri, is truly one of the most talented pianists ever to grace this planet. Kendra has been a welcome addition to my life, and I hope as the years go by, we continue to grow and learn about each other. Betty and Loren McQueen are my patron saints. Kenny and Mitch King provide a quiet calmness to the family. Granny King is larger than life—the matriarch of hillbillies. Barry and Peggy Carney are the epicenter of activity, and pretty good swing dancers, to boot. My cousins—Chip, Scott, Jenny, Ali, Randy, and Danielle—are never far from my thoughts, although a great distance separates us.

Lastly, I want to thank my uncle Dennis who passed through this world far too quickly. He was a scholar and a biker, but he never quite found his community here on Earth. Still, I'd like to think he's looking down on me, smiling, knowing that through him, I've found the courage to strike out on my own, and forge my own way through this world. Ride strong, Hot Dog.

—Brad King

Thanks to my family, to everyone who read our early drafts, and to the scores of people whose infectious love of computer games informed and inspired the reporting for this book.

—John Borland

Prologue

The Beginnings

On a cool fall afternoon in 1972, a trio of Minnesotans pulled into Lake Geneva, Wisconsin, a picturesque lakeside town about an hour north of Chicago. They puttered through the four-block downtown, pulling into a driveway just a few streets outside the tiny main street drag. Two of them, Dave Arneson and Dave Megarry, anxiously rechecked their bags as they emerged from their car. They'd driven 350 miles just to show off the board games they'd made themselves. If they'd forgotten anything, it was too late to go back, but they wanted to make sure all their materials were in order.

Lake Geneva then, as now, was an unlikely gaming mecca. A resort town with a population of 5000 people—that figure quadrupled in the summer, when people came to swim in the lake's uncharacteristically clear, rock-bottomed waters—it had been better known as the summer home for wealthy families such as the chewing-gum Wrigleys and the home-appliance Maytags. Now it was home to 34-year-old Gary Gygax, a game player and game writer whose peripatetic energy and immense curiosity had already earned him a prominent place in a community of Midwesterners fascinated by military and history-themed games.

Arneson and Gygax had met before, at the GenCon gaming convention that Gygax had started in Lake Geneva a few years earlier. The two had collaborated on a sailing game called Don't Give Up The Ship. Now Arneson was working on a new adventure game with a style of play that was as close to theater as it was to the typical miniature soldier battles. Megarry, too, had been trying out a new board game, played more conventionally with dice and cards, but set underground in a monster-infested dungeon. Gygax had heard about them and wanted to see both.

"Come on in," Gygax told the visitors. "I'll show you around."

He let them inside, showed them where they would be sleeping, and then led them down to the basement. Gygax had built a sand table there, 12 feet long by 6 feet wide, where a group that he played with almost every weekend held their games. Gygax was the author of a game called Chainmail, which used little figurines to simulate medieval battles. He'd recently modified the game, adding elements of fantasy such as trolls and dragons and magicians that shot fireballs, which not so coincidentally had the same blast radius as the cannons used for other games played on this table. The new version had proved wildly popular. Sometimes as many as 20 or 30 gamers sat around the table playing.

As the sun set, the little group gathered to play at Gygax's dining room table upstairs. A few other people from the Lake Geneva scene had joined them, including Gygax's own 12-year-old son, Ernie. They tried Megarry's game first. The players traversed a board made of graph paper, running into monsters and fighting them with magic spells. "I said, 'Wow, this is a great adaptation.' It was Chainmail in a dungeon," Gygax remembered later.

Arneson went next. A heavyset, spectacled young man a few years younger than Gygax, with a big, mischievous smile, he launched them into something very different. The players had to make characters and give them attributes that would determine how strong or smart they were. Those attributes would help them when they attacked monsters or tried to figure out puzzles in the game. Then the players would act out the characters' roles as they wandered through the swamps of the haunted Castle Blackmoor, doing their best to stay alive. Arneson himself would play the godlike role of Game Master, telling the story of what was happening to the characters at any given moment and letting them decide as a group what to do next. Would they fight the monster? Would they run away? Would one member of the group steal everyone else's treasure and hightail it for a safe house? It was a little haphazard—Arneson kept rules scrawled in a notebook full of loose-leaf sheets of paper, and anything that he didn't know, he simply made up on the spot. He'd been doing this with his own group of gamers for almost a year now in Minneapolis, and he had the style down.

"Deep in the primeval swamps of Lake Gloomey, shrouded in perpetual mist, lies the city of the Brothers of the Swamp…" he started, and the party of adventurers was off.

By the end of the weekend, Gygax and the rest of the Lake Geneva crowd were enthusiastic. Collectively, they saw that something new was in reach, merging the underground dungeon exploration scenario and this improvisational role-playing mode of gaming. Maybe others in the community would be drawn to its fantastic mix. Arneson gave Gygax copies of his notes to work from, and Gygax set to work creating a full set of rules, drawing from these and from Chainmail, and making up new elements to fill in the blanks. By the time he finished a draft of the 150-page rule book early the next year and began showing it around to his friends, he had a name for the new game: Dungeons & Dragons.

"We were having a tremendous amount of fun, but we figured we were crazy," Arneson said, years later. "We had no inkling that this would turn out to be something so big."

* * *

This book is about the phenomenon of *gamers*, and most specifically, the communities of computer game players that have sprung up and matured over the past 25 years. The story starts in this small town, with a group of people who had no desire to play games electronically. Elsewhere in 1972, the arcade video game craze was just starting to build under the fingertips of game designers and players at Atari and elsewhere. The gamers in Lake Geneva, however, weren't interested in moving pixels around a screen. They were concerned instead with storytelling, and with the ability to play parts in their stories together. That desire would ultimately have a profound impact on the development of computer games and the communities of computer game players. The high-tech story of computer game communities is about people searching for a place that feels like home, surrounded by others—even if they are only virtual representations on a computer screen—who understand them. This story is necessarily intertwined with the rise and spread of home computers and the Internet, but its seeds were planted here in Lake Geneva.

It's almost impossible to overstate the role of Dungeons & Dragons in the rise of computer gaming, even if the game itself was originally all pen, paper, dice, and notebooks. Scratch almost any game developer who worked from the late 1970s until today and you're likely to find a vein of role-playing experience. Some of the biggest computer games have explicit roots in D&D. Richard Garriott's long-running Ultima series was originally based directly on his high school D&D games. The 1996 hit Quake was named after a character in the long-running D&D games played by the developers at id Software, and Quake was originally conceived as a medieval-themed role-playing game. Indeed, without Gary Gygax and Dave Arneson, computer gaming communities would likely look radically different than they look today.

Gygax wound up publishing Dungeons & Dragons in 1974 under the imprint of a new company called Tactical Studies Rules (TSR) started by himself and a few associates. He'd expected it to be a success, although in the war gamers' highly specialized world, that usually meant sales of about 8000 copies. He and his friends had optimistically forecast a big hit—which meant selling maybe 50,000 copies, making it a near-record breaker. The game reached far beyond their expectations, spreading largely by word of mouth across college campuses around the United States. By the time it had been out a year, Gygax and his partners were revising TSR's estimates. Maybe it would ultimately sell a million copies, they thought, stunned. Even that was well short of the truth. By the early 1980s, when Dungeons & Dragons and similar games reached the peak of their popularity, the number of people playing role-playing games in the United States was somewhere between four and five million, Gygax estimated.

Those early role-playing communities had roots in earlier games, just as computer gamers could later look to Gygax and his kin as predecessors. Serious, adult-oriented war games, using toy soldiers, had become popular in Germany in the late 1800s, and the games spread across Europe and America. Even committed pacifist author H.G. Wells had been a devotee, writing a book on the subject called *Little Wars* in 1913. In mid-century America, a game publisher called Avalon Hill started releasing strategy games based on the Civil War, Revolutionary War, World War II, and other battles, helping to initiate a renewed interest in war gaming; Gygax and Arneson had been among the devotees of that company's games, and their local groups in Lake Geneva and Minneapolis were dedicated to that type of play before the advent of role-playing games.

Paper gamers, as they would come to be known after the rise of the computer age, served very much as prototypes for the kinds of digital communities that would come later. The players were mostly male, mostly young, and mostly white and middle class. Computer researchers and programmers—a demographic that seemed drawn in disproportionate numbers to fantasy novels like J.R.R. Tolkien's *Lord of the Rings* series—loved the game. They played it in its original form, and because their medium was code and computer, not paper and dice, they tried to replicate its magic on their machines. Throughout the 1970s, digital versions of the game appeared on university and other publicly accessible networks, and spread quickly through programming circles.

Paper games were heavy on violence and fantasy, as computer games later would be. In the best cases, storytelling and genuine role-playing defined play, although these elements varied with the quality of the imaginations of people running the games. In Gygax's mind, at least, it hasn't been an accident that so much of gaming tradition has been centered on violence, from chess to war games to D&D to Quake, nor that players tended to be males.

"Games tend to answer a lot of deep instinctive things," he says. "Maybe it's men's male aggressiveness that makes them want to play games. There's a competitive aggressiveness to games, even Monopoly. You're there to win."

But whoever was playing, Dungeons & Dragons created the kind of communities sustained by simple physical presence. The games were played in garages, basements, and dorm rooms across the country by small groups of people. The fact that their games took them outside the mainstream of American popular entertainment culture helped solidify their bonds. Over the course of a night, a weekend, or even months—amid piles of empty soda cans, pizza boxes, and more than a few "roaches"—players worked together to get out of each dangerously lethal situation their Game Master threw them into.

The spread of D&D-like games onto computers and computer networks changed the boundaries of the paper game. It opened up geographic borders, linking people from around the world in ways barely imaginable before. It gave storytellers, now in the form of programmers and game designers, a much wider palette on which to paint their universes, changing the dynamics of narrative fiction. It gave the players themselves the opportunity to interact with the story, changing the games in ways developers never intended.

* * *

Gamers, though, don't play alone. This book delves into the computer and video game communities that resulted from that flowering of technological and creative imagination. It's about the people who made and make them up, and the people who have created the games that make them possible. It focuses on one developer, a Texan named Richard Garriott, whose own story stretches from the moments of his exposure to computer programming and Dungeons & Dragons to the present. But the real subject of the chapters that follow is the broader population of gamers: the people who play, the people who create, and the people who sustain gaming communities in one way or another.

This book doesn't cover the entirety of video and computer gaming culture. Many different strands make up that history, and this book focuses on the parts of the culture that we believe best tells the story of the rise of today's vibrant digital gaming communities. At virtually all times covered in this book, sales of video games for home console platforms such as those made by Atari, Nintendo, Sega, Sony, and Microsoft far outstripped most of the computer games we're writing about. The histories of those games and those cultures have been told with grace and thoroughness elsewhere. Interested readers may want to pick up a copy of Steven Kent's *The Ultimate History of Video Games* for the most complete history of the arcade and video gaming industry available. The history of the *industry* side of computer games is well illustrated in Rusel Demaria's *High Score!*

But as has happened in the nongaming technical world, the "geekier" side of computer gaming culture has blazed a trail that the mainstream is following now. The types of games, and most particularly the types of communities, that have sprung up in the wake of home computing and Internet connectivity are bleeding into the arcade and home console market. In Asia, "PC Bangs"—a kind of arcade room where people play games on networked personal computers—are largely responsible for the growth of online game communities populated by millions of people. The same phenomenon is taking off in the United States, although in the U.S., the cyber cafes are often populated with more action-oriented games than are their Asian counterparts. Home video game consoles now have network connections, and the same games that spurred the growth of sprawling online communities on the PC are finding their way to Sony's PlayStation 2 and Microsoft's XBox.

This book will make no broad claims about who gamers are or why they play—nor may this type of generalization be possible, given the increasing breadth of gaming communities and the diversity of games available. This is not a book of psychology or cultural anthropology. But we hope that by the time the reader finishes the book, he or she will understand how gaming communities can play an important role in peoples' lives, even if it seems at times that players are simply staring at screens filled with scenes of violence and bloodshed. The content of these games can often play a secondary role to their socializing effects.

It might sound a little grandiose, referring to computer games as a sweeping, socializing force. These are just games. But really they're not so different from many other components of modern life. Much of what we do with our lives—from organizing our music and movie collections so visitors can see what we like, to joining recreational sports teams—is about finding other people who like what we like, and making the connections that make us feel less alone in a hurried world.

For millions of people, computer games have provided an opportunity to find other people who share similar backgrounds, stories, hopes, and dreams. It may seem strange to think of computer game communities in the same light as sports teams, writing groups, or ordinary offline friends, particularly if you've never logged on to hunt digital terrorists in a cyber cafe or listened to a bard flirting and singing songs in the EverQuest land of Norrath.

But for gamers, those virtual worlds are now just an extension of the real world.

Part I

The Rise of Digital Gaming

1

Together

Richard Garriott flopped onto his bed in the small, two-bunk dorm room at Oklahoma University and surveyed his options. There didn't seem to be many. His parents had dropped him off here, seven hours from his home and high school friends, so he could attend a seven-week summer computer camp. He could think of more tedious-sounding things, but this camp was already high up on his list. He was used to summers full of weird art projects and near total freedom, and the little bit of programming he'd previously experienced hadn't captured his imagination. He kicked the bag he'd flung on the floor as he'd come in, a new feeling of dread washing over him. Already, this felt like a lonely place. He was trapped for seven weeks with computer nerds.

The 16-year-old was actually looking forward to tinkering with the machines using his rudimentary programming skills, but he didn't think it was worth losing almost his whole summer. This was the summer of 1977, and while computers were still out of reach for most of the country, Richard's parents had wanted to make sure he was on the cusp of the technological revolution. The family—and really, most of the kids that Richard had grown up with—already lived in something that looked a little like the future, with rocket scientists and astronauts as their neighbors in suburban Houston. His own father, Owen, was an astronaut and had temporarily shared the title for the longest space flight any human had ever taken. Owen had taken his whole family to Palo Alto, California, for a year of study at Stanford University in 1976 (Richard's parents had gotten the

11

computer religion after this). Richard had done some work on the computer terminals that had been placed in every classroom in Palo Alto's technologically savvy high school, but he hadn't been nearly as impressed as his parents.

Despite his trepidation, the Garriotts packed their son off to O.U. The other camp kids didn't share his mixed emotions. Before long, there was a knock on his dorm room door. He roused himself and answered it. A small group of boys was there.

"Hi," one of the boys said.

"Hello," he replied, a bit intimidated but determined to make friends while he was here.

"Did you say hello? Nobody from around here says hello," one of the boys said, frowning a little. "You must be from Britain, so we'll call you British."

Richard had been born in England, but his parents had moved to Houston when he was a baby, and he had no discernable accent at all. He had no idea what the boy was talking about. This certainly wasn't helping to quell his desire to run down the hallway, down the 10 flights of stairs, and out on the highway toward home.

"Okay, you're British, then," the boy said, tagging him with a nickname that would follow him for the next 26 years. "Welcome to camp."

He realized what was happening. It was a welcoming committee, and simultaneously a naming committee. In this group, he'd be known as *British*. Fine. The group moved on to the next door, repeating the sequence. Knock. Answer. Bestow a nickname. Move along. Resigned, Richard followed as the group made its way down the boys' corridor, through the main lobby, and into the girls' corridor. By the end of the circuit, everyone had a new name.

The rest of the day was taken up in meetings. Meetings about rules. Meetings about courses. Meetings about the campus. The day, which had started miserably, had begun looking promising when he'd met the girls, but had turned sour again until he found himself in the common area after dinner. There he noticed a small group of students huddled together at a table playing some kind of game, surrounded by soda cans and crumpled candy wrappers. He was intrigued. He'd already decided that the way to make the best of his time at programming camp was to try to make a game, and it looked like these others might be allies.

He sauntered over but didn't say anything, hovering for a minute behind the person who appeared to be leading the game. This boy had a stapled pamphlet laid out on the table in front of him, and he was slowly describing a landscape and scenario. The other players responded in turn, describing actions—exploring, opening doors, even fighting monsters. Every once in a while someone would roll some weird-shaped dice that would resolve some conflict. Richard was confused. There was no game board or little pieces to move around. If this game had rules or an immediate objective, they certainly didn't seem obvious. The players were simply talking about fighters, dragons, dwarves, elves, and magic. It sounded a little like the books he'd read earlier in the year, J.R.R. Tolkien's *Lord of the Rings* trilogy.

After several minutes had passed, Richard leaned down, tapped the leader on the shoulder, and asked him what they were doing.

"It's Dungeons & Dragons," the boy responded, not looking up. "It's a role-playing game." That didn't help much. Richard had never heard of the game, and he associated role-playing with his occasional acting in local theater. He stuck around for a little longer, listening to the game unfold, while the Dungeon Master—that was the leader's title—wove the tale. Other students drifted over, too, and before long the original group had to stop and explain in more detail.

Richard soon joined a game, and others did as well. By the second night, the little lobby was filled with several gaming groups, all telling each other stories of dragons and skeletons and orcs. Girls were as eager as the guys to play, and they threw themselves into playing their characters with just as much bravado. The role-playing helped them talk to each other in ways that shy high school kids might have had trouble doing otherwise. It was a little silly at first, pretending to be a dwarf or elf or magician, and "British" Garriott exchanged embarrassed grins with other players more than once, but once the stories started flowing they lost themselves in these magical worlds.

After the initial social awkwardness faded, other barriers fell. Among the first to go were the rules imposed by the gender-segregated halls. The college-aged chaperone tasked with keeping boys and girls apart moved one of the female students into *his* room, and the other girls and boys quickly paired up. One enterprising student figured out a way to jimmy the locks that kept them out of the closed half of the dormitory, and soon the theoretically off-limit rooms had become hideaways or clubhouses for couples and gaming groups. Richard and his summer girlfriend laid claim to a particularly choice room with a door labeled "The Crypt," written in dripping, blood-red letters, and an interior with a full-room mural depicting a swamp creature about to abduct an oblivious half-naked woman.

Programming, though, was the reason the teens were there. They were learning to control computers. They worked in the FORTRAN computer language, feeding punch cards into the big machines as a means of programming them. The programs they learned were simple, certainly not enough to fulfill Richard's vague notions of writing a game, but they hinted at a vast potential power.

Just as powerful was the shared social experience. People spoke the same language here. For the students, it was the first time experiencing this sense of community. They shared an implicit understanding that computers, programming, technology, fantasy, and role-playing games were okay. They weren't nerdy, dorky, or strange. The group just accepted these as perfectly logical and natural parts of their day, in the same way athletes practiced after school or cheerleaders did routines between bells. For Richard, the environment would prove to be deeply influential and bitterly hard to give up at the close of the seven-week camp.

"It was a summer of programming and girls," Richard would say later. "It was one of those pivotal moments. A lot of firsts happened there."

This series of collisions and discoveries would echo in the back of Richard's mind for the next 26 years, and in the process would help him transform the course of computer gaming as much as any other single figure in the business. The mix of computers, community, and game play he found in Oklahoma was a heady one, and the moment he left campus he resolved to mesh them further. He vowed to use his newfound power over the computer to create dungeon worlds as rich and frightening as anything Tolkien or the teenaged Dungeon Masters had come up with. The history of his efforts to repeat and extend his experiences here would ultimately shape the history of computer gaming and gaming communities.

It would take only a few years before "Lord British" was one of the most widely known figures in the young computer gaming pantheon, and his work would become only more influential from there. Large communities of players and programmers would build around his games. He, like other developers, would give game players a common language, give them a sense of shared and individual mastery over their environment that was often missing from their everyday lives. As computer game players grew from scattered pockets of programmers and computer hobbyists into sprawling global communities, his games and influence would be felt throughout. If his own profile was ultimately eclipsed, it would be because his experience and passions had become assimilated by the wider world.

He would play with the elements discovered in that 1977 summer camp—programming and role-playing—for the next quarter decade. But he was already familiar with the feeling of community he found here. It was no accident that this would be a running theme in his life and in his work. It had been a part of his life from the beginning.

* * *

Richard grew up in a Houston neighborhood just a hop and a jump away from Johnson Space Center, where the National Air and Space Administration (NASA) influence could be felt everywhere. His father, Owen, was a former Stanford physics professor and Navy officer who had been tapped by the manned space flight program in 1965, and the Garriott family had quickly become a part of the tight-knit NASA circle. Their own immediate circle—Richard's two older brothers, Randy and Robert; a younger sister, Linda; and Helen, Richard's free-spirited artist mother— was even tighter. They'd all shared the national spotlight briefly in 1973, when Owen went up in Skylab 3 for 59 days, doubling the amount of time any human had been in space. Growing up in that kind of environment tended to undermine any kid's sense of the impossible.

The Garriott household had long been a mix between a mad scientist's laboratory and a surrealist artist's studio. Richard's father, a thin, mustachioed man with an angular, serious face, had routinely brought home expensive government toys from NASA headquarters, tinkering with them for days on end and taking them apart to see what made them work. When he emerged in the evenings from his study, he often brought with him the coolest science project imaginable. In the mid '70s, years before weekend warriors would know what night vision goggles were, he brought home a prototype that the boys immediately strapped on and used to chase each other across the dark lawn outside.

One night, Owen appeared with a pair of glasses with special prisms that reversed the wearer's vision, flipping the world 180 degrees. If someone reached out their right hand, the glasses would make it appear as though the person were reaching with their left. The distortion was mind-wrecking for a time after the wearer donned the glasses, making it impossible to accomplish even the simplest task, like grabbing the handrail on the staircase. The space agency was using cats to test the glasses, studying how long it took the mind to adjust to radical vision problems, but Richard and his brothers were happy to serve as unofficial test subjects.

"It was like magic," Richard said later. "There was always something at our house. I didn't realize that this wasn't necessarily true in other places."

It was rare that Owen had the time or the inclination to work closely with his youngest son. Robert, Richard's serious-minded older brother, was closer to the reserved astronaut. When Richard and his father did work together, the results were impressive, however. Late in Richard's high school career, the two teamed up on a science fair project they dubbed "Wave Propagation with Computer Analysis." Owen had taught and studied electromagnetic theory and ionospheric physics, and he showed his son a little about how light and radio waves moved though air, water, and other substances. Richard, by that time, knew enough programming to create a fairly sophisticated simulation of radio waves' motion on the computer. Their combined efforts helped Richard win the U.S. National Science Fair and place fourth in an international competition.

If the practical-minded Owen was forthcoming with his scientific knowledge, he was decidedly less so with his own experiences, at least with his boys. Despite constant questions, Owen seemed reticent to talk about his trip into space. "My dad has never told me anything about being in space," Richard said, leaning back in his office chair years later and shrugging his shoulders slightly. "He once said it was kind of like scuba diving, but he never said anything with any kind of emotion."

The young Richard was much closer to his mother, an artist whose interests took her from pottery to silversmithing to painting and well beyond to conceptual art. Her garage workshop was always open to the kids, and Richard in particular took frequent advantage of the open-door policy, working with his mother on clay sculptures or little metal designs of his own. These were the little diversions, however—Helen thought big, and she wanted her sons to be just as ambitious. She taught the boys to be totally committed to their projects, a lesson the brothers willingly followed.

"I like to think that I do big projects," Richard said. "But I definitely acquired that drive from my mother."

There was the time, for example, that Helen helped Richard and his brother Robert with their Boy Scout model building. The trio decided to build an airplane in the backyard, starting with two-by-fours, shaping the skeleton, and then paneling the sides. They rigged the wing flaps with a pulley system so they could be opened and closed using a handle in the cockpit, which also came with a working gearshift and a movable steering stick. That was good, but it lacked a certain realism. They had completely jerry-rigged the entire plane, using what little knowledge they had about planes and their overactive imaginations, but it didn't fly—a fairly important prerequisite for planes. They wanted to build something that did more than just sit and look impressive.

The inspiration for something better came at the dinner table, where the boys would on rare occasions get a glimpse of life at NASA. One evening, Owen mentioned tests astronauts had to endure before being allowed into the cockpit of an actual spaceship. One of the toughest tests involved a G-Force accelerator that simulated the crushing effect of gravity several times stronger than Earth's—similar to what they would feel as their capsule catapulted out of the atmosphere.

At that point, a light bulb went on in Richard's head, and "The Nauseator" was born. Four feet long and two feet wide, the structure was built to spin whoever climbed into the little box 360 degrees, with the motion meant to be controlled by motors. They built the controls, which consisted of two joysticks that would in theory guide both horizontal and vertical motion. At the time, the boys believed they could turn this into a game, in which the "astronaut" could control the movements.

The engineering for the electronically controlled joysticks turned out to be far beyond the boys' capabilities, but the project wasn't a total waste. Brute force still worked where technology had failed them. Their friends would climb in, strap themselves down, and then with the help of three friends, the boys would spin the device in all directions, giving the astronaut the dizzy feeling of a plane spiraling out of control. In the anarchistic realm of childhood, this was something like the ultimate game. There was no point, other than not to throw up, and by those standards there weren't many winners. In the end, the thousand-pound behemoth took up much of their garage and was, in Richard's words, "staggeringly dangerous."

"We'd just spin the rings and you'd come out and recover feeling pretty good," Richard's older brother Robert said years later, half-giggling at the memory. "Then you'd get this stomach thing going after about 10 minutes, just when you thought you were going to be fine, and you'd just throw up all over the place. It was really staggering. Ten minutes. Every time."

These were the elements to which Richard added when he came home from Oklahoma with a newfound desire to make computer games. It proved to be a short step from the Nauseator to games that would sweep up dozens of people in his neighborhood, and put him on the path to a starring role in computer game history.

* ❋ *

With summer nearly over after the camp's end, Richard spent his waning free days building bike ramps and tree forts with his sister Linda and friend Keith Zabalaoui, who lived in a house behind the Garriotts'. But Richard couldn't shake the feeling he had had while playing D&D with his fellow students.

When school started up, he decided to start a group of his own. That first day, he tracked his friends down one by one, pitching them on the idea of a weekly role-playing game. He cornered Bob White. Then Elizabeth Froebel, Chuck Bueche, Rene Hans, and Zabalaoui. One by one, they said yes, although few had any idea what the game Richard was chattering about entailed. But, like Richard, they were a bit geeky and they lived close enough to get to his house easily. They agreed to come over Friday, four days away.

Amped, Richard paced around the house on Friday evening. Word had spread throughout the school, and his small gaming group was now closer to a dozen. He'd spent the week huddled over his notebook paper, mapping his fantastical world. His mother, in particular, had loved the idea, and she prepared dinner and snacks. As the gamers arrived, Richard led them back to the formal dining room table, which the family rarely used. It was large enough for everyone to stretch out and eat while Richard wove a fantastic story. Hours passed, and the group continued playing, laughing, and talking, oblivious to the dawn sun peeking through the curtains and unaware of their heavy eyes.

Monday morning, the weekend gamers found each other before the school day began, anxious to relive their weekend game and plan the next one. Throughout the day, they'd see each other in the hallways, classes, and at lunchtime, and conversation turned to the game. Other friends overheard and poked their noses in, asking questions. Richard preached the game's virtues, as did the others. The next Friday, several more gamers showed up. The week after, another batch. Before the end of the first month of school, two games were underway—one in the formal dining room and one in the family's living room.

Word continued to spread throughout the school, first to the science and math geeks, and then, oddly enough, to other social cliques. Throughout the day, people would wander up to Richard and ask if they could spend the weekend with him. He was more than happy to have them. By winter, games were being played throughout the house, eventually forcing Helen out of her garage art studio. In its place, she set up two large ping-pong tables, minus their nets, to accommodate more gamers.

The Garriott home became ground zero for weekend gaming. Adventures would stretch into early Saturday mornings, and after brief rest periods for food and catnaps, they'd slowly pick up again in the afternoon. With so many players, the weekend gaming sessions took on a diverse personality. What started as a small group of hard-core geeks turned into a social cornucopia. By early 1978, parents started showing up with their kids. The front porch became the recreation area for smokers and drinkers. The group garnered enough attention that the notoriously conservative Boy Scouts even asked Richard's eclectic group to become part of their organization.

The games quickly gained Richard a new reputation. He'd never been unpopular, but he didn't participate much in school activities outside the science fair. Athletics didn't much interest him, and social clubs weren't really his bag. He was one of the ordinary students that roamed the Clear Creek hallways, desperately trying to get through the day so he could go on to more interesting events. The weekend games changed that. He was Lord British now.

The stars of the weekend games were the Dungeon Masters, the storytellers who devised the adventures. The best game leaders could transport a room full of players sitting in a living room in Houston back in time to an ancient place where anything was possible. The only limitation was the imagination of the players, and these gamers, in particular, had grown up in a place where the impossible was already routine.

Richard didn't excel as a DM; his interest lay in other areas. Every Friday, he'd take his spot at the formal dining table, ready to follow Bueche or White's lead, his mind drifting to the computer. He'd already started writing computer games at school, scribbling programs in his spiral notebook, and he based those on the stories and characters that developed in these weekend games. They might have been simple single-player computer games, but they carried the echoes of his friends and his own community from the very beginning. It was the interaction of players that had made his D&D games so powerful, and he wanted to replicate that somehow.

In that desire, Richard had hit on an essential truth: Even if he spent long hours alone in front of his computer writing code, the games he was starting to create were essentially social in nature. He'd spent his life in a family and a wider community of friends and neighbors who supported each other in the craziest projects they could come up with. His weekend role-playing games and the computer games he based on them created their own tight communities. As he grew older and his games touched hundreds of thousands instead of just dozens of people, those communities would be replicated on a larger scale.

＊ ＊ ＊

As Richard began programming in 1977, the same inspiring collision of influences—Tolkien's *Lord of the Rings* series, Gary Gygax's Dungeons & Dragons role-playing game, and the power of computer programming—was being replayed across the world. In a way, all three influences were about magic, even if the last was a technological wizardry. Fantasy novels immersed readers in worlds where evil and good both had significance. It was an increasingly compelling idea in the late 1970s, when Vietnam and Watergate and the rest of the real world's disillusioning events had watered down the idealism of the previous decade with cynicism and discontent. Spreading from college students outward to other communities, Gygax's game in turn gave people a way to act out the roles of the fantasy books they loved.

Computers added a new dimension of power to the mix, giving players the ability to use their own imaginations to drive the game. Computers allowed people to control this new digital environment, and the games gave them the ability to wander through fully formed worlds, without interruption from a Dungeon Master. Even the earliest games had an incredible power to grasp people's wondering attention and spit them out hours later, wholly unaware of the passage of time. It could be something as simple as Pong, batting a blob of light back and forth across a digital field that barely qualified as the representation of a ping-pong table. It could be the later adventure games like Richard's that let people delve into the worlds of dragons, orcs, and treasure.

The weekend D&D games in Richard's house, low-tech as they were, contained all the seeds of later computer gaming communities. Like any community—a family, a neighborhood, or a collection of gamers—they fed off the diversity of their members. The storytellers created the worlds. Others, from Richard's mother to the people who brought their books and dice, made the games run. The players then lived in those worlds.

The later computer gaming communities fell into much the same mold. They would have their urban planners in the persons of the game creators and storytellers. Those creators' worlds would work on the same principles as any city's new neighborhood: People would visit if the worlds sounded interesting, and if people liked them—if, in the case of games, they were fun— then people would stay.

These virtual communities would have their architects and construction companies. In game worlds, these infrastructure builders would be the hard-core coders, the 3D modelers and graphics engine programmers, even the T-shirted guys happily stringing wires to connect computers so that people could play together.

Ultimately people would wander in to look at the new neighborhoods, to test out the infrastructure to see if it was a place they wanted to stay; if they liked what they saw, they'd settle down and start playing. They'd put down roots, make friends, form groups that could be as tight as family. They would develop their own mythologies and oral histories about the people who had been there before them, and about people who had heroic adventures as defined by their adopted community's standards.

What would make the computer game communities that developed over the next 25 years so dynamic would be the feedback that occurred among all of these groups—planners, builders, and players. For the most part, the games wouldn't be like Monopoly or poker, where the rules were set, the implements of the games were handed down from above, and the games went on as they always had. Computer game worlds would constantly evolve, pushed by new advances from the technology developers and by new ideas from the players themselves. Years later, it would not at all be unusual to find little pockets of settlers in a game world using it for something wholly different than what its creators intended.

These colonists would be among the first to establish communities that were wholly digital, that interacted and fought and loved and had sex and killed each other all virtually, first through text alone and later with the help of increasingly realistic graphics. Gamers wouldn't be the only people to found digital communities, certainly. But they would consistently test the boundaries of whatever digital media they encountered. They would be the immigrants, off to foreign shores to find a better world, even if for only a few hours a day. They would take what they came across and build something new, impose their own rules and lifestyles on it, and the worlds they found would change them right back.

For Richard, all this would start simply, with 1500-line programs running on a new invention—the Apple II home computer.

2

Machines at Play

Richard walked into Houston's Clear Creek High School's main office on the first day of school his junior year, asked to see the principal, and sat down. The previous year, he'd finished the school's only computer-related class, a basic math accounting workshop that occasionally gave students the opportunity to tinker with equations. He'd nearly passed out from boredom each day. His programming skills now far outshined any other students in class, thanks to his Stanford and recent Oklahoma camp training. There was little left at the school he could learn from their meager computer department. Fortunately, his science fair success convinced the administration that, unlike other students, he worked well when left alone with his own projects. Now, tapping his feet, waiting to see the principal, he'd see just how far he could push that success.

A secretary waved him to the back. He walked in the office and sat down, launching into a long rant about his proposal before the principal uttered so much as a "hello." His pitch was simple: He'd conceive, develop, and program fantasy computer games using the school's computer, presenting the principal and the math teacher with a game at the end of each semester. There wasn't even a computer teacher there to grade him on his skills. To pass the class, he simply had to turn in a game that worked. If he did, he'd get an A. If it didn't, he'd fail.

It was an easy sell. To the school administrators, making a computer game was an educational activity and nothing to be feared. Richard smiled as he walked out of the office, pulling one of his favorite spiral notebooks out of his book bag and labeling it D&D 1 as he walked down the hallway. By the time the bell rang for first period, he'd already started writing lines of code.

His initial plan was to build an epic story based on parts of the adventures that went on at camp in Oklahoma. As Richard's own D&D group grew, he began incorporating those tales as well. He'd already started working on a language of runes, mystical-looking symbols that were much like Tolkien's Elven script; he fleshed this out and built it into the games. That was enough to start a dungeon. He spent his free period at the Teletype keyboard in the math lab, which connected to the central mainframe. Personal computers were in their infancy and his school didn't have one. Like in most institutions of the day, students instead had access to a central machine through various remote connections—keyboards and terminals called a Teletype—that they could use to input code.

A few weeks into the school year, Richard had grown frustrated. He'd had limited access to the Teletype, which meant he spent most of his "programming" time going over code in his head, trying to anticipate problems before they happened. Considering the electronic wonderland in his home, the situation was intolerable. Owen, however, didn't see much future with video games, and he ignored his son's constant pleas for an Apple II computer, the first commercial home computer that had just hit the market. The frustration continued building, until Richard couldn't take it anymore. He marched into his father's den one evening, his eyes twinkling, notebook in hand.

"Dad, if I can make this game work at school, without any bugs, then you buy me an Apple II," Richard said, handing his dad the D&D 1 notebook with 1500 lines of code, scribbled symbols, and charts outlining the mathematical rules for determining the results of combat.

Owen laughed. He'd long ago stopped doubting that his son would give up attacking a problem until he solved it. "If you can make it work without any flaws," he said, "I'll split the cost with you."

Satisfied, Richard stood up and walked out, a grin spread across his face. It was a devil of a deal. The game was nearly finished, save for a few bugs that needed working out. The computer was his.

He didn't stop there, though. Throughout the year, he'd burn through notebooks, labeling each one sequentially—D&D 2, D&D 3, until he reached D&D 28. Whenever he hit a snag, or if he came up with a better idea than the one he was working on, he'd start over with a new version of the game. He would flip through his most current notebook during other classes, scribbling notes and ideas on the cover. He was obsessed with making a game that mirrored those weekend roundtable games.

With the final bell of his junior year, Richard had aced his independent study projects and nearly worked out the idea for his first real game after 28 tries. The stories were falling into place, largely inspired by his home games of D&D. His BASIC programming was solid. Even the language he was creating was nearly complete—in fact, he had tested it in classrooms throughout the year, writing cheat-sheets for himself in his runic script all over notebooks and desktops and using them under the uncomprehending eyes of his teachers during tests.

But for every step forward in his programming skills, Richard faced an ever larger obstacle to creating the type of gaming experience he had enjoyed in the University of Oklahoma's common area and now in his own home. His simple games didn't live up to the social experience of playing with a community of people led by a storytelling Dungeon Master. For Richard, creating the game was just as fun as playing, but even a single-player computer game was fundamentally about sharing the experience with friends. Playing basketball alone on a court was practice, but playing with a group of people was a game.

Great storytellers could transport players into the game, showing them lush worlds where anything was possible. But there was little excitement in sitting alone at a terminal. Richard hadn't figured out how the computer could solve that problem.

＊ ＊ ＊

This collision between computers and game players was already an old one by the time Richard first started typing D&D code into his school's Teletypes. For nearly two decades, university computer departments had been continuously populated by a playful subculture of programmers who saw games as a valuable way of testing the limits of the giant new machines to which they'd gained access. In this early environment, the distinction between players and designers was often moot—almost anyone with access to a computer also had the ability, and often the desire, to create new games or modify old ones.

"Games and programming both reward elegance," later explained game designer Will Wright, who would create the best-selling Sims games of the 1990s. "Games are about exploring sets of possibilities. When you're designing something, a software program or a game, you're doing the same thing."

The first real computer game to spark a lasting community was created by an unruly group of students at the Massachusetts Institute of Technology in 1961. The computer science program there was one of the most advanced in the country, with brilliant minds studying topics ranging from artificial intelligence to database construction. This particular group, associated with the campus's model railroad club, was simply in love with the ability to manipulate the mainframe computers in unconventional ways, and its members spent virtually all their free time playing. They created a series of software programs that had little to do with their official curriculum, ranging from the whimsical to the intensely practical.

Among these was a game they called Spacewar!, which had two spaceships stalk each other around a screen, firing torpedoes while trying to avoid the gravitational pull of a sun in the center of the screen. It looked much like Atari's Asteroids would many years later, minus the giant rocks. At the time, it was a stunning leap forward in graphics technology, which was virtually nonexistent. It also was fun. MIT students gathered for all-night tournaments, and the game quickly spread to other campuses and computer facilities.

As the years went on, each new wave of students found ways to improve or modify the version of the game created by their immediate predecessors. Tens of millions of dollars in U.S. Department of Defense funding poured into the computer research labs at MIT, Carnegie Mellon, and Stanford, earmarked for serious research, while recipients of the funding spent hundreds of hours figuring out better ways to model space battles. As early as 1963, Stanford administrators ordered students and faculty to stop playing Spacewar! during daytime hours.[1] In 1973, *Rolling Stone* magazine reported that IBM had instituted a total ban on the game and then had had to rescind it when its employees complained after a few months.[2] In that same *Rolling Stone* article, reporting on the Stanford "International Spacewar Olympics," writer Stewart Brand said: "Reliably, at any nighttime moment (i.e. non-business hours) in North America hundreds of computer technicians are effectively out of their bodies, locked in life-or-death space combat computer-projected onto cathode ray tube display screens, for hours at a time, ruining their eyes, numbing their fingers in frenzied mashing of control buttons, joyously slaying their friend and wasting their employers' valuable computer time."

When Gygax's Dungeons & Dragons game rippled through these university circles during the mid-1970s, programmers immediately saw the potential for new computer games. In many ways, D&D was already like a computer program, overlaid with a dungeon setting. The game progressed on an *if-then* model that was familiar to programmers—*if* the character slays the orcs, *then* he is allowed to open the door and find the treasure. Many of the game's critical moments, from combat to success in picking a lock, were determined by rolling dice—the physical world's equivalent of a computer-generated random number.

Students and other programmers already primed by reading *Lord of the Rings* saw in Gygax's game a rich source of material, and they began work almost immediately trying to translate it into code, bits, and bytes. Many of these programs would be almost immediately forgotten. Some, like Richard's games, would be deeply influential on generations of games and game programmers to come.

Two parallel computer networks served as highways for the spread of these games and as early hosts for communities of game players. ARPANET, the public university and research network that would ultimately evolve into the public Internet, was home to much of this development. A separate, private network called PLATO, first developed at the University of Illinois in the early 1960s and expanded throughout the United States in the 1970s, carried much of the most advanced technology of the time and attracted some of the most dedicated game hackers.

For all of his futuristic experience with computers, Richard was oblivious to most of what was happening on these networks as he grew up. Although he occasionally tried out a new game, for the most part he kept his nose buried in his notebooks, building virtual worlds in his head. Other programmers he would later work with were already seeing these network games and falling in love, however.

One of these figures was a quirky programmer calling himself "Dr. Cat," who would weave in and out of Richard's personal and professional life for the next few decades. In 1977, Cat was a high school student in South Bend, Indiana, still using his real name of David Shapiro, and his mother was a professor at the local Indiana University campus, where they were trying out a connection to the PLATO network. "My mom had access to this and told me about it," Cat said later. "She said no one was using it on Saturday or Sunday, so I immediately rode across town on my bicycle to try it out."

A friendly hacker who was guarding the trial terminal told him that if he wanted to play a game, all he had to do was type the words BIG JUMP into the keyboard. He did, and immediately a list of more than 300 games scrolled down the screen in blurry orange text—space games, adventure games, and quite a few titles that were obviously inspired by Dungeons & Dragons. Cat was thrilled; he returned the next day to spend hours devouring as many of the games as possible, and then he pedaled across town to tell the local bookstore owner who had brought Dungeons & Dragons to town about his experience. D&D was at the university, too, but on the *computer*, Cat excitedly told the older man.

Cat's high school brush with PLATO was typical in more ways than one—finding games on a network supposedly dedicated to dry research and education topics often opened people's eyes to a quirky, creative side of computing culture for the first time. Moreover, people wanted to share their discoveries, tell other people about this new thing they'd found, and especially let other people play games they'd written themselves. Word of mouth, like Cat's message to the bookstore owner and the helpful hacker's instructions for Cat, was the best advertising.

Many of the most influential games were written at about the same time that Richard was starting to write his own early programs. Despite the deep graphical limitations of the networks and screens of the time, several games (including titles such as DND, Orthanc [the name of the evil wizard Saruman's tower in *Lord of the Rings*], *Oubliette* [French for *Dungeon*], and Avatar) displayed simple line drawings of dungeon maps similar to the graphics systems that Richard would develop over the next few years.

These games proved incredibly popular with the research and student communities on the PLATO network, inspiring some of the same kinds of tensions that Spacewar! had in the late 1960s and early 1970s. Cat later told of a pair of enterprising Indiana hackers who had become obsessed with Avatar, one of the most advanced of the D&D spinoffs in the late 1970s. Anxious to let their characters improve in the game, they'd driven all the way to PLATO's home on the University of Illinois campus, somehow made their way into the central operations room housing the machine where all the Avatar files were stored, logged into the computer, and changed their characters to make them all the highest level possible and give them the most powerful weapons available.

"It was so blatant, they were quickly caught," Cat remembered. By the time he arrived at Indiana's Bloomington campus in 1980 as a 17-year-old freshman, an automatic "Enforcer" program had been installed to make sure none of the students there could waste PLATO network time playing games. He started to write a hack to get around the block but then realized there was another way: One of the computer lab's system administrators was a dedicated game player, and whenever he was on duty, he would simply turn off the Enforcer.

Cat and other students in the know spent dozens of hours timing their visits to the school's computer lab to coincide with this staffer's hours, fighting their way through line-drawn dungeons, fighting battles for the soul of the galaxy against *Star Trek*'s Klingons or Romulans, or programming their own games at one of the system's terminals. Other administrators at other schools pursued similar attempts to stop the games from taking up so much computer resources, usually with similarly little effect.

Outside PLATO, the wider ARPANET was entering its own adolescence through this period in the 1970s. Programmers in university research labs and a handful of elite private companies were creating the basic networking and data-transfer technologies that would evolve into the Internet and the World Wide Web years later. Many of these programmers were also game players and writers. Some of them would be deeply influential on Richard as well, although the Houston high school student had little idea of their existence as he launched into his own series of homemade games.

A few early games fired imaginations nearly as much as Spacewar! A simple game called Hunt the Wumpus, written by Gregory Yob in 1972 for the Berkeley-based People's Computing Company, was translated into several computer languages and spread quickly and freely around university computer departments and research companies. Presented with text descriptions of a dodecahedron-shaped maze ("If you don't know what a dodecahedron is, ask someone," the game's cursory instructions read), the player's task was to hunt and shoot the "Wumpus," a mysterious creature which had a taste for the player's flesh. Other hazards included playful giant bats and bottomless pits. A sample of a very short game might have run something like this:

>BATS NEARBY!
>YOU ARE IN ROOM 2
>TUNNELS LEAD TO 1   3   10
>SHOOT OR MOVE? (S-M)? M (the player has chosen to move)
>WHERE TO? 1 (the player has chosen room 1)
>ZAP--SUPER BAT SNATCH! ELSEWHEREVILLE FOR YOU!
>YYYIIIIEEEE... FELL IN PIT
>HA HA HA - YOU LOSE![3]

The spread of Dungeons & Dragons through programmers' circles would quickly give adventure gamers a taste for more complicated games of exploration and fantastic worlds.

A talented young programmer named Willie Crowther at the Boston-based computer company Bolt, Beranek and Newman (BBN), which was involved in creating much of the early ARPANET's basic technologies, was one of that city's early D&D players. Not long after the release of Gygax's game, his marriage began to fail and he separated from his wife. In a bid to maintain contact with his two daughters, he decided to write a computer game for them, basing it in part on the pen-and-paper dungeon exploring he'd done, and partly on the real-life spelunking he and his wife had avidly pursued. His wife, Pat, was immortalized in spelunking circles for finding a critical passageway connecting two segments of the world's largest cave. Willie turned parts of that cavern into the setting for his daughters' game, which he dubbed Colossal Cave.

Crowther's Colossal Cave lacked even the simple graphics of Spacewar! or the Pong-style games just beginning to sweep the market. Like Hunt the Wumpus, it was all text, and like D&D, it relied on players' imaginations to fill in the most visceral elements of the world. Because he wanted to let ordinary nonprogrammers like his daughters play the game, Crowther made the game respond to natural language commands such as "Go North" or "Take Stick." The details of the environment itself were drawn from the weird beauty of the real Mammoth Caves of Kentucky, from the soaring domes and twisting narrow passageways called "crawls" to a massive column of orange stone based on its real-life counterpart.[4]

Crowther's project, released in 1976, turned out to be one of the most influential computer games in the medium's early history. His girls liked the game, he said in later interviews. But it turned out that other game players liked the adventure, too. Crowther put a copy of the game on a computer at Boston University, and the code spread quickly as programmers made copies and passed it around. At night, players installed it on the giant computers they worked on during the day, and other people would find the code there, start playing it, and then pass it along to others on the ARPANET.

A few months later in 1976, a first-year student in Stanford's graduate computer science program, Don Woods, stumbled across a copy of Crowther's game. A friend of Woods' had been working on a project at the Stanford Medical Center when he found the game and tried it out. Both men thought it was a blast—wholly unlike any other game they'd played. Woods liked it enough to want more. Crowther was still credited in the much-copied code, but without any contact information. Woods was too much of a programmer's programmer to let a simple hurdle like that stop him. He sent an email to every one of the 60-plus host machines then on the ARPANET looking for a "crowther@(thatmachine)." One mail didn't bounce; he'd found the author. After a short exchange of emails, Crowther readily gave Woods permission to modify the game.

Woods was a game player, but unlike Crowther, he hadn't played Dungeons & Dragons or any of its spin-offs. It didn't matter. His first task was to debug the code, eliminating rooms that had entrances but no exits, for example. He streamlined the way the code worked, trying to eliminate programming features that could give inconsistent results. But he also began adding puzzles to the game, in hopes of making it a little more challenging to play. "Crowther had really developed the program more as an 'explore and find stuff' game than as a 'solve the puzzles' game," Woods said years later. "I wanted to make it trickier so it would take longer for a player to 'finish' the game." That model, along with a wry sense of humor in responding to players' commands ("Don't be ridiculous" the game would tell someone that tried to eat a lamp, for example), made the final game enormously popular—and enormously influential on the style of later game writers.

When Woods re-released the game as Adventure on the ARPANET in late 1976, and again with improvements in 1977, players around the country were entranced. "You are standing at the end of a road before a small brick building," the game opened. "Around you is a forest. A small stream flows out of the building and down a gully. In the distance there is a tall gleaming white tower." The first step into the building, or down the road, led players into the most widely developed computer game world any of them had ever seen.

Crowther and Woods' game quickly proved a stepping-stone for other programmers interested in creating these new D&D-influenced worlds. Hundreds of other games were created; the work of one group at MIT stands out for the influence of its games and the commercial impact the team would have a few years later.

By early 1977, Adventure had made its way back to Boston, to the same department where Spacewar! had been created 16 years previously. Just as that game had, Adventure captured the imagination of the programmers at MIT, and many of them spent weeks trying to solve the game (one tongue-in-cheek estimate of the game's influence said that Adventure had "set the entire computer industry back two weeks").

One team of MIT students, led initially by a former political science student and committed D&D player named Dave Lebling, decided they could do better. Lebling had already worked on several games, including a network 3D exploration game called Maze, in which several people at once could wander around a labyrinth trying to "shoot" each other. Almost immediately after playing Adventure, Lebling started writing a command *parser*—a software package that could understand "natural language" commands such as "go north" or "pick up the treasure."

Another pair of students, Marc Blank and Tim Anderson, used Lebling's work to create a rudimentary four-room prototype of a new game, similar to Adventure with all-text descriptions. It was a simple world that contained a band that played "Hail to the Chief," a bandbox, a "peanut room," and a "chamber filled with deadlines." They showed it to Lebling, who tested it, found it promising, and almost immediately went on vacation for two weeks.

The others decided to turn the prototype into a real game in his absence. Blank, Anderson, and another student named Bruce Daniels started mapping out a more complicated world, with puzzles and problems scattered throughout that would make it a real game. They dove into all-night programming sessions, barely stopping to eat or sleep, and by the time Lebling returned, they had a real prototype. Lebling pitched in, and by the end of the summer of 1977, they had a functioning version of the game. The world wasn't nearly as large as it would grow to be over the next two years, but it was recognizably the game that would come later. Players entered the "Great Underground Empire" to contend with the forces of Lord Dimwit Flathead the Excessive, and found the deadly Grue in dangerous dark corners of the world. They called their project "Zork," but that wasn't intended to be the game's real name. That was a simply a hacker-slang nonsense word they often used as a name for unfinished projects. This time, however, the name stuck.

The game's Adventure lineage was evident from its first moments. "You are standing in an open field west of a white house, with a boarded front door," the game opened. "There is a small mailbox here." Entering the house would provide the player entrée into a dangerous underworld, where thieves and monsters abounded. Walking into a dark room would result in a message reading, "Oh no! You have walked into the slavering fangs of a lurking grue! **** You have died ****."

They put the game on MIT's computers, and there it quickly gained a following well beyond the school itself. Many people could use the school's big mainframes at the same time and the access software had been written with the idealistic mores of the programming community in mind; it had almost no security provisions built in. As a result, anyone who could use a modem and had the right equipment could call up the MIT computers, log in, and browse around to see what might be interesting. That wasn't a large number of people, even in the late 1970s, but it was enough to have created a little community of "Net randoms" who found their way to the students' game to try it out. These early players ranged from MIT artificial intelligence luminaries to 12-year-olds in Virginia who'd gained access to a computer and a modem.

About halfway through the process, the group decided to name the game Dungeon. That didn't go over well. TSR, Dungeons & Dragons creator Gary Gygax's company, claimed trademark rights in the name. The Zork team checked with lawyers at MIT, who said they ought to be able to keep the name, but not wanting to take any chances the team decided to name the game Zork after all. In the meantime, however, the source code for their game had been downloaded from MIT's computers by a clever hacker at Digital Equipment Corporation, who'd figured out how to break through the authors' attempts to encrypt it. Another programmer took the source code and rewrote it in a different computer language called FORTRAN so it could run on machines other than the giant mainframes. That unfinished version of the game kept the name Dungeon and wound up spreading around the ARPANET as a separate game.

Zork wasn't initially intended to be a commercial product. But as the game was being finished in 1979, some of its main programmers were putting the early touches on a plan to create their own company. They didn't know what they wanted to sell, exactly—they just knew that they were smart, creative people who surely could offer the world something and have fun doing it. Lebling and Anderson were part of this group, as was the assistant director of the lab, Al Vezza. Everyone kicked in a little money of their own to start the company, and they settled on InfoCom as a name. After deliberation, a home version of Zork was launched.[5]

"Would you shell out $1000 to match wits with this?" read one of the company's subsequent full-color magazine ads, showing an absurdly primitive, pixilated, red video-game-style monster against a black background. They were determined to make a virtue of their dependence on text, even as Atari and other home console games sold millions of machines by emulating the graphics of arcade games. Another ad depicted a glowing brain, reading: "We unleash the world's most powerful graphics technology."

Dozens of other companies were starting up in similar circumstances, many of them finding their path to computer games through the same nexus of programming glee and role-playing games. Richard Garriott was finding his path the same way, even if his early programming days took place wholly away from this networked world.

* * *

While university students swapped programs online, Richard was concerned only about getting his own computer. He'd completed his game, winning the bet, and his father told him that before the end of the summer, the family would get its first computer. Richard was ecstatic, although the waiting proved tedious at best. In the summer after Richard's junior year, his father walked through the front door, hands wrapped around the Apple II computer box. Richard nearly ran over the astronaut. He'd been working on D&D28B, the latest and most advanced version of his continually evolving game, but the going was tough during the summer, since he was cut off from the school's Teletype.

Now, with the Apple II safely hooked up in the confines of his home, Richard began to see less of the outdoors. He tore into the machine, poking around the instruction manuals and prodding the machine with simple code. He came across Escape, a simple game which asked players to find their way out of a maze. He popped it in the tape drive (very early computers stored data on magnetic cassette tapes rather than floppy disks and CD-ROMs) and watched as lines began appearing on the screen, giving him an overview of the labyrinth. Hardly a challenge. The answer was appearing on the screen as he watched. But just as the map finished, the screen went black, and he found himself looking down a long hallway, drawn with vector graphics—long, straight lines from the edge of the screen, connecting in the middle, which gave the illusion of depth and allowed him to wander through the maze with a first-person perspective.

"As the maze dropped down into that low perspective, I immediately realized that with one equation, you could create a single-exit maze randomly," he recalled. "My whole world changed at that moment."

Geek-speak aside, the player was almost literally inside the game. Instead of a perspective that gave him an overhead view of a game map, Richard could see exactly what his character could see. The possibilities for computer gamers—or, more specifically, for the complexity of his own dungeons—suddenly opened up. His games to this point had included graphics, but he had used simple ASCII text—asterisks, parentheses, and ampersands—to denote objects in the game. As he now walked down hallways, turned corners, and ran into dead-ends, he realized that a computer could transport players viscerally into the hero's experience, something even the D&D games couldn't do. Here on screen, a player took control of the hero—*became* the hero—as he tried desperately to escape.

He played for an hour, trying to figure out how the game worked, looking at the code. Then he stood up, grabbed a notebook, and started sketching out dungeons, scribbling his own code, and revamping 28B. When players went into a dungeon, they'd have limited sight, just as they would if they were exploring. They'd see what was in front of them and nothing else. It would be like an Alfred Hitchcock film, where the audience filled in what the director didn't show them.

There was a downside, though. His new vision took him into unfamiliar mathematical territory. Instead of fiddling with equations, he'd previously spent much of his time working out programming problems. Now his programming problems required mathematical solutions. When a player turned left, he realized, he would need to see the same part of the maze from a new compass point. Imagine a character standing at the end of a hallway, facing south. The player would see both walls bracketing the corridor. Turn directly east and he would be facing the wall, but without actually moving. The computer would need to track the player's movement and redraw the perspective as the player faced directly into the wall. That required a complex series of equations to redraw a stationary picture from four directions.

It drove him crazy. For days he sat around, doodling in his notebook, trying to visualize the creatures that would inhabit the new world. Helen occasionally appeared over his shoulder, and before long, she was next to her son, drawing. Richard sketched out ladders, bats, skeletons, and chests using geometric shapes, but it was his mother who helped him create 3D graphics by using perspective. For instance, to create the illusion that a corridor ran off into the distance, objects had to appear to get smaller relative to the position the character was standing in. A treasure chest several feet away would become increasingly larger as the main character walked towards it. It was a simple concept for an artist, but not quite so immediately obvious to a high schooler. Once he was satisfied, Richard wrote the graphics code, using geometric equations to plot the lines needed to draw those shapes. Next he needed to create the dungeon where these creatures would live. He tinkered with the math that created the Escape maze on the

Apple, but he wasn't sure he'd gotten it correct. Owen solved that, whipping out a few trigonometry equations, assuring his son that he was on the right path.

Graphics in hand, Richard was ready to go after the game code just as school started up. This year, he thought, he'd wow his teachers with his independent project. He even got a helping hand from administrators— while the old Teletype remained, the school's principal persuaded the school board that he needed an Apple II to help with his administrative duties. Richard had unfettered access to a computer at school and at home. He attacked the code relentlessly, writing the game by hand, debugging as he went.

He had a built-in test audience on the weekends that was anxious to help him. The D&D games picked again up when school started, and during breaks, Richard would snatch his friends Chuck Bueche or Bob White, part of his first D&D gaming group in Houston, to evaluate his latest work. They'd sit at the computer, Richard hovering behind them, watching as they skulked through his dungeons, battling demons and searching for treasure. D&D28B made him the Game Master—after all, he'd written the story—and he watched as his friends traveled through the adventure.

By this time, Richard and Elizabeth, the young woman whom he had asked to play in the first Dungeons & Dragons weekend game the year before, were spending much of their time together. An avid gamer herself, she'd drive over during the weeknights and watch Richard write his game. Engrossed, he'd sit inches from the screen, pecking in code with his girlfriend's arms wrapped around his waist, her head resting on his shoulder. He'd bang away for an hour, shake her awake, step back, and watch as she played his game. It wasn't necessarily the most traditional foundation for a relationship, but it was certainly good for his productivity. Once again, he found gaming mixed well with pleasure.

Programming the game had become a community event. His father, his mother, his game group, and his girlfriend each added something to the experience, helping him build a rich world that operated with a limited, but rudimentarily realistic software engine. Even his friend Keith, one of the first people to join the D&D group, sketched a knight walking into a dungeon, which Richard used as cover art. The game was finished before the first semester was over. He'd completed his first real game. He dubbed it Akalabeth, a mystical-sounding word he believed he'd made up (but which sounded suspiciously close to "Akallabeth," a word in J.R.R. Tolkien's fictional Númenórean language).

The game was done. It could have ended there. High school was over in 1979, and the D&D group fluttered into the wind. Computer gaming was a nice hobby, but Richard had already been accepted to the University of Texas, located three hours north in Austin. He'd decided to major in electrical engineering, just as his father had done. His whole life, he'd been surrounded by the best technical minds in the country, but none of that was going to get him a job at a game company. For all intents and purposes, there wasn't even a game industry around. The real programming action was happening on the coasts, at MIT and in Silicon Valley in California, hundreds of miles away.

He'd heard tales of the West Coast Computer Faire and the Homebrew Computer Club, both in Silicon Valley, two of dozens of computer hacker groups that made up the heart of the emerging home computer industry in 1979. Here, hackers shared information with each other, toting their homemade computers to meetings, where they'd show off programs, hardware innovations, and new operating systems. For hackers and programmers, those years in the Valley are remembered fondly as the "Golden Era of hacking," and it was there that Steve Wozniak had created the Apple II, the computer Richard would use religiously for years.[6]

Stuck in Houston, Richard took a job working at a local ComputerLand store. At least he'd be around computers. It wasn't long before his boss found out that he'd created a game. Richard set up an Akalabeth demonstration, and the store manager loved it. He persuaded Richard to publish it. People would actually pay money for the game, his boss said. It was good enough that it might even help persuade people to buy a computer to play it.

Self-publishing didn't take much work. Richard made his own packages, spending $200 on Ziploc bags and photocopying for the cover sheet and manual. "Beyond adventure lies Akalabeth," the black-and-white, hand-drawn cover by his mother read. "10 different Hi-Res Monsters combined with perfect perspective and infinite dungeon levels create the world of Akalabeth."

He worked with limited funds, and fearful that he'd end up with a mass of unused, $5 disks, he produced only 16 actual copies of the game. He hung the ziplocked packages on ComputerLand's wall and waited for customers to discover the magic. Fifteen copies sold. It wasn't much, but Richard was thrilled with the sales. Fifteen strangers had wandered into a store, looking for something—anything—to make their computer more interesting, and they'd chosen his game.

A bigger twist in his personal plot was on the way, however. While the Akalabeth games slowly disappeared from the ComputerLand wall, his boss had packaged up the last copy of the game and sent it off to California Pacific, a game company looking to capitalize on the home computer boom. Richard was so excited that his game was selling, he hadn't much noticed that a copy of the game was missing.

A few weeks later, he got a phone call at home. The man's voice on the other end wanted to talk about Akalabeth. Richard didn't recognize the voice, which confused him. As far as he remembered, he hadn't spoken with anyone about the game outside of his gaming group and his boss at ComputerLand. The man introduced himself as Al Rimmers, the owner of California Pacific. He wanted to fly Richard out to California to talk terms. "You need to publish this game professionally," he told Richard. "This could be big."

By the time the phone call ended, Richard's heart was thumping. Twenty minutes before, he was thinking about what he was going to do next. Akalabeth was two years' worth of programming, but he had never meant it to be a real product. Selling the game still felt a little like a joke. Sure, he was proud of the game, and of the packages hanging on ComputerLand's wall, but this was completely different. This wasn't two dozen disks for people in Houston; this was the big leagues. It was like taking a job in the mailroom at IBM and having the president of the company stroll into the basement, inviting him up to the executive suite to talk strategy. He was overwhelmed.

He talked to his parents about the phone call and the potential for his game to go nationwide. Together, they decided he should go. He was thrilled; in just a few years, he'd gone from a gaming geek to a computer programmer with a vision. He wanted to re-create the weekend gaming experience that had evolved at his house: the camaraderie, the excitement, and the total immersion players felt when they entered the world of a great storyteller. Now, it looked like he might get the financial backing he'd need to build that grand world and bring it to the emerging computer culture. "Until that point, I'd never considered gaming a career," he said years later, sitting in the office of his second game company. "I had been happy just doing what I had fun doing."

He was in for a surprise. Instead of the warm and fuzzy hacker culture he'd heard so much about, he was about to enter a fly-by-night, haphazard world of entrepreneurial business. Some of the people here would be programmers like him, while some would be people who sniffed money in this growing new field.

The early hackers' day was already coming to an end, as academics left their labs and hobbyists left their basements for the lure of business profits. By this time Apple, the largest home computer maker of the time, had sold close to 40,000 computers, but it was on track to sell twice that many the next year, and sales would keep going up from there. Tens of thousands, soon to be hundreds of thousands, of regular people suddenly had computers in their homes.

Scores of other programmers were coming almost simultaneously to the same realization. Those people buying computers were also buying software. More people would be playing games. And that meant there was money to be made. Even more important, it meant that hundreds of people like Richard might suddenly be able to make a living from a hobby that had so pleasantly taken over their lives.

3

Building Community, Building Business

For Richard, the allure of being published and actually paid for his game was secondary. As his plane rolled to the gate in California, his heart pounded. In just a few hours, he envisioned himself standing face to face with Bill Budge, one of his programming idols who published games for California Pacific.

Budge had first made his name by writing a Pong-style game called Penny Arcade, which he traded to Apple Computer in return for a printer while still a graduate student, and which had initially caught Richard's eye. The game also caught Al Rimmers' eye at California Pacific, and Rimmers immediately hired Budge to write Space Album, which computer hobbyist magazine *SoftTalk* ranked as its eleventh most popular game in 1980. Over the next few years, Budge would come to even more prominence as the author of a 3D graphics system for the Apple II and the self-published Raster Blaster pinball simulation and Pinball Construction Set, which let players create their own virtual pinball tables.

At this point in 1979, Richard already felt a connection with Budge, even though they'd never met. In fact Budge was one of the few programmers Richard admired. The older programmer seemed to have similar ideas about how to make games, even if Budge's products were worlds away from Richard's Akalabeth. Both were concerned with taking games from another medium and translating them to the Apple computer, with all its limited graphics and technical capabilities. Budge's work to date had largely been focused on arcade-style games, but his success had been undeniable. Richard was already running into trouble figuring out how to move paper role-playing games to the computer screen, and he hoped that Budge's experience and expertise might help him.

"These guys publish Bill Budge," Richard repeated to himself. His heart pounded as he walked down the long tunnel at the University Airport. Memories from his year-long exile in Palo Alto flashed through his head. The computer culture had been springing up all around him, almost literally in his backyard, and he'd barely been aware of it. He'd spent most of that year dismissing it, longing for Houston. Now, Rimmers, the owner of California Pacific, was waiting for him at the airport.

Richard emerged from the walkway to see Rimmers, as promised, holding a handwritten sign with Richard's name on it. Amazing. The plan was to head back to the California Pacific offices, where Richard hoped he would run into Budge. Instead, Rimmers took a detour.

"I have to make a stop first," Rimmers said. "It's too late to get you back home anyway."

They drove to a one-story apartment near the airport. Rimmers hopped out of the car without explanation, and Richard, feeling a bit uneasy, followed. He'd grown up next to NASA, where there was barely any drinking and certainly no drugs, but life in California was different, particularly among young developers who found themselves with more money than they knew what to do with.

Rimmers introduced him to a tall, scruffy man, and the two disappeared into the back of the house. Shaken and jet-lagged, Richard stood in the middle of the room, his heart racing. "Houston wasn't the Bible Belt. It was just that that kind of thing wasn't heard of," he remembered later. His publisher had disappeared into the back room, Richard was 1700 miles from home, and he didn't know anyone else in the area he could call. It was a bit unnerving. Eventually, he settled uneasily on the couch and fell asleep.

Rimmers shook him awake at the crack of dawn, and as quickly as they'd arrived, they were gone. Ghost-white, Richard climbed into the front seat. The gangly youth who'd grown up surrounded by artists and scientists convinced himself that everything would end well. When they finally arrived, the California Pacific office, a small building with few offices and fewer people, turned out to be a disappointment. Although the two would eventually meet, his idol Budge was nowhere to be found. The company contracted for most of its work, so there was little overhead and few full-time employees. It was the antithesis of Richard's experience both in Oklahoma and in Houston. There was no community here, and he had no desire to stay. He'd been half-scared out of his wits since he got off the plane. He signed his contract and left as quickly as he could.

Still, with Akalabeth finished and a contract in hand, Richard couldn't complain. "I had never thought of making games as a business," he said. "It was always just what I did."

A few days after he returned home, he called Ken Arnold, a boy about his age whom he'd met while working at the computer store. They'd decided to work together on a new game, and Richard wanted to get started as quickly as he could. Time was short. He was leaving for the University of Texas in just a few weeks, and the three-hour drive to Austin would limit their ability to work together.

For now, however, he and Arnold were determined to make a better version of Akalabeth. The basic structure of the game remained the same—hack and slash, hero adventure—but the two didn't want to replicate the experience completely. The weekend D&D games had formed the backbone for Akalabeth, but now he wanted a grander experience, something worthy of Budge, with a lush world and player interaction. Arnold began constructing a basic graphics subroutine using Assembly—a computer language Richard hadn't bothered to learn—while Richard hammered out the rest of the game's particulars. When they were finished, Richard thought, they'd have a game that every D&D player would want to play.

Meanwhile, Akalabeth was starting to sell. Eventually, the game went on to sell 30,000 copies, netting Richard $5 per copy, and bringing him a cool $150,000—about three times what his astronaut father earned in a year. Not bad for a school project.

* * *

These steps were taking Richard into an emerging community of computer developers around the country, who were slowly finding—like he was—that the magic they worked on their machines almost wholly for fun could also be profitable. The budding gaming industry was drawn from a loose assortment of science-fiction and fantasy fans, hard-core programmers, and other motley assortments of creative-minded people with a knack for learning simple computer languages. Many of them would find in each other a shared passion and wonder for the machines they were working on; for them, it was the equivalent of the shared experiences that had molded Richard's earlier communities.

In these early days, isolated pockets of like-minded people often wound up working on the same type of projects. In Texas, Richard had little sense for what was happening on either coast, although he saw many games as they were released. Most American programmers who were unaffiliated with universities or research institutions had little idea of what was happening overseas, where one of the most advanced attempts to bring role-playing communities onto a computer network was happening. As the threads of all of these projects wrapped together over the course of the next few years, many of the lessons from around the world would find their way into Richard's own work.

For now, the computer games business that Richard was entering was a decidedly amateurish enterprise. The computer software companies of the late 1970s and early 1980s were haphazard outfits, often launched by people who had started programming as a hobby rather than as a profession, and who had gradually fallen in love with computers. Broderbund Software founder Doug Carlston, at the time a lawyer in Connecticut, later told of writing games for his RadioShack TRS-80 computer largely as a hobby to support his own computer habit. He wasn't concerned about royalties, but most publishers would pay for games by sending free copies of all the other software they published, and that was more than enough reason to write a program or two, he said. "I'd send the software off, and get 30 or 40 freebies back in the mail," Carlston remembered.

Computer software publishing companies were often tiny affairs, run out of homes and dorm rooms, and taking out ads in local publications or one of the growing number of national hobbyist computer magazines. They were hungry for software—particularly games—to sell, and some of the more obvious business rules that would develop later in the industry's history were simply ignored. Carlston, for example, often sold the same program to two or more publishers. A lawyer by day, he told his correspondents at the companies clearly that the games had already been released elsewhere, but few cared. It helped that most publishers had little ability to distribute their wares nationally—at the time, only a few chain stores sold computer software, and most sales were regional or occurred through the mail. There was little likelihood that the same game, released by two separate companies, would show up sharing shelf space somewhere. Crowther and Woods' Adventure was a beneficiary of this phenomenon, released for the Apple II by Microsoft, Apple Computer, and Frontier Computing.[1]

In these early days of hobbyist computing, many games didn't come from what would now be viewed as a traditional "software publisher." The most popular pre-1980 game for the Apple II, according to *Softalk* magazine, was a Space Invaders rip-off called Super Invader, distributed by the popular *Creative Computing* magazine in 1978. The founder of that magazine, David Ahl, had earlier written a book called *101 Basic Computer Games*, which in 1979 became the first computer book to sell more than a million copies.[2]

But as more people started buying computers, and then looking for software to run on them, this scattered little circle of hobbyist developers started seeing royalty checks roll in, and the hobby began turning slowly into a profession. Richard's surprise at seeing Akalabeth suddenly selling thousands of copies wasn't unique, even if its scale was somewhat exceptional. Budge's first game with Rimmers earned him a surprising $7000 in his first month.[3] Carlston, too, suddenly saw royalty checks start trickling in from publishers he'd almost forgotten about—first hundreds of dollars, and then thousands. Like hundreds of other part-time programmers of the time, he began thinking that this hobby might actually be a career. Certainly it was more fun than practicing law.

The years 1979 and 1980 proved important ones in the formation of several key gaming companies. Carlston packed his computers into his Chevy Impala early in 1980 and drove across the country, winding up in Oregon, where his brother, Gary, lived. The two agreed to start publishing Doug's software themselves. They called the new company *Broderbund* (*broder* means *brother* in Swedish, while *bund* is German for *alliance*), and the company started off with barely $7000 in working capital, mostly donated by family members. Sales were slow at first, hampered by distribution difficulties. Doug drove across the country again, stopping at retail outlets wherever he could find them, trying to sell his company's software. The tactic worked, and he saw it as a formative vision of what the computer industry of the time was like. "It was as if it had been left to geeks to create the universe. It was kind of warm and fuzzy from top to bottom," he said. "The people who were running the stores were the kind of people who wanted to invite me home and show me all the hacks they had running on their own computers."

InfoCom's Zork was also released for the Apple II in 1980 by an outside publisher, although the game did poorly until InfoCom's ex-MIT programmers took control of distribution themselves. Sirius Software was formed in Sacramento, California, by a Vietnam veteran and computer store manager named Jerry Jewell, who had found in college student Nasir Gebelli a brilliant programmer with a talent for bringing arcade-style games to the Apple. On-Line Systems, later to be renamed Sierra On-Line, released its first game that year. That company would touch Richard's life more deeply than the others.

On-Line Systems was the product of a collaboration between husband and wife Ken and Roberta Williams, both of whom were new to computer games in 1980. Ken had begun as a temperamental corporate programmer with little interest in games but with ambitions of creating his own company. His decidedly nontechnical wife, Roberta, had fallen in love with a copy of Crowther and Woods' Adventure, and she decided to write her own adventure game called Mystery House. After initial skepticism, her husband pitched in and added a graphical element that pushed the boundaries of Apple II display technology beyond anything that had been done before. They toyed with taking it to a "real" software publisher, but then they decided to keep all the profits and took out a magazine ad for their "Hi-Res Adventure #1." They made $11,000 in the course of the next month. On-Line Systems was renamed Sierra On-Line when the Williamses moved to a little town near the California Sierra mountain range not long afterward.[4]

These publishers grew to be part of a small circle of friendly companies. Many of the companies and their founders grew to know each other well, developing a sense of community that would stay intact throughout much of the 1980s. They met at trade shows like the West Coast Computer Faire and AppleFest, and they spent time together away from the shows when they could. The Williamses hosted a series of rafting trips over the years that would often draw 50 to 70 people from various companies out into the woods for water fights. The programmers were drawn together in large part by a shared sense of purpose—and occasionally by a beautiful and incredulous sense of having lucked into their new lives.

"We were all in it out of a sense of wonder," Carlston remembered. "All of us either had no lives before or had thrown them over because of these stupid machines. We hung out together because we were all the same sorts of jerks."

That didn't make them good business people, however. Some of their companies did very well, borne aloft by their own programmers' talents and a market hungry for whatever software it could find. The computer games market was a tiny fraction of the billions of dollars being spent on arcade and home consoles like the Atari, but it didn't matter. For the most part, these people were in the industry because they simply loved pro-gramming on the temperamental new machines, and the draw of bigger money elsewhere simply wasn't a factor. Real-world business concerns would swamp some companies, and would undermine the hackers' cul-ture in others, but as these companies started, financial and accounting is-sues were simply new problems to be solved as quickly and painlessly as last week's graphics hack.

"Most of these guys were in the industry because they loved it," Broderbund's Carlston said. "It was a very hackery kind of thing. You didn't go to business school, you didn't read the rules; you were just going to go out there and figure it out. It was a blissful ignorance of the real world that united everybody."

* * *

Richard and Arnold certainly fit that mold, even if they existed only on the margins of this West Coast computer culture at first. Unconcerned with distribution and contracts, the two had started work on Ultima, the name for their planned follow-up to Akalabeth. (Originally titled Ultimatum, the pair's game became Ultima when they realized a board game already carried their original title.) They plotted a story in which the player would try to stop an evil wizard, Mondain, from wreaking havoc throughout the land of Britannia. They didn't have much time together to finish the project. Just a few weeks after returning from California, Richard piled into the car with his parents and headed three hours north to Austin's University of Texas, where he would try to master the more advanced arts of computer programming.

The environment in Austin wasn't promising at first. Gone were the weekly games of Dungeons & Dragons and the physical community that had developed over two years and become such a source of inspiration for him. With few friends in Austin, Richard spent several weeks sequestered in his room, tinkering with the new game. He was cut off from people and miserable. On weekends, he'd drive back to Houston, holing up in his house with Arnold, knocking ideas back and forth, but nothing was really jumping out at them. By the time Richard came home for the Christmas holidays at the end of 1979, he was depressed. He was too far away from Arnold to get serious work done. Too much commuting meant that he wasn't acclimating up north, either. He made a New Year's resolution: It was time to explore Austin and find interesting people and groups to join. They had to be there somewhere.

Computer programmers and gamers had little social cachet at the time, so meeting anyone proved a bit difficult. He latched on to the fencing team, but there was little time for social interaction there. He picked up a campus newspaper one day after class and found an advertisement for a group called "The Society for Creative Anachronism." Each week, these people would get together to re-create medieval society, complete with full garb, role-playing, and sword fighting. It sounded interesting, he thought. In a way, they were the real-life manifestations of the Dungeons & Dragons games he'd played and the computer games he hoped to create.

The SCA was a curious group started in the shadow of a different kind of renaissance. It had been formed on the weird streets of Berkeley in 1966 by a handful of science-fiction and fantasy fans who wanted to bring to life the worlds they had been reading about, complete with the sense of honor and trust they felt were missing from the '60s. By the late 1970s, the group had spread nationwide. The Austin chapter had existed since 1977, and was started by Steve Jackson, another game designer who was getting ready to start his own company out of the large metal barn behind his two-story house when Richard arrived on the scene. A longtime paper gamer, Jackson wanted to create a hybrid of the war games released by more established companies like Avalon Hill and Simulations Publications, Inc., and role-playing games like Gygax's Dungeons & Dragons.

That was business, however. The SCA was more about something different—part fun, part philosophy, part medieval craft. Over a bottle of whisky, SCA members would discuss the guiding principles of chivalry they thought should rule not only their weekly fencing matches but also their lives. It quickly became a safe haven for the science-fiction crowd, the paper gamers, and the computer programmers—three distinct groups who were starting to realize their common interests. For Richard, the mix of creative community and anachronistic philosophy would be seductive in both his personal life and his gaming activity.

Fittingly, Richard stumbled across the SCA while he was tooling around an arcade by the university's student union. After reading the SCA's newspaper ad, Richard tracked down the group in Waterloo Park, a grassy area southeast of the university, where it held weekend gatherings and fencing matches. Two fencers were thrusting and parrying when he arrived, and he watched with a practiced eye. He'd already become a reasonably good fencer, and he thought he might be able to beat at least one of them.

The two fencers were David Watson, then a 30-year-old craftsman, and 20-year-old Greg Dykes, Watson's roommate. Richard asked to join them, and the trio soon became inseparable during the Sunday afternoon fencing sessions. They practiced constantly, challenging the others to epic duels over any issue that came up, no matter how trivial. When Dykes, known as Dupré in the Society, became agitated over Richard's insistence on calling him "Super Duper," he challenged Richard to a duel on Watson's front lawn. Richard quickly dispatched Dykes, winning the right to use the nickname for six months, after which the challenge would be reissued.

The older Watson was the odd man out in the trio, but his meticulous attention to detail and his eccentric personality meshed well with Richard's interests. When Watson was a graduate student in history at the University of Texas in 1970, he had taken apart a crossbow he purchased at a gun and knife show and tried to improve it by using information from a book written at the turn of the century. The endeavor proved unsuccessful, but Watson had spent much of the intervening time learning how to craft crossbows that would actually function.

"The four of us, David Martinez joined the regular foursome, really all hung out and camped together at almost every SCA event," Dykes later remembered. "We got into the philosophy of the group. We'd sit around drinking and talking about proper behavior, the rules for living your life, and honor. Sure, there was some straight tavern stuff too, but we always did things with a certain style."

Richard found much inspiration for his game in this crowd. He used the group's honor code as the backbone for later games, creating mythical heroes and quests for his adventures and tying those into the game. To make believable characters, he used his friends in the game. He showed up at Waterloo Park one day, notebook in hand, tapping people on the shoulder and asking them, "What would you like to say in my game?"

"The thing about the characters is Richard takes the best qualities from these people, from our friends, and he's used them in the game," Watson said years later over tea, his belly hanging below his belt, popping through a black leather riding jacket. His goatee and receding hairline peppered with gray, the glory days of sword fights were now long behind him. "When Dupré"—regarded by his friends as a good-hearted but flawed man—"is the Paladin, there is truth in that."

Richard also got feedback from gamers among the SCA crowd, particularly Jackson. The two talked more abstractly about SCA-related issues and medieval combat than about computer game theory, but it was helpful. Jackson was interested in the computer games, but he was so focused on his own projects that he never dug deeply into the world that Richard was helping create. "I have always been very interested in the computer game world, but through bad decisions, bad luck, or both, I never got very far into it," Jackson said years later.

Meanwhile, California Pacific, mired in financial trouble, pestered Richard for his latest game for nearly a year. But Richard refused to ship the game to the company until he felt it was finished, late in 1980. Soon after Richard delivered the finished Ultima, the company hit the financial skids. The game was distributed around the country, but by the time Richard was starting to expect royalties, the company had stopped returning his phone calls. It took him some time to realize that it had gone out of business.

While the failure meant he was once again adrift in the gaming world, it proved useful in some ways. He turned to his brother Robert to try to squeeze royalties from the defunct publisher, but it proved to be impossible. Freed of their influence, and with a growing name as a successful game writer, Richard realized he had some leverage to get a better deal the next time around. He started working on a sequel to his Ultima game and began looking for another publisher.

＊ ＊ ＊

Elsewhere in the world, the desire to re-create the community feeling of paper role-playing gaming was taking a different form. The most advanced project was announced in the United States with a teasing cross-Atlantic email that went out across MIT's Zork email list in 1980. "You haven't lived 'til you've died in MUD," the short message read.

MUD stood for "Multi-User Dungeon," and its British creators were taking the line of gaming started by Crowther and Woods' Adventure and the MIT programmers' Zork a step further. Like Lebling, Blank, and the rest of the InfoCom crew, MUD's authors were creating a rich, often funny, text-based world in which players could explore, find treasure, and fight monsters. However, MUD was online, and that opened up a world of possibilities that few others had achieved. Many gamers could play at the same time, exploring dungeons together and battling each other, or they could just hang out chatting. The authors of that transatlantic email, Essex University students Roy Trubshaw and Richard Bartle, would soon be known in computer circles around the world.

The game had grown out of much the same desire for a community gaming experience that had fueled Richard when he left behind his first D&D group in Oklahoma. There, he'd finally found new friends who enjoyed the same entertainment he did, who spoke the same language, and who enjoyed fantasy and role-playing. Leaving that group would bother him for years. Bartle, in particular, had felt a similar sense of being out of place as he went to college and set out to do something about it.

Bartle had grown up in a tiny town called Hornsea on the English coast of Yorkshire, where there simply wasn't much to do. His father had been an avid board game player who quickly instilled the love of dice and competition in his two sons. As Bartle grew older, he started reading science-fiction and fantasy books, and he started playing increasingly more advanced games at home with friends and through the mail.

In 1975, the 15-year-old sent away for a copy of the Dungeons & Dragons rulebook, and he quickly fell in love. He brought together a small group of other Hornsea gamers, and he was soon leading them through fantasy worlds of his own creation. He started writing a small gamers' magazine for local gamers, and in the last two years before college he took over a national 'zine called *Sauce of the Nile*, dedicated to gaming, where he printed rules for a swords-and-sorcery game he had created, called Spellbinder.

Bartle was obviously smart, but he didn't apply himself much to school. The games called, the 'zine called, and his computer classes called. Ordinary schoolwork wasn't enough to hold his interest. He passed his college entrance examinations easily enough, but unspectacularly—relying on "flair, rather than hard work and revision," he later said. The scores were enough to bring him to Essex University, a school about an hour northeast of London with a good reputation for research, however.

Essex in 1978 proved to be something of a shock for Bartle. The school's culture and social scene was dominated by a left-leaning political element that felt far removed from the engineering or scientific frame of mind. The student body's political voice was dominated by a far-left Labor Club and the Socialist Workers. Ordinary Communists were viewed as "sellouts," Bartle remembered. That made it hard for people like him—smart, creative, and funny as he was—to fit into the campus mainstream. He liked computers, and that was enough to put him in a dangerous category in the eyes of much of the student body. Programmers were social misfits, able to master the mysterious beasts in the basement that no self-respecting radical had any business playing with, at least in those days. Computers were still seen as tools of a bureaucratic, Big-Brother mindset, rather than an artistic, or better, a revolutionary, tool. "All scientists were regarded as nerds, and computer scientists were the nerdiest of the nerds," he said later.

If the bitterness never quite wore off, the sense of isolation quickly did. In Bartle's first week at the University, he met Roy Trubshaw, the secretary of the student Computing Society, and the pair hit it off. Bartle joined the group, eager for more time on the computers there, and quickly became an integral part of the little subculture. He'd gone to the school expecting to major in math, but he quickly abandoned that path to concentrate on computers. Plenty of people were better mathematicians than he. The same wasn't true for programming.

Like Lebling's group at MIT, the Essex Computing Society had found its way to Crowther and Woods' game of Adventure and was collectively captivated. Trubshaw loved it for the programming. Bartle just liked the game. They and others in the student group talked about creating their own version, but better and more complex. The cave game was too simple, allowing just a single player at a time to wander through the text-based environment. But that wasn't how people played games. Compare that to Dungeons & Dragons, where at least half the fun was getting a band of people together to go adventuring. What if groups of people could all get into the caves at once?

Trubshaw began working on the infrastructure for that kind of world in late 1978, ultimately calling it the "Multi-User Dungeon." The name was a reference to the hacked single-player version of Zork, which was floating around the Net at the time. Trubshaw made a database that would remember what was inside each "room" as people were in it, that would allow different people to be "in" the room at the same time, and that would make sure that if one person picked up a chair, for example, it would stay picked up for everyone else. By 1980, his last year at Essex, he had the basics of the project down. It had taken him most of his third and final year there to get this far, and it had distracted him enough that his degree project had all but fallen by the wayside.

Trubshaw's first version had 100 locations and a simple set of commands. He called it a game, but it had really been more of a programming exercise. When the elder student left in 1980, Bartle took it over and "gamified" it. If it were to be a world, it needed inhabitants. If it were to be a game, it needed to be *fun*. "My aim was primarily to attract players: a world with no inhabitants is no fun at all," Bartle said. "I understood that not all people would want to game when they got there, but its being a game would draw them in."

Bartle's first task was to make the world bigger. He expanded MUD and added a long list of new commands, allowing players a wide range of actions. He added tasks, puzzles, and ways to improve a character's skills and power. Before long, he had created a working game. Points were awarded to players who discovered treasure and dumped it into the swamp, where no one else could get to it. Points were awarded for killing wandering monsters, or "mobiles," as they were known. Lots more points were awarded for killing other players. The game included a goal worthy of a newly created world: players who got enough points could become wizards, or even arch-wizards, with power to get behind the scenes of the game and exert godlike power over the world or even over other hapless players.

The message that Bartle and Trubshaw sent to the Zork email list at MIT in 1980 brought a few curious Americans into the game, but it was difficult for them to spend much time online until the transatlantic data network had improved. More, at least at first, came from Britain. The university had allowed Bartle and the Computing Society to open the school's computers to outsiders, at least in the middle of the night—but that restriction barely mattered. Singly and in small groups, people took up residence in MUD. The community that developed was tight—certainly as close as in the games that Gygax, Garriott, and Bartle had played with pen and paper— and almost wholly digital.

The relative anonymity of the digital community helped create improbable mixes of players, bonded by their connection to the game. Because MUD was a role-playing game, players could be whoever they wanted inside the game, and their status in real life mattered little. In Richard's early games, people he knew had found their way into the story as fictional constructs. In Bartle's MUD, the people he knew *were* the game, and these people became one of the first communities to bond wholly inside the context of a game world.

"Jez" was one of those players. In real life, Jez's name was Jeremy San, a 15-year-old prototypical bedroom hacker living at home. His computer equipment was rudimentary, to say the least—he didn't even own a modem cable, and so hand-connected his 300-baud modem to his computer with ordinary wires. They weren't shielded, so the screen on his computer flashed into gibberish every time his younger brother used his CB radio in the bedroom next door, he remembered later.

When he stumbled upon MUD, he found the social aspects of the game were the most compelling. "Most players in MUD went there to converse and play with other players," he said later. "The game itself was quite good, but it was the multiplayer angle that made it addictive and compelling. The unpredictability of having real human opponents, as well as AI (artificial intelligence) ones, made it incredibly enjoyable." Nevertheless, the hacker in him drove him to achieve "wizard" status by solving puzzles and completing adventures. With his new power, he found he could spy on other players, travel invisibly around the world, and generally act as a benevolent or malicious god toward players who hadn't achieved his exalted status. For a 15-year-old in his bedroom, it was an enormous thrill.

He quickly became a standby, popular character in the world, serving as storyteller, gossip, and collective memory for the others who routinely played. He spent hours a day online, sleeping by day and playing by night, cutting classes when he went to college, or leaving for lunch to catch a few extra minutes of sleep in his little Datsun Cherry. As a result, his grades weren't stellar, but he was already working on the side doing computer consulting work for companies including British Telecom, and he had started his own games company. (The company and his interests proved lasting; in 2001, he was honored with an Officer of the British Empire award from the Queen for his long work in technology.)

Much of the world's character was due to Bartle's influence, Jez said. Bartle was god—literally, god the creator in the context of the MUD world. "He was omniscient and omnipresent. He seemed to know everything that was going on, and he ruled the game as if it was his creation and he had just created the Earth, and we players were the Adams and Eves of the place." Bartle trusted others who had "made wizard" with the ability to change and modify the game, so players felt like they had a stake in the world itself. That helped keep players in the game even after they'd reached the highest level possible. To Jez, Bartle seemed to be an "extremely nice and funny guy, very articulate and creative. He was quite a bit arrogant, but deservedly so. He'd regularly tell me his IQ was very high, something like 170 or 180," Jez said. "This was extremely annoying, mainly because it was probably true."

The text-only world opened up the games to players' imaginations, which sometimes ran towards the bizarre, but that served to create better legends.

One of the game's most famous denizens was Sue the Witch, who dialed in to MUD from South Wales and played long hours every night. She worked her way to the game's highest rank in just four weeks, and then she became what Bartle later called MUD's "greatest player." Spending up to six hours a night online, her phone bill reportedly topped 1000 British pounds a month. Particularly popular because she was female in a community that was predominately male, she was always online, always willing to help, and always upheld the MUD's social ethos to the point of angering some other wizards. Bartle trusted her implicitly. While other players met face-to-face, even if only infrequently, no one ever saw Sue. She claimed, in handwritten letters to some of the players, that she was agoraphobic. Jez was one of those who corresponded with her, and they developed a close relationship. She sent him pictures and tapes of her favorite music. Occasionally, Jez or someone else would talk to her on the phone, but conversations were always short.

After long months playing, Sue disappeared. She sent a cursory note indicating that she was going to Norway to be an *au pair*, and then she stopped corresponding altogether. Some of the players were worried; this didn't sound at all in character for the Sue they knew. A few of them finally tracked down her address in South Wales and made the trip. A woman answered their knock at the door and gave them the bad news: Sue's real name was Steve. He'd been playing as a woman since the beginning, letting his wife—whose real name was Sue—answer the phone calls. He was gone, but not in Norway. He was in prison for defrauding a government agency, the woman said. Crestfallen, the players returned home.

All of this gender-swapping was expected. In interviews long after the release of the game, Bartle said he had set up the flexibility of the game's role-playing system to encourage his fellow programmers at Essex to explore parts of their nature in ways they might not otherwise feel comfortable doing. One of his own first characters, used to test and debug the game, was named Polly. The persona was used in part to test the ability of the database to handle female characters after being created with solely male personas, but he said it was also used to encourage other people to explore other characters.

MUD's fame quickly sparked successors and imitators. While Bartle tended the first MUD, and then created a company that would operate its successor, others followed his lead. Source code for the original began popping up on university systems around the world. Other programmers created different software for doing roughly the same thing, and before long hundreds of these text-based worlds, populated by hundreds or even thousands of people, were scattered across the world, living on university servers, bulletin board systems, or the young commercial online services like CompuServe. Some of these kept Bartle's swords-and-sorcery theme. Some used other inspirations, drawing from science fiction, Western, or movie themes. Many of them weren't games at all and simply served as venues for social interaction or theatrical role-playing. Some were even explicitly sexual, with text-based actions describing graphic pornography of every conceivable variety.

All of them were played over the networks or online services to which most people had no access until much later, however. For most gamers, the commercial single-player worlds of Richard and his peers would remain the main exposure to computer gaming they would have for years to come. The networked game advances being made by Bartle and his successors, along with the lessons they learned about the way gamers interacted in online worlds, would ultimately prove deeply influential for Richard.

* * *

Back in Austin, Richard was still looking for a way to bring his next game to market. Figuring he had little to lose at this point, he put the word out in the gaming industry in 1981 that he was a free agent. If he didn't get a job, he'd stay in school. If a deal did come through, so much the better.

Initially, it appeared as if Richard would have little trouble finding a publisher. When word got out that he was on the market, game publishers began contacting him. He'd already shown that he could publish a game—two, in fact—so he asked for a huge amount of money by prevailing industry standards. He wanted a 20 percent cut of the game sales, a figure that was practically unheard of at the time. Programmers were already a dime a dozen—publishers could find any smart kid and teach him how to program an Apple II in a few weeks, having him or her churning out a new version of Space Invaders in no time. Companies were making money, but none wanted to give Richard too much of it, particularly when he took 18 months to finish a game.

Richard wanted more than money, though. He wanted the game to be right this time, to be more than just a disk in a baggie. This was a *world* he was creating, not just a diversion, and that meant a few things had to happen to bring it to life in the right way. He also wanted to package the games differently. Until this time, games were shipped in ziplocks. Richard wanted his next game in a cardboard box, splashed with medieval graphics on the cover. He wanted his manual included. And he wanted a cloth map included so that players could get a visceral sense for the world that the computer graphics still were too simple to portray. He and friends had sat through Terry Gilliam's movie *Time Bandits* over and over again, scribbling details of the time portal map that the anarchic little bunch of midgets had used to bounce around history. He liked that idea, and he wanted to use it in his own game.

When publishers heard that pitch, the offers dried up quickly. Nobody wanted to deal with an oddball who played with swords and spoke of medieval truisms that should guide their lives. On top of that, they wondered why he wanted to include a cloth map, a manual, and a box. Those were expensive. This was a computer game they were distributing, not some kind of weird tabletop thing with painted lead figurines and dice. If Richard took 20 percent, profits would fall sharply. Publisher after publisher turned their backs on him. Who needed that kind of headache when simpler games were easily had?

Sierra On-Line's Ken Williams saw potential in the young programmer, however. By this time, Williams had been working with programmers who were even younger. He knew how code-slingers' minds worked, and he knew that Richard had something that most of them didn't. For a product as potentially valuable as the Ultima franchise, Williams decided to give up more than he was used to. He signed Richard to a contract for Ultima II, and he let the programmer go to work. He had enough games in the pipeline that he could afford to give the next Ultima some development time. Richard, in turn, began drafting a story that picked up where the first Ultima left off, featuring the wizard Mondain's apprentice, Minax, seeking revenge on Britannia.

The relationship worked marvelously as long as Richard stayed in Austin. But it began to turn sour in the summer of 1982, almost a year after they'd starting working together. Richard still hadn't finished the game.

By this time, the Williamses had moved their operation into the California foothills and bought a house, where a growing group of programmers could stay, dormitory style, while they churned out game after game. To kids who'd never had much of a community before, this environment was better than camp. They got paid, they got to play with their beloved computers all the time, and if an occasional stress-related blowup occurred, it could all be taken in stride. Richard relented and joined the Sierra team's community for the summer.

"When I was working on Ultima II, I didn't know machine language very well at all," he said later. "I was always calling up there for help, so I went up there, even though technically I was freelancing for them."

Again, Richard found himself a fish out of water. He rarely attended the weekend parties, and he didn't make many close friends there. His friends were back in Texas, not in the California mountains. "From a personal standpoint, I really liked Ken Williams," Richard said, "but I didn't really fit into what was going on up there. I'm not sure they liked me."

The game, however, proved to be a success when it was unveiled at that year's San Francisco AppleFest conference. Richard attended as Lord British in full medieval garb, a nod to his friends in the Society for Creative Anachronism. Soon afterward, he packed up his suitcase and headed for Houston. School was about to start, and he needed to get back.

When Williams subsequently offered him what he thought were less than desirable terms to translate the Apple II version of Ultima II into a game that would run on the young IBM PC, Richard decided to cut off his relationship with the company. It was time to strike out on his own. He hadn't been so impressed with the companies he'd seen so far, and he figured he could do better.

That decision helped catalyze the decision to leave college. The experience with the Williamses, and his own success, had reinforced Richard's tendency toward independent-mindedness. His computer classes in Austin were proving to be infuriatingly slow—or at least irrelevant to what he thought he needed—and he was anxious to do his own work. His annoyance came to a head when a professor in one class introduced assembly language programming for the latest Apple II, which used a 6809 processor. It was an important subject, one that would theoretically help Richard in his own work and if he wanted to get a job as a serious

Apple programmer after graduation. But his work had used a different kind of processor, the 6502, than the class was using. It was a less advanced unit, but it worked for him. The work he'd done with it had made him hundreds of thousands of dollars.

He refused to learn what the new processor could do. Why should he? He completed his assignments, but he refused to include the latest features of the new processor in his work. His professor wasn't amused and knocked points off Richard's grade for each successive sign of intractability. With each dropped point, Richard's motivation waned until he finally hit bottom: an F in the class, and a determination to get out. He just couldn't take the demands of the professor seriously.

It was time to leave in any case. Before Richard had even set foot on campus, his mind had been in Ultima's land of Britannia. Other worlds called, and he wanted to get to work building them. Without a job and without a degree, Richard sat down with his brother Robert and hatched a plan. He'd leave school and they'd start their own company, they decided.

But the pair had to overcome one powerful obstacle: an overachieving NASA astronaut parent who hadn't ever been completely at ease with his son's fascination with computer games. Now here was Richard, the computer genius of the family, coming home with his tail between his legs because he had failed, of all things, a programming class. Quitting was clearly the right choice for Richard, but, as Robert said later of their father, "We were pretty sure he was going to kill Richard."

Instead, their father surprised them: He cut another deal with Richard. The games-writing business just might make sense, he said, but only as long as they were making money. The practical-minded father was sure that this computer games boom was a fad—a profitable one, and one in which an unfocused college dropout could make lots of money, but a fad nonetheless. With their father's conditional blessing, the two brothers launched Origin Systems with $70,000, which Richard fronted largely from the profits from his first game.

"When this ends," Owen told his son, "you'll go back to school and get a real job."

4

Brave New Worlds

Out of school, Richard moved back into his parents' Houston house. Along with his friend Chuck Bueche, he set up residence in the loft of the family's three-car garage—the one they'd built four years ago after Helen's art space was commandeered by the weekly Dungeon & Dragons games. The space was mostly barren—a few desks and cots peppering the room. They gave their new company Origin Systems a motto full of hubris: "We Create Worlds."

The reality of Richard's company was much less impressive than that initial claim, but the little group was nonetheless promising. He gathered a close-knit collection of friends who could help create and sell the games. Robert, now living in Massachusetts with his wife, Marcy, would handle the business operations, commuting between New England and Texas. Mary Fenton, a customer service representative from Sierra On-Line, joined the team, and Jeff Hillhouse, an ex-college basketball player and fellow Sierra On-Line refugee, came with her.

Like any startup, it was a ragtag operation with little money and meager management. What they lacked in resources, they more than made up for in pests, Hillhouse recalled later. "My first look at the living quarters..." he said, his voice trailing off. "I'd never slept on a cot before, but that turned out to be all right. But if I left anything in the trash at night, I'd wake up and hear a scuffling, a rummaging. Houston has a reputation for huge cockroaches, and when I worked for Richard I found that the reputation is true."

They took up residence in Origin's computers, too. The sweltering Texas heat and the ungodly humidity wreaked havoc on the Apple II. To combat the pest problem, the programmers would remove the computer tops each night, prop them up against the wall, and allow the motherboards to cool down. The warmth acted like a homing beacon for the roaches. The employees' morning routine often consisted of peeling fried bugs off the computers and wiping up any water that had leaked through the windows in the course of the night.

One night, a few months after they'd settled into their new digs, the doorbell rang as they were having dinner with Richard's mother. Richard got up, sauntered through the house, and opened the door. Standing in the doorway was his brother Robert, who'd flown in from New England, and a stocky man who was built like a fireplug—a bit round through the chest, with a long, bushy beard flowing off his face. He introduced himself as "Dr. Cat from Indiana." Cat had sent Robert a note after seeing an advertisement announcing the formation of Origin in a gaming magazine published by Steve Jackson. As Cat walked by, Richard gave him the once over, which did little to set his mind at ease. On the newcomer's feet were fuzzy bear slippers and he was wearing a Watchimal—a watch hidden in a stuffed animal that wrapped around his arm. A stuffed dragon perched on his shoulder.

Richard was flabbergasted. He'd never heard one word about this from Robert. Origin Systems was barely a company. They were just a bunch of kids crammed into the Garriotts' garage, and here Robert was already hiring new programmers without so much as consulting with him.

Still, Dr. Cat was a believer, and after being grilled by the rest of the team, they realized he sounded like a pretty good programmer, too—exactly the type of person the team needed. He had an encyclopedic knowledge of the game and computer industry, young as it was. It was clear that he'd never fit into the corporate environment that Richard, too, was desperately trying to avoid. Over one of Helen's home-cooked dinners, the group decided to add one more misfit developer to the team.

With his team in place, Richard made the decision to leave the confines of the garage, strike out on his own, and rent a small office in Houston. Without the safety net his parents provided, he was going to face the bumps and bruises of life. Some would prove to be minor setbacks, while others would be major problems. They were in many ways indicative of the changes that were going on in the gaming industry itself. No longer confined to universities and hacker garages, computer and video games were becoming a powerful force in popular culture. The rise of computer games, particularly role-playing games, even threatened to drown the paper-based games that had spawned them. The broader home video game industry was wavering on the brink of financial disaster as the industry pioneered by Atari headed into a crash that would ripple into smaller computer businesses.

Chaos, both personal and professional, was on the horizon. The industry was changing, Richard was changing, and gamers were changing. Each was maturing, growing more complex as the initial thrill of the technology receded. As with any adolescence, this growth spurt would carry with it growing pains.

✳ ✳ ✳

Although he was in Houston, Richard's continued connections in Austin (where he would eventually relocate his company several years later) helped signal what would become a substantial change in that city's gaming industry—digital or otherwise. In 1983, paper games like Dungeons & Dragons were hugely popular in gamer circles around the world. Back then, computer hackers and programmers gathered for long nights of battle, and Austin was no different. But even then the attraction of video and computer games was beginning to eat away at their popularity. Warren Spector, a game designer who would ultimately play an influential role at Origin and in the wider game industry, saw this change happen firsthand.

Then a graduate student in Radio, Film, and Television at the University of Texas in Austin, Spector fell in with a group of writers—science-fiction writer Bruce Sterling, *Austin Chronicle* editor Nick Barbaro, and their friend Walter Simons. The members of the group were mostly unknowns at the time. Sterling was working on his first novel. Barbaro headed up the weekly newspaper in town. But they enjoyed each other's company. Once a week, they'd order food, gather at Sterling's central Austin home, and hunker down for an evening of gaming.

Sterling, the Game Master, would spend his week weaving an intricate tale, creating maps and long story arcs. When the players arrived, they'd gather in his living room, around the dining room table or floor, and Sterling would open up the game, describing the scene.

However, in Austin, as elsewhere, the game nights were starting to get cluttered with video games. The group, largely technophiles who wanted a first crack at emerging technology, would boot up computers, home consoles, and anything else that they could use to play games. Quite a collection of equipment appeared for these sessions—the Apple II, the Atari 2600 and 5200, Intellivision, ColecoVision, the RadioShack TRS-80. On any given night, small pockets of players would gravitate to living rooms around Austin, particularly when new games hit the market. That was what brought Spector to the doorstep of Bill Wallace, another Austin gamer. Wallace's living room was wired with a RadioShack TRS-80 and the Atari 5200, each of which were often surrounded by anxious gamers.

Spector knocked on the door one evening, expecting a quiet evening of playing out the latest games with his pal. Wallace ushered him into the living room. Inside, other visitors crowded around the television. Nobody batted an eye as the two came in and took their places. The lights were out, and the only illumination came from the 20-inch TV, in front of which Nancy Sterling, Bruce's wife, sat cross-legged with controller in hand. The screen was filled with black space with an octagonal series of bars running from the edges of the screen, forming a circle in the middle. It was the image of a cockpit.

She swiveled the joystick, and as the screen turned, the men sat rapt, an occasional "Oh!" cutting the silence. She was, for all intents and purposes, flying a spaceship. The game, Star Raiders, changed the way Spector looked at video games. "That was just a magic moment," he remembered later. "We were all surrounding this woman, like cavemen, watching this game. And these were Ph.D. candidates, writers, scholarly people, all staring at this game." For Spector, the moment was similar to Richard's first look at the maze game inside his original Apple computer. The first-person perspective offered something much different from their D&D adventures. This was less of a story and more of an adventure, in which the player had direct control of a far more visceral experience.

The game group may have sparked Spector's imagination, but it certainly wasn't paying his bills, and that was quickly becoming a problem. As fun as these nights were, gaming was just a hobby, something interesting to pass the time between his classes and the undergraduate communications course he taught while working on his master's degree. University budget cuts forced him to give up his teaching job in the summer of 1983, however, and that meant no money. Without a job, and with few prospects of finding a radio or television gig flexible enough to keep him in school, he hit up his gamer friends for work.

It was a good time to look, particularly in Austin. Richard's friend Steve Jackson had his paper gaming company up and running now and was producing successful—if not very profitable—games. Jackson gave Spector a job, but the student quickly realized it wasn't terribly secure. Even at the peak of paper gaming's run, Jackson's company was a bootstrap organization competing against larger gaming companies for the paper gaming market.

Every dollar counted in those days. "It was total chaos working there," Spector said. "If you spent $1000 badly, you were in serious trouble." One month, a dozen underpaid workers would huddle together, working into the wee hours of the night. The next month, double that number would be working, contractors brought in to help fill the orders for Car Wars and Illuminati, two popular paper games.

Paper gaming wouldn't go away; it would exist in smaller, dedicated pockets of players in the United States, even decades later. But change was in the air, and Spector got his own glimpse at just what this meant a few weeks after signing on with Jackson. Taking a break to stretch his legs, he wandered out of the barn where the company was run behind the house. He noticed a black Mitsubishi pull into Jackson's driveway. It was an odd sight, particularly here. Most of the workers drove rundown beaters, if they had cars at all, so he walked up closer to the house to get a better look. The door swung open, and Spector's mouth dropped as Richard Garriott stepped out of the car, dressed in black slacks and black shirt, with silver necklaces hanging across his chest and his signature single braid falling down his back. The visitor walked to the front door, knocked, and Jackson, his longtime SCA friend, ushered him in.

"That is a success," Spector thought, shaking his head as he walked back to the chaos of the barn.

That contrast was playing out across the industry. Jackson's company and Gygax's TSR (now without Gygax at the helm) would keep publishing games for years. But computer games' ease of play and visceral appeal increasingly contrasted with the hyper-detailed rules of paper games, and consumers' hearts and dollars began flowing towards Richard's style of storytelling. Exacerbating the trend, each generation of paper role-playing game seemed to complicate its rule system, driving out all but the most dedicated gamers.

Digital games were having their own difficulties, however. After years of stellar growth, the home console video game market faced almost total financial collapse in 1984, thanks to bad business decisions and an oversaturation of low-quality, arcade-style games released by companies more anxious to cash in on the latest fad than build a lasting business.

The Atari 2600, Intellivision, and Magnavox Odyssey, all gaming platforms that plugged into the humble living room TV, had built huge followings by parlaying popular arcade titles into home console games. Software companies had boomed on top of those platforms' success. By 1982, just a few years after the home-gaming gold rush got under way, Activision had grown from a small startup to pass Atari itself as the premier home-gaming development company, bringing in $150 million in sales. That same year, a second generation of consoles was being released with new technology that closed the gap between computers and consoles, including the Atari 5200, General Consumer Electronics Vectrex, and the ColecoVision.

Those machines couldn't save the industry from its own excesses, however. Poor business decisions at Atari—ordering 12 million units of a poorly written Pac-Man game at a time when only 10 million Atari machines existed, for example—helped send the company spiraling into financial chaos. By the end of 1984, Atari's sales figures were off 30 percent and its parent company, Time Warner, had sold off pieces of the company, hoping to recoup at least some of the losses it had incurred.

The computer gaming industry, though, was starting to take hold, thanks to the popularity of such systems as the Commodore Vic-20 in 1981 and the Commodore 64 in 1982. The latter would go on to reach 20 million households in less than a decade. They gained such popularity that users created public domain software programs that they traded freely through bulletin board systems. For many, the user-friendly system became more than a business machine; it was a newfound source of entertainment. Added to the increasing popularity of the Apple II, these systems buoyed the burgeoning computer games market. The companies that emerged to feed this market's hunger for software—California Pacific, Broderbund, Automated Simulations, Sierra On-Line, and Origin Systems, to name a few—resembled the chaotic structure of Steve Jackson Games through the late 1970s and early 1980s. But like Jackson, most of those programmers were more concerned with their medium than with money.

* * *

Origin Systems' Houston tenure would last less than a year. The company was eating up much of Robert Garriott's free time, and he started pushing for a change. He was spending three weeks each month in Austin while his wife, Marcy, whose career at Bell Labs was taking off, stayed in Massachusetts. She was on the fast track to the upper echelon of management, expecting a promotion in two years that would allow her to move anywhere she wanted in the country—but for now, she was stuck in New England.

Late in the fall, Robert arrived in Austin with a proposal. If the programmers would move to New England for three years, after Marcy's promotion came through, the group would decide on a permanent home. After a short debate, the ragtag crew decided to pack their bags and move to Massachusetts together. Within a few days, they were on the road.

"We were thrilled with the idea, because it would end my commute," Robert said later, recalling his wife's joy about the move. "This was going to end that separation."

Once again, Richard was pulling up roots; but this time, he was going to take everyone with him. He'd progressed far enough in the industry that he wouldn't be leaving his gaming buddies behind. Richard loaded up his car. The others did the same. Two volunteered to drive the rental trucks full of equipment. They'd head north, through Arkansas, head for New York, and turn east to Massachusetts. No problem. Pile everything into trucks, cars, anything with wheels and drive north, right? People did it all the time. It quickly turned into a white-knuckle adventure.

It took them only a day to hit snow. At first it was funny, trying to keep seven cars together through the rough weather. They saw it as an adventure—a few hours of real-life thrills, like the kind they wrote into their games. They had walkie-talkies that kept them in touch as they slid back and forth across icy roads, and they all managed to make it to the same hotel that night to laugh about beating their first winter storm. Trouble was, none of the drivers knew anything about snow. The Indiana-born Cat might have known a bit, but he'd trailed away from the company not long after arriving, and they were on their own.

"The move itself was a disaster," Richard remembers. "We had seven people, and seven vehicles. Some people were driving rental trucks, and this was in the dead of winter. By the time we got to New England, these southern Texas drivers, with rear wheel drive and no experience on snowy roads, had terrorized drivers across America."

The hard roads along with the drive was a portent of things to come. Richard's parents were hundreds of miles away, and he was responsible for a little community of seven people who'd followed him across the country because they believed in his vision. The complexities of real life were fast approaching, for Richard and for gamers at large.

✳ ✳ ✳

In Massachusetts, Richard, Chuck Bueche, and Mary Fenton rented a large, three-bedroom, two-story house that sat up against the woods. Richard, armed with a bank account filled with profits from his first three games, turned his home into a virtual funhouse. He grabbed his two roommates, climbed into his car, and hit the local shops, outfitting the house with $10,000 worth of electronics—stereos, televisions, and computers, enough gadgets to satisfy the team of programmers who'd braved the northern winter.

Monday came before they could unpack the equipment, so much of it sat still boxed up in Richard's room while they all sped off to work. The thick woods turned out to be the perfect hiding place for thieves, and the first-floor glass door, which faced the woods, proved to be little deterrent. When they arrived home that night, the trio found the place had been ransacked. Perturbed, but undaunted, Richard called the police, filed an insurance claim, and when the check came in, replaced every piece of equipment that had been stolen. Unbelievably, thieves broke into his house a second time, this time carting off everything on snowmobiles. A neighbor spotted the heist and phoned the police, who gave chase unsuccessfully on foot. The insurance company, now wary of Richard's penchant for losing everything in his house, decided that instead of issuing him a check, they would purchase everything for him.

The neighborhood at large wasn't much comfort. The Austin newcomers didn't seem to speak the same language as the staid, small-town locals. Richard and his band of merry programmers set off to the local bar as often as they could, figuring they'd fit in soon enough, but the locals seemed to distrust their Texan openness or apparently frivolous lifestyle. The southerners quickly found themselves isolated, forced to make their own fun.

This new world was proving much more complex than Richard had ever imagined. Adding insult to injury, it was bitterly cold. Within two months, the Origin Systems team was ready to leave Massachusetts, but they were stuck in this winter wasteland. There was only one escape: diving into developing games, the point of being there in the first place.

With nothing else to distract them, the business got off to a flying start. Ultima III was released that year as the first Origin title. It quickly became Richard's biggest hit to date, even if it was little more than an updated version of his previous hack-and-slash games. No matter, though. The first order for the game tallied 10,000 units, netting the company $350,000—enough to make them profitable all at once, if they could somehow manage to manufacture and distribute that many games. After all, Origin Systems still consisted of just eight people: five programmers, two customer service representatives, and Robert. If the company was going to survive, they were going to have to fill the orders themselves.

Every night, the group sat around Richard's house watching television and folding boxes. During work hours, they copied disks one at a time. After the games were boxed up, they used a shrink-wrap machine to finish the job. Once the games were shipped, the team of programmers took over the massive customer service job, handling phone calls from users—people getting stuck in the game to those with defective products.

Richard's mind was swirling with activity now as he set to work on his next game. He was thrilled to be on his own but miserable about his surroundings. His house had given him previously untapped freedom, but robbers had twice invaded it. His sense of uncertainty translated into the games, as well. The simple graphics of Akalabeth and the "Ultimas" still bore little resemblance to the images of the world of Britannia he painted in his head. He'd envisioned his games much more like the role-playing at the Society for Creative Anachronism—events where people would gather, socialize, duel, sing, and commune—and he still wasn't sure how to achieve that feeling.

"I wasn't sure if I knew what I was doing anymore," he remembered. "It was a time that I just sat back and tried to figure out who I was and what I was going to do next."

His internal journey, though, would again manifest itself as one part real-life role-playing and one part computer gaming. In August, three months before Halloween, he decided to transform his home into a haunted house. He enlisted the aid of Hillhouse and Bueche, along with other programmers who could spare their time at night, and they started planning. For Richard, this was all part of the culture of gaming. Whether he was sitting around a table creating fantasy worlds, sitting in front of his computer roaming around dungeons, or building real-life amusement parks, the principle remained constant: Build a world where people can play.

The team spent weeks strategizing. A project like this had to be done right. Richard laid out the internal floor plan for his house, first crafting the longest pathway possible through the house from entrance to exit, and then determining what they could do in each section. They carted in bales of hay and crafted mutilated bodies, monsters that could be controlled with electronics, and spooky sounds. Before long, the front lawn looked like a video game, and inside the house, every turn and closet was used as a launching pad for some concocted horror. A staircase that climbed three stories was turned into a winding tower with walls of cardboard painted like stones. As a group ascended the tower, Richard rigged it so that one member of his team could yank a rope and collapse the walls, resetting them for the next group.

He loved it all. It wasn't his life's work, but it was letting him stretch, letting him see people's reactions to the physical manifestations of his imagination. "It's not terribly exciting putting together a video game," he said later. "You release it and hopefully it sells well. What you rarely hear is positive feedback. It's mostly negative feedback. With the haunted house, you are standing there watching people going through. It's a real-life performance. It's like writing a song. You play it and they clap. In our business, you don't get that."

Over the years, as his vision of gaming became more focused, so did his haunted houses. He often spent six months and hundreds of thousands of dollars planning elaborate pranks. (After the development team moved back to Austin a few years later, and Richard moved into a huge castle in north Austin, his haunted houses took on legendary status. Like the townsfolk in *Willy Wonka and the Chocolate Factory*, Austinites clamored to get invited to his manor for a trip, in which every year, increasingly sophisticated fright devices made people literally pee in their pants.)

Richard's creation shocked his New England neighbors, particularly in its aftermath. Robert—even years later—winced when he talked about it, bowing and shaking his head. His house next door was the "neat" one, with a meticulously kept lawn. "You have to understand," Robert said, "Richard would roll his garbage can down to the curb, let it get emptied, and then leave it there until he needed it again. So, you can imagine what happened when he had the mess of a haunted house."

Never particularly good about cleaning up after his experiments, Richard had thrown himself back into his computer work after Halloween, leaving little time for pedestrian thoughts like picking up after himself. Soon afterward, when winter set in, trouble began. It was one thing to leave a garbage can on the curb for a week, or say, Christmas lights strung up until Valentine's Day, but it was quite another when the winter freeze came in and turned the hay bales into blocks of ice. Even that wouldn't have drawn as many raised eyebrows from neighbors if these ice bales hadn't still had remarkably realistic-looking decayed body parts sticking out of them at disturbing angles. As the snow came, Richard's yard became a virtual graveyard for monster and human body parts, with heads and bloody arms peeking out above the snow.

Robert and his wife were mortified. But Richard didn't care, and he even took a little pleasure at the disgust of his neighbors. He wasn't here to make friends, after all. His goal was to create a game where people could come together, where new communities would form. Sometimes, that was messy.

* * *

Now that he and Robert were handling their own distribution, the brothers were also handling customer feedback, which meant they were discovering just how completely Richard's games had struck a nerve with players around the country. For the first time, Richard heard from thousands of people playing his games. Fan mail, as well as hate mail, was coming directly to him. Maybe it had come to the publishers before and had simply never been forwarded—he didn't know. "I'd had very little feedback for the first two games I'd done, but Ultima III was different because we'd basically published that out of our garage," Richard said later. "When I started getting mail, everyone was telling me they were having a great time playing my games, and I began to see people reading things into my games that were simply statistical anomalies in the programming. They thought I was putting messages into the game."

He heard from more than just fans. One person accused him, on the basis of the red demon with fiery wings spread across the cover of the game, of being "The Satanic perverter of America's youth." He was in good company; conservative Christian groups of the time were also attacking Dungeons & Dragons, accusing that game of encouraging worship of the occult, violent behavior, and suicides.

The mail started Richard thinking. If people were reading this much into his games without him actually putting messages there, the games were clearly vehicles for provoking thought. Maybe he should use that power. He didn't want to be dogmatic about any particular message, but he was developing a more complex vision of the universe, and maybe it was time to put that into the games.

The success of his early games had all been basically drawn from the thoughts and experiences of his high school years, living at home with his parents. Even when he'd been away at college, he'd come home frequently and had done much of the work at his parents' house. The first Ultima trilogy had essentially been expansions of the world of Akalabeth, itself the culmination of the simple D&D games that he'd worked on all the way through high school. Now the realities of life—the bills, break-ins, disappointments, haunted houses, even the office rubber band fights—were coalescing for him into a vision of an ambiguous world, where actions had real consequences. Until this time, most games had allowed their protagonists to engage in any actions they wanted with little consequence to themselves or the wider game world beyond the obvious life and death, winning and losing. Maybe a "hero" should be held to higher standards. The most evil characters in the games usually wanted nothing more than a little old-fashioned world domination. By contrast, the players came into the world, killed virtually everything they saw, stole money from anyone or anything that had it, and walked off with smiles on their faces. Who was really the evil one, after all?

He decided to introduce a system of ethics and morals into his game world. He wasn't interested in teaching any specific lesson; instead, his next game would be about making people think about the consequences of their actions. He locked himself away with books of literature, poetry, philosophical concepts, and a white board, bound and determined to break life down into its fundamental principles. It was very much a programmer's approach to moral philosophy. "I starting writing down all the virtues and vices I could think of, throwing them on a white board," he said later. "Many of them were overlapping. But what I started to see was that all the virtues and vices were derivatives of truth, love, and courage, just like the characters in *The Wizard of Oz*."

The game would incorporate eight tests that covered the virtues of honesty, compassion, values, justice, sacrifice, honor, spirituality, and humility throughout the adventure, although none of this would be immediately obvious to the player. Gamers would visit eight cities, each representing some combination of the virtues. In each place, they would have two missions: one quest they'd been told about, and one test they didn't know about. Players who controlled the Avatar—the main character—and failed the moral components, found themselves unable to complete the game as effectively as if they had acted in line with the land's system of virtues. It was the computer-game version of the question, "If you found a million dollars, would you turn the money in?"

Throughout the game, Richard threw in little hints that the world no longer accepted the simple hack-and-slash mentality without consequences. For example, outside one city, a blind merchant repeatedly offered characters items that they needed for successive elements of their quest. When players purchased an item, the merchant could tell whether she was being paid enough money. If only one coin rattled in her tin cup, she'd make a comment that the player was being a bit cheap. If the player threw in two, she'd say nothing, even though it wasn't really enough. Many players quickly realized this and dropped in as little money as they could, saving their funds to buy more powerful weapons or magic items.

Unbeknownst to them, the old merchant was remembering their avarice. No simple two-dimensional computer monster, she had a long memory and a temper to match. Near the end of the game, the player turned out to need the help of the blind woman again. Approaching her with little inkling of trouble, the players asked for her assistance. If they'd been cheapskates throughout the game, she had only bitter words for them. It was too late to apologize. If they'd paid her enough throughout, she helped graciously.

Fundamentally, Richard wanted the worlds to engross, to suck in players the same way *Lord of the Rings* was for him an absolutely believable world. It wasn't that it had to be like the real world; but the world nevertheless had to be in certain elements: The characters had to be believable, or at least exhibit some rudimentary sense of motivation. Plots and stories could be simple—most epics were—but they had to sweep up the player with a sense of urgency. He was seeing that the more the non-player characters built into the world—not simply by dying or giving up cash, but with complex consequences recognizable from real life—the more compelling the world would be.

Richard was taking a gigantic risk with his new game. The fate of the company rode on his shoulders. If Ultima IV failed, Origin Systems would likely hit the skids, putting them all out of work, thousands of miles from home. During the programming, his stomach would cramp up, forcing him to lie down, trying to calm his nerves. "I thought people might completely reject this game because some folks play just to kill, kill, kill," he said later. "To succeed in this game, you had to radically change the way you'd ever played a game before."

For the first time, Richard was getting a taste of the business side of video games he'd rejected before, and he didn't like it. He sometimes longed for a time when he wouldn't have to worry about taking responsibility for the young company.

He was in for a welcome surprise, however. His instincts about how to make the world more compelling proved accurate. The game, released in 1985, was his first to top the best-sellers list, selling more than 200,000 copies—a considerable sum for a computer game of the time.

Robert Gregg, a longtime Ultima fan who was then in his freshman year studying computer science at Carnegie Mellon, remembers the game as a major leap forward in the industry. In school, he'd been writing little dungeon crawl adventures like Ultima II himself, but the new game showed that the stakes were now higher.

"You had to be able to actually write, not just code," Gregg remembered later. "When the scripting and interaction got to the level that you actually stopped and thought about the moral implications of what you were doing, computer games started to leave the realm of games that involved little more than tapping buttons and moving characters and actually became art. The game was commenting on society, and on the observer himself, just like other forms of art. That was the most exciting part to me—watching the emergence of a new form of art, coming right off the computer."

✳ ✳ ✳

By 1987, it was time to decide where Richard's company would go. The team members had fulfilled their promise to stay in New England, and now it was time to figure out what would be next. The original team assumed that would be back to Austin, then a thriving, hip, *warm* town. Robert had another trick up his sleeve, though. Richard and his group of programmers thought they would be the only ones voting on the move, but by now, the company had moved offices, relocating to a larger office space in New Hampshire, and hired 40 employees. Most of the newcomers were local residents hired by Robert. Any vote that included the whole employee base was likely to result in a resounding defeat for the programming team. The prospect incensed Bueche so much that he quit the company, packed his belongings, and moved back to Austin.

The brothers fought constantly over the issue, with Richard threatening to quit the company if he wasn't allowed to move back to Texas. Arguments spilled out of closed-door meetings and into Origin's hallways. On several occasions, Richard insisted he'd start his own game company and leave Robert high and dry in New Hampshire without any games to publish. Tension around the office was thick as San Francisco fog. It got so bad that the brothers brought in their parents to mediate. Richard eventually got his way, moving game development operations back to Austin, while the manufacturing, publishing, and marketing teams stayed in New England.

In Austin, the team took up in a small office, with 15 desks along one lone hallway. Richard quickly began reassembling a team. It was difficult. Few video game companies were located within 500 miles of Austin, and certainly none had the star power of Richard Garriott. This was a paper gaming town, but many of those gamers were growing restless. Denis Loubet, the artist who had helped with the box art on the original Ultima, jumped at the chance to join Richard, and left his job at Steve Jackson Games. Talented new programmers, including Chris Roberts, creator of the popular Wing Commander series, also signed on.

"Chris would sit down in a room, and he would describe from beginning to end, in every detail, a game that he'd be working on, and I'd go 'jeez, why couldn't I think of that,'" Richard said later. "I'm a researcher. I go through massive amounts of data and pull out little pieces of inspiration. I consider that an incredible amount of labor, but when I finish, I can tell you everything about my world. Chris can just sit down in a room and do that off the top of his head."

Slowly, the New Hampshire team started transferring down to Austin, and by 1988, when Ultima V was released, Robert moved the remaining operations to Austin. Ultima V continued the company's success, with Richard exploring what happens when dogmatic leaders use positive virtues as a force of social engineering. In the game, Lord British has been captured by the evil Shadowlords. His replacement, Lord Blackthorne, has turned the religious virtues into law, punishing anyone who doesn't follow the strict code of behavior. The player, taking on the role of the Avatar, must rescue Lord British and restore order to the kingdom.

That same year, Warren Spector, now in Lake Geneva and working for TSR, the company in charge of the D&D franchise, packed up his office and came home to work for Richard at Origin. "He knew we were changing the gaming world, and that we weren't making games for kids," Spector said. "This was like a family, and he was a visionary. He saw what the games could be."

They worked hard, but the atmosphere was fun, at least in these early days. They played laser tag in the hallways after nightfall and went on spontaneous rock-climbing trips in the middle of the day. If every company was in some respect a reflection of its founder's personality, Origin was certainly a reflection of Richard Garriott. "He was a lightning rod for other guys that wanted to be just like him," remembered Broderbund founder Carlston, whose own company was more sober-minded. "It was a 24/7 kind of lifestyle thing. As long as you were dealing with a whole bunch of young singles, it was more important how you played, and that you lived and worked and played all in one place."

By this time Richard and his team were hard at work on Ultima VI, the last in the Avatar series, which would complete the second trilogy of games by taking the lessons from versions IV and V and flipping them on their head. In the final installment, the Avatar began the game tied down upon an altar surrounded by gargoyles, with a sword raised over his body. It appeared as though the valiant warrior would be killed. The player escaped and then faced the task of figuring out why anyone would want to kill such a righteous person. The player, convinced the monsters were evil, was drawn into battles with the demons who tried to kill him. Eventually, the truth came out. The actions the Avatar had taken to defeat his opponents in the previous games had caused earthquakes and devastation in the monsters' subterranean home world. Their religious texts, found in the course of the game, prophesized the coming of an outworlder that would destroy their race, and they—quite naturally, it turned out—had done their best to prevent their version of Armageddon. The player found as he played that he had become something like an antichrist instead of a hero, and he faced the task of saving the creatures' world without also destroying his.

The gritty game forced players to evaluate the consequences of their actions on other cultures, a theme Richard was only then beginning to explore. In fact, much of his life to this point had been about learning how to assimilate into new cultures—whether creating gaming nights at his house, fencing in medieval garb in the SCA, or embarking on a five-year journey in New England. His games reflected that thinking as well, increasingly forcing his characters and players into moral dilemmas without disclosing the tests until it was too late.

He was tinkering with the idea of pitting players against each other, too, something that would potentially make players think even more about their actions. For years, he'd linked computers together in Origin's makeshift offices, first in Massachusetts, then in New Hampshire, and now in Austin. Networking, along with some clever coding, allowed players to go through Ultima adventures together, although the computers back then weren't powerful enough to make joint adventures very enjoyable. It took 30 seconds for the graphics to be redrawn on the computer screen, for example. The Internet games Richard would ultimately create would help spark global culture clashes—but for now, he had to focus on the immediate problems at hand.

As they worked on Ultima VI and other games, the Origin programming teams continued to blaze away on code for the Apple II, still their primary focus, even this deep into that machine's decline. They were also creating versions of their products for the Macintosh, Atari, Amiga, and the Commodore 64. Richard toyed with the idea of porting the game over to the IBM PC, but after testing the machine, he decided to ignore the cumbersome device. Surely nobody would waste their time with such a clunky, slow computer, he thought.

"We looked at the IBM PC and thought it was a piece of garbage," Richard remembered later. "We had six games in development at that time, and we decided to go with the Apple and then convert the games to other systems. But we were a small company, and by now Electronic Arts and other large corporations were getting really big. They could afford to miscalculate a platform because their other sales would make up for it. We were small, and the industry wasn't about being small anymore."

Before the game was finished, it was clear that the company had miscalculated. Money was getting short. The company was overextended, and it was increasingly apparent that the bet against the IBM had been the wrong way to go. For the first time in his life, Richard could sense failure, and it nearly incapacitated him. He and Robert huddled together to discuss the finances on a daily basis, and Richard spent many of the meetings curled up in Robert's office, guts wrenching from stress.

They had one chance to save the company. Robert pooled together all the resources he could. They had $1 million in credit from the bank. Richard had $500,000, but he'd just bought a house, his castle in north Austin, and Robert had some money put away. All told, they had enough money to last about a year, which would get them within 30 days of the release of Ultima VI, the last and most controversial game in the Avatar trilogy. If the game tanked, or worse yet, if any delay cropped up in the publishing cycle, Origin Systems and its 80 employees would be dead broke—and Richard and Robert would be in the hole for $1 million.

"We sat down and had a big strategy meeting, and we calculated our sales and added up everything we had in the bank—ten years' worth of savings," Richard said, wincing. "I was paying off a house, so I was going to lose my house if this didn't work. We chewed our nails. We had financial meetings every day. My stomach was in constant pain, and I'd just curl up in the corner."

Despite the looming financial crisis, the game came out on time. Like the previous Ultimas, it wowed the gaming public and gave the brothers a reprieve. Still, this wasn't an environment either could stand. They needed some insurance that if one game failed, they would have two others ready that would pick up the slack. Only three possible scenarios could help them accomplish this: find venture capitalists who would invest money in exchange for sizable control of the operations; purchase smaller companies to diversify their game business; or sell the company to a large corporation.

The first option was quickly dismissed. The venture money would only be a stopgap. Eventually, the money would run out and they'd be in the same position. Plus, neither could imagine willingly turning over a large part of the business they'd built themselves. The second option felt more palatable, since it would leave them in charge of Origin. For two years, they looked around, targeting businesses, doing economic analyses, and meeting with developers, and they eventually realized that adding more people to the fold would simply add more pressure to the bottom line. Richard's stomach couldn't take that.

Instead, he threw himself into developing Ultima VII, the first game he'd create for the newly dominant PC. Whatever their decision, Richard knew that the company still needed him to crank out a new Ultima. The latest game had a simple concept—an evil character called the Guardian was trying to take over Britannia by establishing a new religion called the Fellowship (an homage to Tolkien's first *Ring* book, *Fellowship of the Ring*), and the Avatar had to expose the group. The game, though, would be anything but simple. Instead of building one large, complex game, he broke it into separate parts. After releasing The Black Gate in mid-1992, Origin Systems released an additional game called Forge of Virtue, which built upon the Ultima VII story.

Meanwhile, Robert was courting larger game companies. Some of these were making buyout offers that would have made the brothers millionaires ten times over, but they were reluctant. Ever since Richard's experiences with California Pacific and Sierra On-Line, they'd been skeptical of outside help. Finally, begrudgingly, they decided to sell their company to Electronic Arts, one of the premier gaming companies in the world in 1992. The company had originally been built on the premise that its programmers would become stars, and even if that idea had fallen somewhat by the wayside, Richard hoped he'd have the freedom he needed to finish out his third and final set of his planned Ultima trilogy of trilogies. Electronic Arts was big enough that it wouldn't have to depend on Richard to pump out his games on a hard deadline to stay afloat, which was another advantage.

As it turned out, EA didn't really have much interest in Ultima at all. The company would release the third and fourth Ultima VII games, Serpent Isle and Silver Seed, in 1993, but the company's CEO, Larry Probst, was more interested in Roberts's Wing Commander series. The Ultima series, for all its intense following, was already being pushed out of the spotlight by action-oriented console-style games and new genres of play that reduced or removed the role of the storyteller. Meanwhile, Richard would spend the next five years struggling to integrate his company with Electronic Arts, constantly fighting with executives whose eyes were squarely focused on the bottom line instead of the creative goals. He hated it.

Richard sank into depression. He was spending too much of his time playing corporate politics and not enough time developing games. That gave other developers the opportunity to reach out to new gamers—people who hadn't been much interested in computer or console games. Richard began to fade into the margins of gaming culture, much like the paper gamers he had helped displace just a few years before.

* ※ *

The shift to other game genres had been building slowly for several years. The resurgence of the home console, led by Nintendo and Sega, had helped raise a new generation of kids more attuned to games like Super Mario Brothers, which—though a complex graphical world—were more action-oriented than Richard's role-playing games. Fighting and shooting games were gaining prominence in the late 1980s and early 1990s, ratcheting up the action quotient even more. Richard's games appealed to players older than Nintendo's teen-oriented games, but console company Sega was also going after an older gaming market, offering games with edgy, often violent themes.

The computer game market was changing even more, as the industry's momentum swung unambiguously to the IBM PC and its clones, and the demographic of computer owners expanded. There, too, faster and bloodier games were coming to the forefront. But stranger games were vying for the computer gamers' attention as well. Perhaps the weirdest success was the 1989 game SimCity, created by a thoughtful independent designer named Will Wright. The game was a simulation of urban policy planning that allowed players to control the speed and rules of a city's development, tax policy, immigration, and other components of growth, and then let the city grow organically by those rules. As much or more than Richard had ever been able to do, Wright helped expand the gaming market to a demographic of professionals and casual players who had never been interested in games before.

Wright would turn out to be one of the industry's leading figures for more than a decade, lending a consistently quirky intellectual cast to a business increasingly interested in flash and action. He grew up in Louisiana and Georgia, with a chemical engineer father who encouraged him in scientific projects. The science wasn't his immediate concern, however. "Mostly I built a lot of models," he said later. "Then I blew them up, and built more."

He moved from simple constructions to radio-controlled models, found himself interested in the electronics behind them, and finally began developing a fascination with robotics that never waned. His first computer, an Apple II bought when he was 20 years old, was purchased primarily to connect to the robots he was building. Writing the software that would power robot brains was like model-making taken to an extreme, he found.

He bounced around a few colleges after he finished high school. He took a few classes at Louisiana Tech and Louisiana State University, and then he moved to New York to go to the New School there. None of it inspired him, and when he met the sister of a good friend who lived in California, he decided to move West and be a full-time programmer.

By 1982, however, thousands of programmers had the drop on him, with reputations and experience programming for the Apple. He decided to buy one of the new Commodore 64 machines and learn it instead. "I thought if I was going to stand out, I'd do better to go to a new platform," he said later. The decision paid off. After spending some time learning the Commodore's ropes, he wrote a shoot-'em-up game called Raid on Bungeling Bay, in which the player guided a simple helicopter around a set of islands, bombing factories and towns and whatever else got in the way. Software publisher Broderbund picked it up and published it in 1984, and Wright was on his way to a comfortable place in the industry.

A funny thing happened along the way to success. Wright found himself obsessed by the islands he was coding, building models of little factories and towns that were far more detailed than such a simple game needed. He built another software program to help him design the islands, and he had far more fun using this tool than he did building the actual game. When he'd shipped Bungeling Bay off to Broderbund, he kept working on this island-building tool, seeing how complex he could make the little worlds.

His interest was piqued further after he picked up a book by Jay Forrester, an electrical engineer who had switched careers in the mid-1950s to study the interactions of social groups, elements of the environment, and other complex, seemingly unrelated subjects. Forrester had applied many of the lessons he'd learned as an engineer to these subjects, working out theories that explained how elements of different systems interacted with and changed each other. He'd called the resulting field of study "system dynamics," and he had applied his theories to urban studies, environmental science, and myriad other subjects.

Wright had an epiphany, and began thinking about how he could integrate Forrester's theories into a new game. He pushed the island-building tool much farther than it had originally been intended to go, trying to make a city with elements that interacted with each other in the sense that Forrester had spoken of, a "simulation that was fighting back, or fighting entropy," he said later. Players would take the role of mayor, controlling such features as development policy, road-laying, zoning, and taxation. The decisions a player made would affect the history and growth of the city, leading to population booms and busts, economic surges or recessions, and other signs of a healthy (or unhealthy) community.

It didn't really seem like a game to him at first, but it was a fascinating project. "At first, the audience was just me," he said. "I would get to have a model railroad set that came to life." He had a working version by mid-1985 and showed it to people at Broderbund. They liked it, but they didn't really see how it would be a game. Plenty of simulation games had been written before—Microsoft's Flight Simulator, released back in 1982, was still one of the best-known computer games. But those were still action games. Players were in the cockpit of an airplane, or a car, or even controlling a simple lunar lander as it careened toward success or death. Urban policy planning just didn't sound like it would appeal to an audience of adventure seekers.

Wright put the game on the shelf and moved to other projects. In 1986, his first daughter was born, and he spent a year focusing on her. But the next year, he met another software developer named Jeff Braun, got to talking about the game at a pizza party, and wound up showing Braun the prototype, watching as Braun's eyes lit up. "He was the only person who saw what it could be," Wright remembered later. "Even I just thought it would be a cute strategy game for architects."

The pair decided to start their own company. Braun had some money from the sale of his own software company, while Wright had a little money from the publication of his first game, and with a few other friends they created Maxis. With a little more work, Wright transformed his project into a PC game. The pair talked Broderbund into copublishing the game, and finally in 1989, four years after Wright had finished the first version, it hit the shelves.

But it hit an initial snag, too. People didn't know what to do with the game. Wright and Braun were betting on a new demographic of PC owners who were increasingly buying the machines to use for work, not just as a novelty or expensive game-playing device. It took a little while for news of the game to filter into this more open-minded demographic, but when it did, aided by a few prominent media articles, sales exploded.

So did a few things they didn't expect. This was 1990 and 1991, before there was much of a mainstream online world. Gaming communities were scattered, mostly on university networks, bulletin board systems, and the early online services like America Online and CompuServe. It didn't take long before they saw a SimCity group spring up on America Online. People there talked strategies, talked urban theory, and actually swapped cities, posting their files online so other people could download them.

All of this seemed to be evidence that Richard's time might be passing. The resurgence of the home console seemed to demonstrate that many gamers were more interested in the fast, furious action of arcade-style games than in the slower-paced role-playing worlds. The rise of SimCity indicated that others seemed to want control over their virtual worlds the way Wright had offered it to them. Finally, the unexpected SimCity online phenomenon seemed to show that real potential lay in online communities forming, even without the explicit encouragement of developers.

Three hours north of Austin, in a sprawling suburb of Dallas, two men were about to give people all of those things—and so much more.

Part II

Networked Gaming Age

5

Log On, Shoot Down

Id Software "biz guy" Jay Wilbur sat in front of his computer in Mesquite, Texas, cursing to himself. He was in an endless line, as surely as if he'd been waiting at the post office, and this line wasn't moving. There were dozens, maybe hundreds, probably even thousands of people virtually piled in front of him—a genuine Internet traffic jam. Here was the rub: They were all waiting to get their hands on the computer program he had on his machine, and they weren't leaving until he could upload it to the University of Wisconsin's servers, and he couldn't upload it until some of them logged off.

They were at an impasse. Much of that was Wilbur's own fault. For months, his company had been teasing the game community with tantalizing promises about its new game, Doom. Today, December 10, 1993, was D-Day. Eager fans had bought entirely into the hype. They were convinced this was going to be the biggest thing ever to hit PC gaming circles. The game would put the player in the role of a space marine battling wave after wave of demons released from Hell, armed with a massive array of machine guns, chainsaws, and the ever-popular BFG (Big F***ing Gun). The first-person perspective, stunning visuals, 3D mazes, and lightning-fast action had started a buzz on the Net that had been growing ever since the company had announced it with a press release almost a year before, on New Year's Day.

"Stationed at a scientific research facility, your days are filled with tedium and paperwork," that missive from the company had read. "Today is a bit different. Wave after wave of demonic creatures are spreading through the base, killing or possessing everyone in sight. As you stand knee-deep in the dead, your duty seems clear—you must eradicate the enemy and find out where they're coming from.... See your friends bite it! Cause your friends to bite it! Bite it yourself! And if you won't bite it, there are plenty of demonic denizens to bite it for you!"

No question, Doom sounded like it would top anything that had come before. Few could have predicted just how influential it would also prove to be on game culture; but right now, Wilbur needed to get the game loaded onto a server where people could download it. He'd tried logging onto the FTP site where it was to be released late in the afternoon, and again as evening turned into night, but he was stuck on the outside. He was getting anxious and angry. He contacted the administrator at the university where the powerful server was—in theory—ready and waiting for the files. "I can't get in," he said. "The FTP is full."

The administrator checked the server. "OK, I just added a slot, and you should be able to get in."

In the time it took Wilbur to read the message, somebody slipped on before him. This logjam had no end in sight. "No good," he reported.

The Wisconsin student tapped a few commands into his computer, on the other end of the line. "Try again," he said. "I just added 10 more slots."

Rolling his eyes, Wilbur tried again. Still no luck. The would-be Doom players were *fast*. "This isn't working," he said. "You've got to clear the way."

Sitting in front of their computers around the country, fans were starting to grumble. On Usenet newsgroups dedicated to PC gaming, people were posting angry notes, losing faith that id would deliver that day as promised. Finally one person said they'd managed to log onto the site and had seen a message: "Sorry, the incoming directory is full, no one can upload any files until it's clear." A collective digital groan went up from the people waiting online. Was the game never going to appear?

Enough fans got the message, however. They realized some of them had to get out of line and unclog the connection, or they'd never get the game. Slowly—painfully slowly—connections began to drop off and Wilbur was able to start uploading the file. That only served to feed the frenzy. As soon as parts of the game were available, people started downloading the file before Wilbur was finished uploading it. It was a digital riot, as anxious gamers started grabbing and pulling at the files as quickly as they could. The attention slowed file transfers to a crawl. Ready to throw his computer out the window, Wilbur called the administrator back, frustrated.

"OK, OK, I know what to do," the administrator said. With a few simple keystrokes, he effectively barricaded the doors of the digital room, locking out everyone who was trying to log on from outside the university. The move angered many who had been waiting all day long, but it created the necessary breathing room. Wilbur's upload finally sped up, downloads began in earnest, and the age of Doom (several hours behind schedule) had come at last.

The game would explode like a rocket shell in the collective consciousness of PC gamers, changing the way that people thought about the computer as a gaming platform, and inspiring whole industries of imitators. The first-person perspective captured the imagination of gamers everywhere, just as it had for Richard Garriott when he'd peeled open the Apple II box years before and watched the Escape maze appear before his eyes. The "shooter," as Doom clones would come to be called, essentially took the kill-fast-or-die concept of Space Invaders and blew it up into a fully realized 3D world defined by its demonic creatures and blood-spattered walls.

Beyond these basic game mechanics, it did more than any other single title to usher in an era of networked games and gamers. With Doom, and even more so with id's later games, the digital playing field moved from the machine underneath a player's fingers into cyberspace itself, as players increasingly learned to battle each other online. Communities coalesced around the game and its successors, fed by id's repeated decisions to help players modify and extend the games with almost unprecedented ease.

In a way, id was simply in the right place at the right time, creating a popular network-capable game at precisely the moment in technological history when home computers were joining the networked universe in droves. Other companies were releasing networked games, but id's developers provided a unique mix of game-writing panache, the ability to see and take advantage of trends just a step ahead of their rivals, and a corporate ideology that valued giving players as much power over the gaming technology as possible. The combination of all these laid the infrastructure for passionate networked gaming communities on a scale that had never been seen before.

The core figures behind id's early years, the ebullient John Romero and the taciturn, ultra-focused John Carmack, were a *yin* and *yang* of programming. Each was a visionary in his own way: Romero was a talented programmer and game designer who believed in games and gaming with a missionary fervor. He communicated that infectious optimism to his company and the world. Carmack wasn't much on small talk, but he became one of the recognized titans of game programming, to the point where even technology industry lions such as Apple's Steve Jobs and Microsoft's Bill Gates would seek his blessing for their products.

Like Richard, each had grown up with a love of programming in general and games in particular. They were a few years younger than Richard but they had still cut their teeth on the Apple II computer. Both counted Richard's Ultima series as one of their biggest early influences—Romero actually went to work at Origin Systems as his first real job in the computer industry, and the first games that Carmack sold to hobbyist magazines in the late 1980s were deeply influenced by the Ultima worlds. Each programmer had a much more unsettled adolescence than Richard; whether that contributed to the far darker worlds they created is hard to say, but it's certain that each of them found programming to be a refuge from unhappiness elsewhere in their lives.

Romero grew up in the small California foothill town of Rocklin. His parents divorced when he was young, and his mother remarried an engineer who helped encourage his interest in programming. He was mostly interested in games, however—first arcade games, and then the mainframe games like Adventure that he found at the local community college in 1979, and finally in writing games for his own Apple II. He moved to England for high school, returning afterward to bounce unhappily back and forth between his separated parents' homes, looking for direction. He was selling his games to hobbyist magazines like *Nibble* and *UpTime*, but wound up working at Burger King and Taco Bell to make ends meet before finally screwing up the courage to go to San Francisco's AppleFest computer trade show in 1987 to look for a real job.

Wilbur, at that time an editor for *UpTime*, remembers the young Romero as one of his top freelancers, even at the age of 18. "He was very smart, a brilliant young man," Wilbur said. "He was very energetic, very happy, very enthusiastic. He just exuded a desire to do nothing in life but write games on the Apple."

The San Francisco trade show turned out to be Romero's first big break. He showed employees at the Origin Systems booth one of the games he'd written, and they were impressed. A few months of persistent calling finally got him an interview at Richard's company, in the New Hampshire office, for a job programming the Commodore 64 rather than his beloved Apple. It didn't matter. "I had never used one, but I told them I was completely confident that I could learn the entire computer in a month," Romero said later. "I said, 'OK, dude, I'll do it. Anything, I just have to get in there.'"

He got the job, impressing the programmers that interviewed him, and moved to New Hampshire. He met Robert Garriott and a host of others he already knew by name and reputation. He watched the newest Ultima being play tested. He wandered around the Origin shipping offices, looking at the stacks of game trinkets, colorful boxes packed full with some of his favorite games, and Richard's cloth maps. For a young hacker who'd been working at burger joints not long before, this was the promised land.

Even then, Romero was restless and ambitious. He lasted at Origin six months. His supervisor quit to form a little startup nearby in New Hampshire and asked Romero to join him. After some soul-searching, he agreed to go. That job, too, lasted just a few months before the startup's Apple-based contracts were canceled, a casualty of the growing market perception that the Apple II was a platform past its prime. In 1988, finally Romero followed his old friend Wilbur to Louisiana, where both were hired by SoftDisk, a company that published monthly discs full of software for Apple and PC owners. After a year there learning how to program for the PC, churning out what he thought were boring utility programs, Romero told SoftDisk's owner that he wanted to start writing games again, or he'd leave. The company's owner agreed to start a new division for him, and said he could look for help.

* * *

Two states away in Kansas City, Missouri, barely making ends meet, a kid named John Carmack was slowly building the skills that would make him one of the weird geniuses of the gaming industry.

Carmack was, and still is, Romero's opposite. A slight, blond man with a baby face and a perpetually distracted gaze, he's as intensely private as Romero is public. He speaks with a verbal tic, a slight gulp between phrases and sentences, and his words flow with the unemotional evenness of code itself. He's as focused as any human being alive, surely; his work days are legendary, and his co-workers have joked that he rarely actually speaks to them. The collaboration between him and Romero would prove explosively productive in its early years; the tensions between their styles and visions would later tear the relationship apart.

In 1989, Carmack was an unknown with few connections to the gaming world. He'd graduated from high school and taken a year of exclusively computer classes at the University of Missouri, Kansas City, but he had found little reason to continue. "All through high school and when I went to college it was really clear that I was the big programmer around," Carmack said later. "I never got the sense that any of my professors was a hot programmer in any way. Obviously they knew some things, but in some cases it was really frustrating. I didn't think they were even on the right track in how you should go about things." Years later he would realize that he could have gotten more out of the college environment, he said, but as a teenager, he simply didn't have the patience to wait.

Carmack had shared elements of Romero's unstable early family life, each of them a stark contrast to Richard's more utopian childhood. Carmack's parents divorced early in his life, and he split his time between his parents' houses. He was a smart kid, taking all the gifted classes available at school, but he had little use for others' advice. His disregard for boundaries or conventional paths brought him quick proficiency in almost anything technical. In other realms, the anti-authoritarian streak in him ran in riskier ways—at the age of 13, he was arrested for breaking into a local school, and he subsequently spent a year in a juvenile reform home.

He knew from an early age that he was a programmer. By the sixth grade he was already writing games. Unlike Garriott or Romero, Carmack wasn't focused entirely on games, but he found they served as vehicles to give him the technical challenges he craved. At his mother's house, he had a Commodore Vic-20 computer that he quickly mastered, but its limitations soon proved maddening. He begged his mother to buy him an Apple II like the one at his high school. At the time of the divorce, his parents had created a college fund for him, and he wanted to raid it to buy the computer, but his mother didn't take his game writing seriously and refused to give in to her son. The conflict worsened the relationship between them that would stay rocky well into his adult years, until he'd proven that game writing could be a serious and very profitable business. "When I was writing computer games, it was *playing* to her, and she didn't take it seriously," he said. "It wasn't until I drove up to the house in a Ferrari that I proved my point."

Stuck with the Commodore at home, he used it as any hacker of the age would, tapping into pirate bulletin board systems and other people's networks. He dabbled in phone phreaking, an activity that involved mapping the secrets of public telephone networks and manipulating them in ways only technicians were supposed to be able to do. He continued to learn the ins and outs of the Apple II, and eventually bought himself a stolen machine, procured cheaply from one of his reform school friends.

By the time he dropped out of college, however, he had his tool of choice. Carmack's grandfather left him about $1500 when he passed away, enough to buy an Apple IIgs. His mother mocked his decision, saying it was stupid to buy a computer when he couldn't even afford a printer. He didn't care. He threw himself into writing his own games. He studied Richard's Ultima games in particular, digging as deeply into the code as the programs would let him, creating his own similar titles. He sold a few of these to some of the same hobbyist programming magazines that Romero had started with. One of them found their way to Wilbur, Romero's mentor who was now working with freelancers at SoftDisk.

Wilbur later remembered the first Carmack game he saw as similar to Garriott's Ultimas—a top-down, swords-and-sorcery role-playing game. It was not wholly original in concept, but it went into incredible detail. Wilbur loved it, but it was far too big for SoftDisk to publish. He asked Carmack if there was anything else he wanted to do, and Carmack mentioned an idea for a 3D tennis game. Wilbur didn't really see how that could be fun to play—it would be a vector line-drawing game, the kind of game a programmer developing a sports game would find interesting, not something that sports fans would necessarily enjoy. Regardless, Carmack went to work and again came up with a surprise.

"I was skeptical," Wilbur said later. "I couldn't really close my eyes and visualize how this would be fun. But it kicked ass. All the physics were right. It was awesome."

Carmack started writing games regularly for SoftDisk. It was quickly clear that this wasn't enough. He was barely bringing in enough money to survive. He didn't ask much—he told his mother that all he needed was enough money for pizza and books, but he wasn't even able to pay rent without borrowing cash occasionally from friends and family. Finally, Carmack decided to make the leap so many others had. It was clear that the PC was beginning to dominate the market, despite being maligned by Apple lovers for its poor graphics, nonexistent audio support, and cumbersome operating system. Any programmer with ambition to support himself had better learn the machine.

"I was programming really fast, and learning a lot, but when I realized that I was just barely scraping by as far as the money I could bring in from that, I decided to make a little bit more money by picking up the IBM PC," he remembered. "What I did was rent a PC for a month and converted some of my Apple programs over to the IBM, and sold them to the other branch of SoftDisk. Evidently that really, really impressed a bunch of the people there, that I could just go rent a PC and learn a whole new architecture. At that point they started pressuring me to go down and interview."

He held off for months. He liked the freedom of working alone, but his consistent destitution was beginning to wear on him. When SoftDisk contacted him about working in its new Gamer's Edge division headed by Romero, he decided he'd take the company's offer a little more seriously.

SoftDisk flew Carmack to Shreveport, as they had with Romero. With little personal stake in the success of the meeting, he didn't take much care to impress. He showed up in a T-shirt and jeans torn at the knees, the same way he ordinarily dressed at home. He talked to the management, but they didn't leave much of an impression on him. He looked at the town a little, but it didn't make a mark. He was from Kansas City, and he spent most of his time working; the place around him didn't really matter.

But when Romero and fellow programmer Lane Roathe took Carmack to dinner, something clicked. They went to an Italian restaurant and talked programming, surrounded by plates of pasta and bread and diners who were surely talking more about local boy and former KKK member David Duke's Senate run than about operating system calls and low-level machine language. The other two programmers impressed Carmack; he loosened up and they talked for hours. By the end of the conversation, he was ready to come on board. "It was really the first time I had met programmers who knew more stuff than me," Carmack said. "I decided to take the job there almost exclusively because I had been very impressed with John and Lane."

Romero was also impressed, seeing Carmack as a perfect addition to the new games team, although he didn't immediately see all of the younger programmer's potential. "I thought he was pretty cool, although he wasn't the raging monster genius he is now," Romero said years later. "But he really seemed excited. He was just a normal guy who was going to learn to program."

The team bonded quickly. Wilbur, Carmack, and Roathe wound up renting a house together on the shores of the nearby lake, just as Richard had done with his team of Austin programmers after their move to New England. It was very much a bachelor pad, complete with a Jacuzzi in the master bedroom. They spent a lot of time zipping around the lake. Kneeboarding quickly became their sport of choice, and their competitive nature soon took over. Each outing became an exercise in adventure, as they pushed to top each other's stunts.

It was clear that Carmack was a little different than the others. The house was filled with entertainment reading: Tolkien's *Ring* series, William Gibson's *Neuromancer*, and other standards of the programmer's literary repertoire. Carmack's reading material tended more toward the details of Intel processors. When he was working on a project, he could barely be interrupted by anything. "When he was programming, there was nothing else but programming," Wilbur said later. "I'm sure there were days where he didn't eat."

Carmack himself was happy. He was making more than he ever had—$27,000 a year—and that more than kept him in books and pizza. He'd been right when he told his mother that was all he needed. He was learning quickly in an environment where his programming was taken wholly seriously. The young Kansas City expatriate was also showing off an ability to create gaming worlds that transcended his ultra-focused technical side. His passion for fantastic worlds was fed each Saturday night as his housemates, along with Romero, gathered for late-night sessions of Dungeons & Dragons. Carmack ran the games, creating a massively detailed, complex world that provided the setting. The world, its history, and characters in fact predated these games; Carmack had created them long before moving to Louisiana, and the characters played by his earlier friends in Kansas City occasionally showed up in those Shreveport lakeside games.

Recreation aside, it took some time before Carmack, Romero, and the rest of the team would find their own voice as a development team. Initially they were stuck working on small games that would be distributed with the Gamer's Edge bimonthly disc. They liked the work. They were good at it. It fed their passions. But it was hardly brain-stretching activity.

The downtime between projects, though, gave them opportunities to explore their own creativity. Carmack had been working on a project using Nintendo's Super Mario Bros., at the time one of the most popular games in the world, as a model. The side-scrolling game, in which the character runs across an environment that unfolds smoothly in front of him, had no direct counterpart in the PC gaming world. Carmack thought he could build something like it. It was an ambitious idea. The PC wasn't much of a multimedia machine yet, and graphics technology was undeveloped enough that many thought that trying to replicate Nintendo's vision on the PC was simply a waste of time.

One night in September 1990 proved to be the breakthrough. Carmack hadn't shown even his closest co-workers the latest versions of what he was working on. Romero went home that day, leaving his workaholic partner at the office. A few hours later, another programmer from SoftDisk's Apple II department, Tom Hall, stumbled over to Carmack's office to see what the whiz kid was working on. With the sun going down and the office mostly empty, Carmack's confidence swelled. He showed

Hall the side-scrolling game engine. To Hall's eyes, it was amazing, rivaling Nintendo's work.

The two put their heads together, trying to figure out how they could best impress the others in the company. Their best bet was to roll it out with a demonstration. Show Romero something big. They snagged one of Romeo's older, simpler characters named Dangerous Dave, and put him in a near-exact copy of the first level of Super Mario Bros. 3, all projected onto Carmack's new graphics engine. DANGEROUS DAVE in COPYRIGHT INFRINGEMENT, they called it. They worked through the night, finally leaving a disk with their work on Romero's desk at 5:00 A.M.

When Romero came into work a few hours later, he popped the disk into the computer. He was stunned. "I knew what we had," he wrote later in an account on his personal web page. "We had our ticket out." He showed it to other SoftDisk employees. Few of them understood his glee. It didn't matter. When Carmack and Hall got back to work, he pulled them into his office and gushed. His old friend, Wilbur, passing by the office, heard Romero expounding on the future, and laughed. "I'm serious," Romero said, and pulled his former benefactor into the office with them.

The team had no grand vision for reinventing gaming. Carmack and Romero had entered the industry considering Richard Garriott's slow-paced role-playing games to be the pinnacle of their art. This moment, however, turned that thinking. They realized they could show off their own respective talents better through increasingly fast-paced action games. Carmack in particular would demonstrate a knack for sniffing out ways that future technology could be used to make a 3D world a little more realistic than his competitors', or make frame rates—the succession of still images that creates the illusion of motion—faster and smoother. These technical innovations, along with what seemed to be a collectively innate sense of how to make basic game play simple and viscerally thrilling, would keep them making action games even when they felt drawn to other genres. It was telling that this first moment of discovery came from a fast-paced game of the kind that was already starting to push Richard Garriott's vision into the background of gaming culture.

At first the team tried to convince SoftDisk to publish the new game. They could take out the obvious Super Mario Bros. graphics and they'd still have a game that would be unlike anything else then on the PC—no small feat. But the company wasn't interested. Carmack's programming required the use of a monitor technology that was still deemed high-end at that time, and SoftDisk was after the mass market.

The team decided to aim higher. Wilbur took the game to Nintendo, sending it to a woman on the legal team there. The message from that company was simple, short, and clear: No. We don't want it. You can't use Mario. Destroy it.

The team pressed ahead anyway, working on their own game largely in secret. Their days were spent working on their SoftDisk games, and they dedicated their evening hours to finishing the game they renamed Commander Keen. They hatched a plan for a new company called id Software. At the time, Hall was the story man. He asked the others what they wanted the game to look like, and then he took their basic ideas, brainstormed for a few minutes, and came back into the room. In the stentorian voice of a 1950s radio announcer, he read the paragraph that would accompany their first game:

> Billy Blaze, eight-year-old genius, working diligently in his backyard club house has created an interstellar starship from old soup cans, rubber cement, and plastic tubing. While his folks are out on the town and the babysitter has fallen asleep, Billy travels into his backyard workshop, dons his brother's football helmet, and transforms into... COMMANDER KEEN—defender of Earth!

All their work was fine, guaranteed to get any game player's blood flowing once Commander Keen's "Bean-with-Bacon Megarocket" blasted off. There was still one important question: Who would publish their game?

The answer turned out to be hanging on the wall in front of them.

Romero had been getting a series of fan letters praising his games for months. They all bore different names, but all were gushing in their acclaim. He'd proudly posted them on his office door. Then something caught his eye: While reading an advertisement in a computer magazine for a Texas company called Apogee Software, he recognized the address. It was the same as the return address on one of the letters. He looked further. It was the same address on all of the letters. They'd all come from the same place. Angry, Romero wrote the seemingly crazy correspondent, demanding to know what was going on.

The mystery pen pal turned out to be Scott Miller, Apogee's founder, and he wasn't crazy. He was simply undercover. He was afraid SoftDisk was scrutinizing Romero's mail, and he wanted to fly under the radar. "I told him I knew how it looked," Miller said later. "But I was just trying to get in touch with a business proposal."

Miller was a programmer and gamer himself. He'd written a few adventure games and published them through on-disc magazines or posted them on university servers and software bulletin boards. Through the middle part of the 1980s, he'd released his programs into the wild, allowing people to distribute them to their friends for free. Embedded in the game was a message that asked people to send money to help support him. The "shareware" strategy, as it was called, did encourage a few people to send money—certainly not enough to quit his uninspiring day job as a computer consultant. Somewhere along the way he had a different idea for distributing his game. He wrote a new game called Kingdom of Kroz, and released it in parts in 1987, much like a serial movie. He gave away the first section for free and then asked people to pay money to get the rest of the game. It was vastly more successful. Suddenly he was pulling in $500 to $1000 a week from the games, nearly enough to support himself as a game writer.

The decade went on, and he continued releasing successive versions of "Kroz" titles. But he started thinking: What if he made this a real business? What if he got other shareware developers on board? He was ambitious enough to start sending a stream of letters to Romero in Louisiana. He wanted to be careful though. SoftDisk was a real company and was now his competition. Romero was a smart guy, Miller thought. He'd figure the trick out.

Miller desperately wanted to publish a Romero game through Apogee's shareware network. After assuring himself that Miller wasn't actually crazy, or at least no more so than any number of other reasonably successful people in the video game industry, Romero sent him a candidate. Miller liked the idea, but when he saw a copy of Carmack and Hall's Copyright Infringement demo, he smiled. That was the one he wanted. The trio asked for $2000 up front. Miller, who had just $5000 in his account at the time—he was spending money as quickly as his new publishing strategy earned it for him, unfortunately—wrote them the check right away.

With a publishing strategy in place, the id team now had to figure out when they could finish the game. Romero, Hall, and Carmack set about a brutal work schedule over the next three months. They recruited another art intern at SoftDisk, Adrian Carmack (no relation to John), to help them with some of the final graphics. Adrian had just barely started learning computer graphics, but he acquitted himself well enough to earn his spot on the team.

Apogee released Commander Keen in December 1990. Anybody could have the first two levels for free, but to get to the rest, players had to pay. Miller's optimism paid off. In January, just a month after the game's first distribution, Apogee wrote them a check for $10,000.

The money cemented their resolve. It was time to strike out on their own. They split away from SoftDisk the next month. Romero and John Carmack informed their boss over lunch that the team would be leaving together. Adrian was coming with them, they added, although they hadn't actually told the intern yet. After lunch, they let the other Carmack in on their plans for him, and he—figuring that if the team he was interning for left, he wouldn't have a job anyway—agreed. Legal obligations to SoftDisk kept them publishing games through the company for more than a year afterward, but their hearts and minds were focused on the future.

❈ ❈ ❈

The team moved around like gypsies as it coded games throughout the early months of its existence. From Shreveport they caravanned to Hall's hometown of Madison, Wisconsin. It was friendly enough, but the bitter winter cold there took them by surprise. They lasted only six months, before moving to Mesquite, Texas, a suburb of Dallas, in April 1992. It was an auspicious choice. A Carmack Street runs through the city, not far west of the little downtown. The town itself had been the home to one of the early legal fights over the morality of video games, although the id developers knew little of the city's history. In their minds it was simply convenient, close to Miller's Apogee and blessedly warm.

New games followed quickly. There were sequels to Commander Keen, most of them released through the shareware channels. The team was also under contract to SoftDisk, and it pushed out a series of hastily written games designed to fulfill these obligations. A few of these games began to lay the technological and theoretical groundwork for their later break-throughs, however. A game called Hovertank drew on the idea of digital warfare that stretched as far back as Battlezone and Atari's Combat. Id, though, created rudimentary 3D graphics and a first-person view, as though the player were looking through the eyes of the character in the game. The dungeon-crawling Catacombs 3D followed. The two games were developed back-to-back, and because of that, the team noticed some-thing important about the worlds they were creating. The combination of the 3D graphics and the first-person view was lending itself to action games in a way that drew players quickly and viscerally into their worlds.

"You could do moody and tense in some ways in a slow-paced game, but the kind of things that really grab you and make you sweat and jump are the kinds of things that really only happen in the action games," Carmack said later. "There were really specific things in the Hovertank and Catacombs games. You'd see people playing a game and they'd open a door and there'd be a great big troll right there, and you'd see them go 'AHHHH!' and jump back. You just never saw that in games before. That's where we said, 'This is powerful, this is what we should be concentrating on.'"

The 3D, first-person perspective that would become the hallmark of their games had its origins elsewhere, much earlier in gaming history. Sev-eral of the D&D-influenced role-playing games of the early PLATO net-work had had simple first-person perspectives like this. Richard's own Akalabeth had had the simplest of line-drawn perspectives. A few games through that early period had even been rudimentary shooters. Maze (also known as Maze Wars), a multiplayer networked game that Zork and InfoCom creator Dave Lebling had helped create in 1974, had briefly been responsible for a huge amount of cross-country network traffic between MIT and Stanford. A similar game called MIDI Maze in 1987 let Atari com-puter users network their machines together and chase each other—each player represented by different colored happy-face balls—around a maze, shooting each other.

It was an Ultima spin-off that brought first-person into the modern age, however. When Richard had taken the programming side of Origin back to Texas from New Hampshire, a few talented programmers had stayed put. They collected a few other like-minded acquaintances and started a new company called Blue Sky Productions. A programmer named Paul Neurath there had been fascinated by the simple first-person perspectives of the mid-1980s role-playing games, and he decided he could do better with modern technology. By summer 1990, he'd created a prototype that Blue Sky displayed at the Consumer Electronics Show in Las Vegas. Origin saw it and signed Blue Sky to create the game for its label. Romero saw it, too.

That game wouldn't be released until 1992, eventually coming out as Ultima Underworld, a 3D, action-packed dungeon crawl that was nominally set in the same world as Richard's popular games. It garnered critical praise and a rabid—if not huge—fan base. "It was the first game that ever gave me a sense of actually being in a real place," remembered longtime Ultima fan Robert Gregg, a Virginia software engineer who later created The Notable Ultima fan site. "I played it the first time with lights out, and several times just got scared out of my wits. You really did get the very creepy sense of crawling around in this dark, damp dungeon, with real inhabitants and nasty monsters waiting around almost every corner."

It was id's next game, released just a week after Ultima Underworld, that sent the industry careening into its love affair with the first-person perspective and its bloodiest manifestations. Romero had suggested basing the game—their own this time, not a SoftDisk release—on the old Apple II Castle Wolfenstein franchise. It turned out to have almost the same game play as Hovertank, although instead of a tank's view, players saw the soon-familiar view of the in-game character's hands holding guns ahead of himself as he stalked though the world killing Nazis, and ultimately Hitler himself. Carmack took a number of technological shortcuts to make the 3D graphics work on the day's average computer. By the standards of the time, the game looked superlative.

Word of the game spread quickly through bulletin boards, the young Internet, and online services like CompuServe. Romero in particular was eager to watch what people said about their creation. He would bring back files full of comments that people were posting online. But they found more than comments—people were hacking into the game and transforming bits of it, changing the way the characters looked (someone created a Barney Wolfenstein, letting players shoot the giant purple children's TV character), changing the way the game sounded, and writing their own virtual mazes to play in. A few people even released tools that would let others hack into the game and create their own game "maps." Carmack was impressed. The hackers reminded him of himself just a few years ago, when he was tearing apart the old Ultima games to get at their secrets. Carmack vowed to help them next time.

"I'd had a lot of fun going in and trying to decipher the internal working of the Ultimas," Carmack said later. "I clearly remember thinking it would have been excellent to have the source code to one of those games I was messing with. So when we were in a position where we had popular games that people were having a lot of fun with, it made a lot of sense to let people who might be in the same situation that I was back then actually have that come true."

✹ ✺ ✹

As the gaming world made these steps forward in perspective and graphics technology, the broader technology industry was in the early stages of a communications revolution. By 1992, more than 3.3 million households in the United States had access to some kind of online computer network.[1] Most people were still using one of the commercial online services that had sprung up in CompuServe's wake, rather than subscribing to direct Internet services. Those online companies had divided up the market demographically. IBM and Sears Roebuck's joint venture, Prodigy, the largest of the consumer services with 1.75 million subscribers, had grown quickly with a low price tag bolstered by brash on-screen advertising. The venerable CompuServe appealed to the techies and information sophisticates, but it was trying to move to the mass market with a new graphical interface. America Online, the new incarnation of the former Quantum Link, was far from the powerhouse it would later become, with fewer than 200,000 subscribers.

A newcomer among these ranks had begun to hint at the promise of networked gaming. Launched in early 1992, the Sierra Network was the first national online service to be dedicated wholly to games and gamers. The service was the brainchild of Ken Williams, the Sierra On-Line founder who had published Richard's second Ultima, and then helped push him into the decision to start Origin. Sierra had never previously been online, but in interviews of the time, Williams said he'd been dreaming of the networked gaming service at least since 1982, and he had simply lacked the capital to start up a national network.[2]

As gaming went, the Sierra Network outstripped any commercially available network play, even though most of the online services had offered some kind of multiplayer networked games for years. Some of these were MUDs modeled after Richard Bartle's invention. Others were games with simple graphics, much like what could be found on PLATO in the 1970s. Modem speeds had made games with all but the simplest graphics impossible to play over the telephone networks.

Sierra launched with a few basic games, such as bridge, chess, checkers, and hearts, allowing people to chat with each other while they were playing. When players signed up, they created a little cartoon of themselves (called an Avatar) that other players would see as they were chatting. The service quickly added a multiplayer flight simulator called Red Baron that allowed subscribers to dogfight with each other in the digital sky. An adults-only LarryLand, based on Sierra's Leisure Suit Larry games, allowed subscribers to role-play lounge lizards while playing blackjack, roulette, and other casino games. MedievaLand opened up a Dark Ages role-playing game called The Shadow of Yserbius.

It was clear as 1992 drew to a close that *cyberspace* (as it was already being called) in general, and online gaming in particular, wasn't just for geeks anymore. Mainstream newspapers wrote breathless stories about the "videotext" services. "You'd better get your tongue around the term 'interactive multimedia,' because it's shorthand for a revolution," *Fortune* magazine gushed, late that year.[3] Cable companies, telecommunications giants, and computer companies were strategizing ways to capture and control this brave new world. Most of the smart money was on the cable companies, whose coaxial cables passing 90 percent of the homes in America could carry more data than ordinary telephone lines. But the big phone companies and AT&T weren't taking that bandwidth deficit as a sign of their own weakness. AT&T was on the warpath, looking for multimedia companies that could help it capture a big slice of the new digital world, even purchasing 20 percent of the Sierra Network—renaming it the Imagi-Nation Network in 1993.

These corporate giants' dreams of a captive, cable-network–like online subscriber base evaporated almost as quickly as they had risen. In January 1993, a University of Illinois computer science student named Marc Andreessen sent a terse email across a handful of techie email lists, announcing that he and a few other students were creating a new graphical program for reading and browsing those corners of the Internet already being called the World Wide Web. Released as a finished program in April 1993, Andreessen's Mosaic took the Internet by storm. The dry world of text databases and research archives suddenly blossomed with pictures and color. More and more Internet service providers sprung up that simply allowed their customer access to this sprawling, decidedly uncorporate, digital Wild West, and the phenomenon of the World Wide Web, dot-com fever, and all the other fevers of the Net-obsessed 1990s was begun.

Carmack and Romero were part of this latter tradition. Their sympathies were with the independent-minded hacker, not the online bridge-player, and certainly not with the big corporations' desire to colonize and control this new cyberspace. As they watched these networks grow, and watched their own Wolfenstein become a cult favorite in PC gaming discussion groups on CompuServe and on the Internet's sprawling Usenet bulletin-board newsgroups, they decided it was time to make their next game multiplayer, and let people play it over these computer networks.

Years later, Carmack downplayed the innovation of this step. "It's an obvious thing. If you've got two computers and you can connect them together, you're going to make a multiplayer game. It's like a law of nature," he said. "If anybody looks at a video game with somebody playing there, the first thought is 'Wouldn't it be cool if I was in there, too.'" They might have done the same thing with Wolfenstein, but their office simply didn't have an internal network. Once they got that up and running, network gaming was a forgone conclusion.

It might have been obvious from a technical perspective. The consequences for gaming communities were not so obvious.

* * *

The team started work on Doom in September 1992, two years after Carmack and Hall had stayed up all night to finish their Mario Bros. style game. They had tried to negotiate with Hollywood lawyers to get the rights to do a game based on the *Aliens* sci-fi/horror movie, but it hadn't worked. The programmers had wanted to keep absolute control over what happened in the game, and the studio wasn't ready for that. Wolfenstein had been a big success by the standards of the computer game industry, but id Software was still far from a household name.

Carmack came up with a different idea. What about basing the monsters of the game on demons somehow released from Hell? They would be just as frightening as any *Aliens* creatures, he argued. Romero later said the idea might well have been spurred by their most recent Dungeons & Dragons session, which had finished when "demons had overrun the entire planet and destroyed the whole game."[4]

The excess of that image—a world and its heroes drowning under a flood of demons—appealed to the team. It might not have been terribly original, but it would certainly serve as the skeleton for a game. Hall got to work on the story ideas. He wrote a set of memos the company called the "Doom Bible," which laid out the basic narrative of the game (simple at its core: Space Marine on Mars must fight his way through demons accidentally released from Hell). The rest of the team started following that plot, working from rough sketches of monsters and level maps.

They sacrificed some things along the way. Initial press releases spoke of amazing detail to the game's graphics, game-play elements that would include a scoring system, and treasures that players would pick up along the way, with evocative names like "Demonic Dagger and Skull Chest." By the next summer they'd decided to simplify things. The new goal would be simple and twofold: Kill everything that moves. Get out alive.

Carmack did keep his promise to feed the online hackers' community that had developed around Wolfenstein. He remembered how much he'd wanted to see the Ultima source code, and if he wasn't quite ready to release that much information along with their new games, he did want to give the hacker-players tools to dig into the game. He contacted one of the Wolfenstein hackers and gave him tools to write a level-builder for Doom.

He built in ways that people could change the look of the game relatively simply. He decided to release code for some of the tools that id developers themselves used to develop elements of the game.

The buzz surrounding the new game climbed to a fever pitch long before it was released, at least on the online forums that followed PC games. Game developers are notoriously late with their work, and Carmack would become legendary for slipping ship dates. This time was no exception. Hard-core Wolfenstein fans spent much time online, on chat groups and Usenet newsgroups dedicated to computer games, speculating about features, mulling over the bits of information that had been released, and joking about the delays. The bombastic promises that id had released to the community were the source of considerable parody. Constant questions asking "Where can I get Doom?" from newcomers who'd heard of the game and didn't know the full story exasperated people on the discussion groups. This bubbling interest wound up producing some of the game's first moments of collective community history, even before the software's actual release.

A few weeks before the release of the game, a fan named Eli Bingham posted a suggestion to one newsgroup. Maybe id should pick a less catchy name for their next game, so there wouldn't be so much crushing prerelease interest. Something like, say, "Smashing Pumpkins Into Small Piles Of Putrid Debris." The giddy newsgroup picked up the name and within hours jokes about the fictional game SPISPOPD were flying. Finally, another player named Seth Cohn announced that he was the official author of the FAQ (Frequently Asked Questions) document for "ego software's" hottest new game, SPISPOPD. People mailed him suggestions for game features, and within a few days he had a long spot-on parody of a real id gaming FAQ, making ludicrous promises for the fictional game. It fooled many gullible people online, who quickly wrote him and asked him for the game. It amused the developers at id, who incorporated the name of the fictional game into Doom itself as a secret cheat code, giving the players extra power.

By the time Wilbur finally got the game online on December 10, the online community was ready to pop with excitement. The University of Wisconsin servers were full for days with people downloading it. Reviews online were ecstatic—although every once in a while, a lone voice worried about the over-the-top gore would pipe up. In the first five months alone, people downloaded more than 1.3 million copies of the free version, more than five times the number who'd ever purchased even the most successful Ultima.[5]

Doom did more than just push the limits of graphics technology. The game, through its ability to let people network computers together and play at the same level, became one of the first widespread commercial realizations of an online virtual reality. The dream of a networked cyberworld had infused notions of online behavior for years, driven by visions spun by a handful of science-fiction authors, San Francisco Bay Area futurists and journalists, and programmers. Doom seemed to many to be a long step forward towards this vision.

Foremost in many peoples' minds were the ideas drawn from William Gibson's science-fiction works and Neal Stephenson's novel *Snow Crash*. Gibson had been the one to coin the word *cyberspace* in a short story called "Burning Chrome" in 1981, and he expanded on it with his 1984 novel *Neuromancer*, depicting a world where those who were trained (and outfitted with the right equipment) could plug themselves into networks of information and soar through it with the skills of an abstract surfer. Gibson later confessed that he'd never been online when his book was released— he'd written the book on a typewriter, in fact, not a computer, and his depictions of the digital universe were fantastic rather than drawing on any specific technology. Stephenson's 1992 book was written long after Gibson's ideas had begun filtering through popular culture, and long after MUDs and other online worlds had begun to feed people's dreams of living and interacting in online communities. *Snow Crash* envisioned the digital "Metaverse," where visitors could log into and roam through a 3D world represented by their own digital "avatars," or imaginative graphic representations of their selves.

Doom brought parts of this vision into existence in a way that stepped well beyond most other commercial games to date. Carmack had again been forced to take many shortcuts to fit his technical vision into the confines of the day's home computer technology, but he had recognizably created a 3D world that people could wander through. The online component meant people could inhabit the same virtual space at the same time. Each little game world popped into existence only as long as at least two players were there. It was a long way even from a text MUD's ability to create a stable world that people could visit, leave, and return to. But the technology, the graphics, and the ability to feel visceral motion and bodies in the world made it a big step forward toward the idea of a virtual reality.

Todd Gerhke, a young programmer at the time in Redmond, Washington, later told of walking in on the early attempts of a pair of Microsoft network administrators to set up a private Doom network, a few months after the game had been released. The two were simply running around the world, testing out what it was like to spend time in the game's environment. They weren't hunting each other yet. They were exploring. Gerhke, who would shortly become a Doom player of regional stature, was thrilled. "I still remember the hair on the back of my neck standing up and getting goose bumps, knowing I was witnessing the future of computer gaming," he said. "I felt like I was witnessing the first flight of Wilbur and Orville Wright."

Richard's Origin Systems team was also floored—but more by the market's response than by the game itself. They'd gotten a peek at the demo earlier in the year and hadn't been impressed with either the story or the game play. "We figured nobody outside of tech geeks would ever want to play this game, and certainly nobody would want to link their computers together and shoot each other," recalled Warren Spector, who got a sneak peek at the game when a team from id had come calling. Richard, who was fast at work trying to integrate his company with Electronic Arts, didn't take the time to check out the game when the id Software team trekked through the office looking for a publisher. Although after its release, he quickly recognized the power of the online games.

"There is no doubt that what they did changed the industry," Richard said later. "It wasn't what we were doing, but it certainly showed us what was possible."

It changed reality for the people at id, too. The game sold incredibly well. Their shareware release strategy attracted hundreds of thousands of people to the game. Over the next few years, they sold millions of copies of the title and its sequel, Doom II, was downloaded tens of millions of times. Money started pouring in. They hired a public relations firm to help them sell the game and sell an image of themselves as creators, and almost overnight they helped change the image of what computer games were supposed to be. "The industry needed a rock star and didn't have one yet," Wilbur said later. "We were all geeks. Before, it had been like the nerds are winning, but nobody knew that. You could talk to your parents about what you did for a living, and if you told them, 'I write games,' the response would typically be, 'Well, you're a loser!'"

Romero in particular thrived in the spotlight. Always the most outspoken of the group, Romero let his hair grow nearly to his waist and started dressing more flamboyantly. The other founders were more private people, although that didn't prevent Carmack from buying the red Ferrari that finally convinced his mother that game-making might be a reasonable career. They never said the words in public, but internally they did: They *were* rock stars now. Everyone was writing about them and fawning over their games. *Forbes* magazine even wrote that id's profit margins made Microsoft look like "a second rate cement company."[6] The group posted that article on their office wall.

The spotlight brought the little company to the attention of legislators and family advocates who were in the midst of a wave of criticism of violent video games. Doom was lumped in with Mortal Kombat and other ultra-violent games as a damaging influence on kids. The id developers didn't pay much heed. "I've always ignored that whole side of things," Carmack said later. "People never want to be responsible for themselves and are always looking for a scapegoat. If you raise yourself up there, you'll be attacked."

What the programmers were paying attention to was the sudden rise of player communities around their games. The multiplayer feature was proving attractive to people who could figure out how to network computers together. Much of this was happening inside companies, as tech support staffers took over their corporate networks to play the games. Tech-savvy home players slowly figured out the same thing, although the equipment and knowledge needed to do this would be beyond most home computer users until Microsoft built simpler networking technology into its Windows 95 operating system.

Other businesses were springing up that would help the spread of this multiplayer phenomenon. Companies were formed specifically to cater to online Doom gamers, making it relatively simple to dial in to the digital version of playing fields where gamers could find other players. People began having Local Access Network (LAN) parties, holding shooting rallies where everyone would bring their own computers, link them together with cables, and play against each other for days.

Carmack's response to all of this was perhaps the most curious of the id programmers. Romero and some of the other developers loved spending time online, going to bulletin boards and chat rooms to see what people were saying, and pitching in with their own thoughts from time to time. Romero's missives in particular were well known for their wild enthusiasm. Carmack, by contrast, had little interest in actually interacting with the communities he'd helped spark.

"I've never really been a big community kind of person. I've always been more of the hermit hacker sort of person," Carmack said later. "I remember thinking about getting an amateur radio license when I was a kid, because I was interested in the technical side of things, making radios and things like that. But the whole basic point about talking to random people you didn't know, I just fundamentally didn't get. It's sort of like that with a lot of these things with computers, too. I recognize these are fairly basic human things that most people get, but I'm not there."

Nevertheless, Carmack and id kept feeding the community what it wanted, and the community grew and gave back. One player, a Novell network engineer named John Cash, sent in critical improvements to the Doom initial networking function—the original turned out to swamp networks with unwanted data traffic—and ultimately came to work for id. New levels and whole new games sprang up on online bulletin boards. The company hired Tim Willits, a Minnesota college student who'd written a few of these "mods," to work on a contract basis, and he ultimately became a lead designer. Doom II came out with some improvements in the technology, and ultimately it became the company's best-selling game. They collaborated with another developer, Raven Software, to make Heretic and Hexen, magic-themed games based on Doom's underlying graphics technology. But the team already had its eyes on its next game. If Doom ushered in the age of networked gaming, the company's next game solidified it as the future.

* * *

Doom had taught the id developers several things. Multiplayer was important. Network play was important. The visceral, bone-chilling nature of a dark first-person view of the world remained vital. By late 1994, id's next big advance along these lines already had a name and at least the beginnings of an idea. It was going to be based on a character named Quake, again taken from one of the id programmers' long-running, epic games of Dungeons & Dragons. The story line was a bit hazy, however. Initially they envisioned it as a kind of role-playing game. The Thor-like character, Quake, would have a magic hammer that gained power as the game went on and as the player gained experience.

The developers were extraordinarily public about their plans, and their excitement shone through. In one early interview, published in the 1994 *Doom II Strategy Guide*, Romero could barely contain his excitement. He conceded that they didn't really have a story yet, more of "kind of a feel for the thing," but that didn't matter. The world itself was going to be amazing:

> We're going to make you feel like you're in a real world. There will be bugs and birds flying around. You'll be looking around, going, 'This is great! Hey, I wonder what's over there?' In Quake, you'll really have to kill things. You won't just press the trigger and hit it, you'll have to really beat the living shit out of the thing until it's dead. So you'll have this huge hammer and you'll pound it into blood paste on the floor, and you're going to have to take awhile, too. You're going to have to work on it. You won't just have this arrow point-and-click kind of thing.[7]

The concept for the game world, as Romero indicated, was initially far more ambitious than it turned out. In one interview, designer American McGee said the team wanted it to be a "graphical MUD," a comment that seemed to promise a sprawling, stable multiplayer world.

The design team started working on a world with art that looked a little like old Aztec temples. They soon switched to medieval castles, leaving behind much of the work Romero had already talked about. They pressed forward for months, modifying it until Carmack and others started worrying that Doom aficionados would take one look at the low-tech fantasy weapons they were creating and go immediately back to their grenade launchers and machine guns. At least one of the lead designers threw up his hands, complaining that he was out of ideas for the medieval theme. Late in the year, they met, argued, and decided to move to the dark futuristic world that would ultimately be home to Quake. But because the artists complained that they'd already put a year of work into the other idea, and couldn't start from scratch, the company decided to keep much of the old look as well. As a result, dimensional rifts wound up transporting players back into medieval worlds, taking advantage of levels that had already been designed. As a story and setting it was somewhat flimsy, but Carmack, at least, had never believed that story and narrative were critical parts of games. Better to make games into activities that, like basketball or football, needed no back story to be fun, he said.

Ultimately, they made the multiplayer version first—or in the parlance of their own gaming community, the deathmatch version. The single-player game could come later, but it was important to make sure the world itself was consistent and powerful. This was the way that Richard, too, had worked through much of his career, developing the world first and later going back to impose an actual story on his games. For a game that the team envisioned would place more emphasis on exploring and killing than on storytelling, this strategy seemed best.

As a game-play strategy, that was sound, but by the time these deathmatch versions were even rudimentarily finished, they proved a daunting distraction. Id's offices in Mesquite at the time were like the offices of other startups of the 1990s, in a rundown building, with no office walls, a fair amount of dust, and folding chairs scattered about. The open office and the energy had everyone moving quickly. The development team huddled around networked computers and ran the game through its paces with their own deathmatch games, screaming and shouting across the room at each other as their digital counterparts were successively pulverized by machine guns, rocket launchers, and lightning guns. There was little exploration going on, but there was a fair amount of killing. Romero and another developer, Shawn Green, were particularly avid players, stretching games out to 50 or 60 kills before stopping. Carmack finally put a "frag," or kill limit, on the deathmatch games, in part to keep them at work. It didn't help. The testing team would finish a bloody game, and a call would go across the room: "Does anyone think this game is finished testing?" A collective "NO!" would ring out across the room.

Throughout this process, information flowed freely to the Doom fan community about the new game. In February 1996, the company posted a very early version of the game online, with only a few of the final features enabled. It quickly spread across the Net, and Quake deathmatch servers run by the players themselves almost immediately began to spring up, a huge advance on Doom network play. A few enterprising code-slingers figured out how to dig into the code and unlock features that the company had intended to leave dormant, including the monsters themselves. A full beta release hit the Net in June, catalyzing the community further, and the game was finally released in August.

Despite being far less different in concept from Doom than originally promised, it quickly soared to the top of sales charts. Some reviewers quibbled that the company should have spent more time on developing an original story. Some complained about the game play itself. Most waxed eloquent about the technical innovations, from the graphic quality of the world and monsters to the Internet play that was already taking off.

Players loved it. Since shortly after the release of Doom, id staffers had been talking privately about "clans of warriors" that might coalesce and play against each other online. Players themselves had come to use the term too. In the days before Quake's full details had been released, speculation had run wild about what could be done with the multiplayer worlds that had been described at different stages of the process. In long-running online discussions, fans came up with wild scenarios of all-out team warfare, with huge armies or clans fighting each other the way they would in later massively multiplayer worlds like Lineage or Dark Ages of Camelot.

This concept of clans already had a history in gaming circles. A few MUDs had begun implementing clan systems in the late 1980s and early 1990s. In that context, clans were teams of players who agreed to work together and were usually associated with killing other players—not terribly dissimilar from the older concept of "guilds." A popular series of games called MechWarrior had also featured clan systems as part of the story.

Even before Quake was released, players began gathering into groups. A few people complained in online forums about adopting the clan terminology, saying it made sense with the MechWarrior story, but made no sense whatever in the Quake world. They were ignored. Clans popped up daily, with names like "Reservoir Dogs," "Clan Vengeance," and "Violent Movement Clan." Some, like an all-star group of Doom veterans called the "International House of Spork," were a little more whimsical, although no more deadly for their humor. Internet news sites dedicated to the game and community listed them, and for a short period of time—until concerns about legal liability over copyright and other issues intervened—Quake clan logos and news were featured on id's own web site.

Carmack had continued the process of encouraging people to create mods, and again the community went wild. The tools he'd released were more powerful than those for Doom, and mod-makers reacted accordingly. He also licensed the underlying technology to a host of other commercial companies, who made their own hit games with software engines that powered the game. Over time, he released the full source code free of charge, and the game found its way into academic research labs and digital animation studios, as nongamers found the software to be one of the best ways to create their own 3D work.

Internally, the rough development process had taken its toll. Romero felt that technology had taken precedence over the kind of creative game design that he wanted to do. Carmack and others felt that Romero was no longer pulling his fair weight. "Romero was going on IRC (Internet Relay Chat) when he should have been working, from my point of view," Carmack said in one interview of the time.[8] The split had been building for a long time, but shortly after the Quake beta version was released, Romero announced with a terse online message that he was leaving the company to start a "new game company with different goals."[9] The rancor on both sides showed up in headlines and interviews across the gaming community for years, and the effects of bruised egos would be felt rippling through the gaming community for at least another half-decade.

From a gaming perspective, the split wouldn't matter, although the industry's version of gossip columns would continue to make hay of the rift for a long time. The work they had done together had already had a catalyzing effect on game communities, and those communities were now in a large part self-sustaining. Romero went on to found a high-profile company called Ion Storm, centered more specifically on design. Its games initially didn't sell as well as expected, eventually forcing the closing of its offices in Dallas. The quiet Carmack continued to build his reputation as a gaming technology genius, releasing more versions of Quake, Doom, and Wolfenstein that continued to soar ahead of most rivals' efforts with each new iteration. But five years after the release of Quake, Carmack was getting a little bored, even if his games were still technologically stunning market hits. "I'm not a gamer anymore," he said in early 2003, as the company was finishing Doom III. He'd turned much of his attention to a new project by this time, an attempt to build a manned low-orbit spacecraft. "This lets me go back to the stage where every day I'm learning something new," he said. "I remember that from my early days of the computer industry, but it hasn't been like that in years."

Nevertheless, Doom and Quake had irrevocably changed computer gaming. The communities of networked gamers they'd helped spawn had gained enough momentum and power to affect the development of games themselves, and these communities stayed active whether or not a new title was due. The networked age of gamers had begun in earnest.

6

Homebrewed Gamers

On a mid-August Thursday in 1996, a carload of young, straggly-looking men pulled up at a Best Western in Garland, Texas, a Dallas suburb. A group that looked like it hadn't spent much time in the sun emerged into the motel's parking lot, dressed in T-shirts and shorts, joking happily with each other. They made their way to the main office, anticipation etched clearly into their features. They may have looked a bit ragtaggy, but they certainly didn't look particularly rowdy. If anything, they looked a little on the geeky side. At worst, an anxious hotel manager might have thought they'd leave a mess of soda cans and pizza boxes behind.

Even so, there was something odd about them, and about the stream of others that pulled up in their wake. They moved into their hotel rooms, doubling or tripling up on rooms the way young people without much money often did. What made these kids so odd, though, were the boxes they were carting in. Big boxes, with computers inside. These weren't just the laptops that businessmen and writers often brought along. These guys had the whole setup—boxy machines and bulky monitors. Lots of cords— definitely more than were needed just to plug in a computer. The manager of the hotel stared, confused. She knew they were coming and had agreed weeks ago to let them use a small ballroom, and they'd explained to her what would be happening (more or less), but it was immediately clear that she hadn't entirely understood. There had been talk of a convention—she understood that. It was the computer games part that got her. Now, too late, she was getting a firsthand view of gamers.

While other cars pulled up outside, Jerry Wolski was inside the hotel's small ballroom, helping set up computers in rows on folding tables, and starting the tricky job of setting up network connections. The tall, thin 22-year-old was a local, a freelance graphics designer from Dallas who'd started organizing this party a few months ago with Kevin Searle and Jim Elson. As the group finished the setup, the Quake games began, the players' eyes focused intently on the 3D world spinning across the screens. Wolski smiled, excited. This was good, he thought.

A few of the other attendees were talking together animatedly, and called him over. "Hey," one of them said. "We're thinking we should challenge the id guys to a deathmatch."

"Let's send them an invitation. Tell them we'll kick their ass. That ought to get them down here," someone else said.

They could find the company's office easily enough. "Yeah," Wolski said. "We can drive it down there personally."

The group looked around for a piece of paper big enough for what they wanted to do, and found a marking pen to write with. They scribbled a message, and 14 of the people there signed it, a good-natured declaration of war against id Software. Wolski, Elson, and a few others jumped in the car and headed for id's offices. They found Suite 666 and walked in the door. Their hearts were pounding—these were their heroes, after all, and this was the place where some of the best computer games in the world had been created. They walked to the front desk, and held the paper out sheepishly. The tone of the invitation couldn't have been more at odds with the meek looks on their faces as they looked around the offices with awe.

The note was short, getting right to its point: "The ops of #quake cordially invite the guys at id to a MAN BEATING."

The event that Wolski and his partners had organized was the very first QuakeCon, and many of the attendees were regulars in an online chat community called #quake, the hardest of the hard-core communities of network gamers. The game players streaming into the Best Western, most of whom were close to Wolski's age, were here to play Quake, and they intended to keep playing it almost nonstop all weekend. The game wasn't even out in the stores yet, but the new id title had already sparked paroxysms of delight inside a vocal segment of the gaming community.

People who'd played Doom and Wolfenstein had waited a long time for the new game. Many of them started trying it out as soon as the company had released early copies, not even official beta copies, onto the Net. Some of them had hacked into that early game and unlocked elements such as monsters that id hadn't intended them to see until later releases. They'd been playing it avidly ever since. QuakeCon was one of the most visible expressions yet of the communities growing around networked games.

Many attendees had met online in a chat network called Internet Relay Chat, or IRC. This sprawling ad hoc network of networks was still the haunt of fairly sophisticated computer users, often used to discuss the most arcane of technical subjects, but it allowed anybody anywhere to set up a chat room on any subject. People could be found inside their own #quake channel at almost any hour of the day or night, talking about Quake, other games, computers, networking, or anything else that crossed anybody's mind. No longer were gamers relegated to neighborhood groups; they'd found a way to connect across states and countries, and for these players, at least, IRC was their home base. Nobody had to follow rules or pass tests to be a part of the group—it was enough to be interested in the game. Once in a while, employees from id—even Romero himself—would stop by and talk about the games.

There were maybe 40 people around the world who were regulars in the #quake circle. They used the chat channel to find games and to challenge each other to deathmatches, but just as often they'd spend time just hanging out. Other people would stop by occasionally, but those core members spent hours there, and they got to know each other well. It didn't take long before someone had suggested actually meeting. They could call the event "#quakeCon," bring their computers, and turn it into a party. Everyone liked the idea. Wolski, Searle, and Elson lived in Dallas, near the Mesquite home of id, and they suggested having it there. Others liked the idea, and the trio had set to work making arrangements.

For Wolski, putting together the event had been one of the biggest thrills of his life. He'd grown up in a small town in Poland, and had come to the United States just five years before. Where turn-of-the-century immigrants had used the daily newspapers to learn about the language and culture, the community of gamers he'd found had been his main means of assimilating in his new country. He'd lived in Los Angeles for a few years, and when he moved to Dallas he found a core of gamers there that had sprung up around id. He spent almost every weekend gaming with groups at somebody's house or at a rented hotel space, or hanging out talking about games. Sometimes he worried about how much he played, but that did little to slow him down. "Ever since I was a kid, I've been very fascinated with video games, sometimes to the point of obsession," he said later. "QuakeCon and its organization was really a dream come true for me."

Their trip to Suite 666 cemented the success. The id developers—along with Carmack himself—agreed to come. Just minutes after they left, a breathless message appeared on "Redwood's Quake Page," one of the first web sites to provide daily news on the game and its community of players.

I just got off the telephone with Tim Willits of id (you were expecting some other company maybe?) a few minutes ago. He wanted me to let EVERYBODY know (because 'I like your page the best' *grin*) that on Friday the 16th (tomorrow) at 7:00 p.m. Central time, JOHN CARMACK and the gang (Tim Willits, Bear, Adrian Carmack, and possibly others) will be attending #quakeCon talking about QuakeWorld, Quake II, and the future of gaming at id Software!!

Directions to the hotel followed.

When Wolski heard of the post, his stomach turned. Suddenly the world knew about the event. They didn't have enough room in the hotel for everyone who accessed Redwood's site. The fear quickly subsided, though, and he started smiling again. This really was big.

Players continued to gather Thursday and throughout the day Friday. It was the first time that many of the gamers had met face to face. There were surprises. Some of the most voluble people online turned out to be quiet, almost painfully shy in person. It didn't matter. They were among friends here. Many had come from Dallas or nearby cities and states, but players gathered from both coasts as well. Six people had even driven all the way from Canada. No matter from where they hailed, they had at least one thing in common: each had a deep desire to play Quake with their new-found friends from cyberspace.

The group, all of them men, spent much of the time in the hotel ball-room, connecting their computers and running around the dark virtual halls of Quake, shooting at each other. It was a different experience play-ing the games in the same room. Many of them had played together on-line. But live, you could feel the impact of your actions. You could hear people swear in frustration when you killed them. You could shout across the room at your opponent. By the time Friday evening rolled around, close to 40 computers were in the room, and nearly 60 people were playing, more than Wolski and the others had planned for. The strain of all those machines was proving too much for the hotel's overworked circuit breakers, and periodically a bank of computers—sometimes even the whole room—would go dark. "F***k!" someone would scream. "I had you!" would come from another dark corner, and Wolski or someone else would have to go talk to the increasingly grumpy hotel staff about resetting the power.

Then came the id-ites. Carmack in his red Ferrari. Romero in his Humvee. The company's new CEO, Todd Hollenshead, was there; Willits was there; and reigning deathmatch champ and designer American McGee was there. They were mobbed by players and spent some time signing mouse pads and CDs. People took photos in front of the Ferrari and the Humvee. Some of the players retired into the ballroom, where they played Romero, McGee, and a few others. McGee won more often than he lost. A group of worshipful technology-minded players gathered around Carmack out in the parking lot, and the ordinarily taciturn programmer wound up answering questions for a full two hours about game design, id's plans for Quake II, graphics hardware, and even about Romero's departure from id.

The crew had brought along some gear that could be given away as prizes at the event: two Quake CDs autographed by everyone at the company, a handful of other games, and T-shirts. Elson, maybe the most practical one in the bunch, quietly mentioned to Carmack and Hollenshead that the event had actually been pricey, when it came down to renting the ballroom and paying for unexpected power costs. Running that many computers in one place was turning out to be expensive, and they hadn't budgeted for it. Carmack wrote them a check to cover some of the costs.

On Saturday came the double-elimination Quake tournament. A Dallas stalwart took top prize. On Sunday was a Doom II tournament. Wolski won this. But people were playing straight through, no matter what else was happening. The energy level was high enough that nobody slept much for two and a half days. When their fingers or eyes got tired, they'd wander around the hotel and talk, remembering stories from the IRC chat rooms, or they'd make repeated trips to the local diner. They sat in the vinyl booths there, nerves buzzing, drinking bottomless cups of coffee until the caffeine had rejuvenated their will to frag. Wolski and the rest of the tired men finally stumbled back into their ordinary lives Monday morning, images of dark underground hallways and coffee cups burned into their memories

Inside the little hotel ballroom, it was easy to feel that something big was brewing. All of these people had been playing games for years. Most of them had been avid Doom players, and at its core, Quake wasn't all that different. Both games were set in post-apocalyptic-looking worlds dripping with sci-fi horror atmosphere, and in both, the point of the game was to stay alive as long as you possibly could while mowing your way through digital adversaries. And even long before Doom, communities of players had gathered around games on online services such as CompuServe or Genie, or on university servers.

Still, Quake was already changing things. The games were on the Internet now, and it was much easier for anyone with a dial-up modem to jump on-line and find a game. Once people found a match, or a server where they could find a good game, they tended to come back, the same way a new-comer to a city neighborhood might find his way back to the same Saturday afternoon game of pickup basketball week after week. Putting the games on the Net meant the game-playing communities were expanding, and that geographical barriers were breaking down. Wolski's group, drawn from around the United States and Canada, was evidence of that.

That tired weekend in the hotel ballroom transformed itself over the next few years into one of the biggest events in the gaming world as Wolski, Searle, and ultimately thousands of others began making the trip to the Dallas suburb every summer. Half pilgrimage to id's home, half convention designed to let people meet the people they'd been blasting into smithereens every night on their computer, it quickly became a barometer for the health of the id gaming community.

These were unabashedly action games, with little of the role-playing or storytelling that were centerpieces of Richard Garriott's Ultima worlds. They were called "twitch" games for a reason: People with the fastest reflexes, who could process information most quickly and turn it into the right combination of digital motion and trigger-finger actions, were the most successful at avoiding the bloody fate of the slow. To be slow was generally to be dead, unless you were a master strategist or simply an incredible shot.

For all of that seemingly vigilante-encouraging content, by the time Wolski and the others arrived at the hot parking lot just outside of Garland, the bloody games that they played had created some of the strongest and most populous gaming communities around. People were drawn to the games initially for the adrenaline rush and the action. These games got the heart pounding, they kept players' attention rigidly focused on the matter at hand, and they were downright *scary*. Mood-altering soundtracks, lightning-quick action, and terrifying creatures populated the games. But as soon as players tried playing other people, something shifted. It wasn't for everybody; certainly many people tried the deathmatches and found them intimidating, or simply no fun. But for quite a few, it was a genuinely different experience.

An element of competition had been missing from the single-player games. Deathmatches turned out to be more than a little like regular, offline sports. The point was to beat the opponent. In the game, it happened to be by "fragging," or killing opponents, as many times as possible, but—as the games' defenders noted—even football is a form of ritualized warfare. Chess itself is a violent game at its metaphorical heart. And, realistically, the worst injury Quake players would walk away with would be a sore hand from gripping the mouse too tightly.

Human opponents were more fun to play than the computer's artificial intelligence, particularly when you could sit in the same room. Screaming at somebody just before you pulled the trigger, sending your opponent into the afterlife—well, that was a big part of the fun. Many people discovered networked gaming at their workplaces, staying long after closing time to play with their co-workers. Sometimes, they stayed to chat with other players online. Most of the games and the online services that rose to support them included a text chat function, which tended to start with lines like "EAT LEAD SUCKAH!" but often moved on to actual conversations about the game and game play and then other topics, until players realized they'd crossed some line to become genuine acquaintances or even close friends, often without even meeting face to face.

To the outside world, this often proved inexplicable. To those standing outside the game community, these were people, often young males, staring blankly into a computer screen with the express and singular intent of killing each other as often and as bloodily as possible. Certainly critics, from parents' groups to legislators, would charge repeatedly during the following years that the activity could be nothing but damaging to players' psyches. But it just so happened that the arena was a fantastic place to make what often turned into deep and lasting friendships—or at least in which to develop a sense of camaraderie and leadership to which intensely computer-focused kids often had no other exposure.

It proved not to be a paradox at all. They came for the competition and the killing, and they stayed for the community. In Wolski's case, the group of people he met playing Doom and Quake and many other shooters he knew stayed together, moving to other games over time, including slower-paced online role-playing worlds inspired in some measure by Richard's work.

"It's very interesting to see how life goes on. People get married, get new jobs, and their lives change, yet one thing remains the same: our common attraction to video games, both online and offline," Wolski said, speaking more than five years after his first event. People he met through the games had helped him start his own web design company, and he now helped organize much larger events. "It's really interesting to me, because I must admit that when I was younger, I was sometimes afraid that my obsessions with video games would maybe affect my professional life negatively, yet it is quite the opposite."

✳ ✳ ✳

Wolski and his #quake crew were to make a lasting impression on the gamer community and on the industry itself with their QuakeCon event, but the gamer community had long preceded that event. Most of the attendees had been drawn deeply into the online gaming circles with Doom, or even earlier. Indeed, by the time Quake was released, many of the community components that would later emerge already existed in embryonic form. Tens of thousands of people were playing Doom online, although largely through specialized online services created specifically for the purpose. People like Wolski were gathering every weekend to network their computers together and play live games against each other. People who had come to Doom as their first real computer game were emerging as superstars in competitive play.

The biggest of those early stars was a boy named Dennis "Thresh" Fong, a gaming virtuoso who served as online gaming's first Michael Jordan, a recognizable superstar who helped transform game playing into something more than just a home-entertainment medium. More than any other single person, he put a face on the gamer community at a time when a curious world was trying to figure out just what this strange new activity was all about. He helped reassure some of those outsiders that gaming might be a reasonable pursuit, that staring into the computer screen and trying one's best to kill one's opponent as quickly and as often as possible didn't necessarily create a homicidal maniac.

Dennis today is a slender, soft-spoken man with glasses and close-cropped hair. His erect bearing and confident, respectful demeanor almost gives him the air of a young military officer, even if virtual rocket guns are as close as he's ever been to a firefight. He was born in Hong Kong, although his mother was an American citizen. His father worked for Hewlett-Packard and moved the family around China for the first years of his son's life. They lived there until Dennis was seven, when they moved to Beijing for three years before settling in the Silicon Valley suburb of Los Altos. Despite the move from East to West, the adjustment was relatively easy for Dennis. He'd spent his formative years in international schools speaking English, and found it easy to be, for all intents and purposes, a typical American kid.

Like many teenagers, Dennis was more interested in sports than computers. He was the family jock, competing in national tennis competitions and starting a hockey club at school. That didn't leave much time for computers, although their house was filled with them, a byproduct of his father's employment with HP. His brothers—one older, one younger—were more in tune with the technology. He just wasn't interested.

When he turned 15, though, his brothers showed him a text-based MUD. That piqued his interest. It was just words on a screen, but that didn't matter. Something about having other people somewhere on the other side of the screen fascinated him. The game itself was run off of Berkeley servers, and it attracted players from around the world. He and his brothers formed their own guild. They called themselves WABAT, an acronym for "We are bad-ass thieves." They lived up to at least part of their name, wreaking havoc in the MUD world. They weren't in it for the chatting; they were competitive players who found it more fun to fight other players than to roam around slaying computer-generated monsters. Before long, the game's operators granted the Fong clan godlike powers, more than they could ever use in the game, simply to cut down on their bloody ways. Having so much power made fighting other people less fun, since there was no challenge in it.

That would all change after Dennis passed his younger brother's room one day and heard the sound of gunfire. He looked in. His brother was playing something that looked three-dimensional, wandering around dark rooms, shooting another shadowy figure, and being shot at.

"Let me try," he said, pushing his way toward the keyboard.

"I didn't know I was playing another person," Dennis said later. "Then I realized it was reacting too quickly and too intelligently to be the computer. I was tripping out. I hadn't played anything like it." The game was Doom. Dennis immediately demanded a copy.

The trio started playing the game together. His brothers showed Dennis how to put the game on his computer and connect all the machines together so their digital marines would appear in the same labyrinthine hallways. This way they could shoot each other to their hearts' content. They pushed each other until they were all very good; then they started looking for other opponents. The brothers found their own way to DWANGO, a new dial-up bulletin board system aimed particularly at Doom players. The company was run by a Houston entrepreneur named Robert Huntley who had taken the old text-based bulletin board services a step forward, configuring servers in a handful of regions around the United States so they were perfect Doom stomping grounds. Players could call up, see who was on their local server, chat with other people online, and then challenge each other to duels. The brothers played on the San Jose server, the one closest to their home in Los Altos. The eldest, Lyle, was the best and before long he was viewed as one of the better players in the country.

Dennis wasn't preternaturally skilled at this game. He was good, but not in the way Lyle was good. There were reasons, of course—his brother played more often and had a better computer than he did. Lyle had been playing the game longer. For a competitive athlete, though, those smacked of excuses. Dennis didn't like losing at anything. The same drive that had pushed him in tennis and hockey was at work here. Doom didn't take over his life; he still played sports like tennis at school, and he didn't let it get in the way of hanging out with friends, but he was determined to improve.

The trick turned out to be in the equipment. Doom, like many shooters, could be played several different ways. The basic idea was simple: The computer screen showed roughly the same view that the character in the world would see. At the bottom of the screen, the player could see a pair of hands holding whatever weapon was active, ranging from a pistol to a rocket launcher. The character's motion, ranging from running forward to spinning around to dancing quickly sideways—called "strafing"—could be controlled variously by the keyboard or the mouse. Most people used the keyboard to control the character action and the mouse to change the direction of the character's sight line.

Dennis had started out using just the keyboard for all of his controls. His brother Lyle was a trackball player, spinning the ball like he was playing Centipede instead of using a traditional mouse. That made Lyle faster. At first, Dennis resisted his brother's attempts to persuade him to change. He was stubborn; he was good at almost everything he tried, and he believed his style was best. Then, when his brother went away to China for a few months on an exchange program in the summer, Dennis decided to try out the mouse. He was almost instantly better and was soon beating people he'd never been able to beat before.

That simple change made all the difference. His brother returned from overseas and immediately found himself trailing his younger brother. He struggled to catch up. He even tinkered with the same mouse-keyboard setup, but it was all in vain. Dennis was too far ahead, and he was soon all but unbeatable.

They played in a few places. A friend had started hosting LAN parties called "Fragfests," where people could come, network their computers, and play Doom. The events grew as others heard about them, and soon dozens of people came to the parties, although unlike QuakeCon years later, these early LANs were more akin to Richard's local Dungeons & Dragons groups. Meanwhile, Dennis was gaining a reputation on the DWANGO servers in San Jose as "Thresh." He had earlier taken the nickname "Threshold" (as in "of pain"), but he had shortened it after finding game servers that wouldn't accept names that long.

By late 1994, Lyle was attending the University of California at Berkeley, and he had switched to DWANGO's Oakland servers. Teams from different cities' servers would play each other; Dennis was captain of the San

Jose team, while his brother headed up the Oakland team. Both teams were among the top in the DWANGO leagues, and they routinely played each other. Dennis almost always won.

This separation gave them an idea. They liked playing through the DWANGO service and had made some close friends that way. But DWANGO had flaws: It was relatively expensive, charging $2 an hour, which added up over the course of weeks and months of play. Moreover, it was difficult for people on different servers to play each other without constantly dialing long distance to the opponents' home turf. That got even more expensive.

They hit on an idea for their own company. A local wireless phone company was running a promotion that gave customers unlimited night and weekend calling for no extra charge. Doing a little digging, they figured out a way to create a call-forwarding service that would let people call a cell phone number with their computers and be immediately forwarded to another number that was connected to a modem. That was all they needed to set up a cheap DWANGO alternative. They signed up with a DWANGO rival called H2H as a franchisee. They rented a small office in Sunnyvale and set up a bank of modems there. They bought a single cell phone plan and set it up so that people could call that number with their computer, be forwarded to one of the modems, and from there be connected to the gaming service.

People streamed into the service, drawn by Dennis's growing reputation. Many of the core players on the Bay Area DWANGO servers were already their friends and routinely played with the brothers in other venues. Their new service operated just as efficiently as DWANGO, and slowly the group of opponents grew.

They made good money with their service—so much so, that they ultimately helped undermine DWANGO's business in the San Francisco Bay Area by 1996.

Dennis, though, was over the initial thrill of fragging people in Doom. He'd mastered the game, but now some of the challenge was gone, much as in the more ordinary sports he played. He didn't spend all his time playing tennis or hockey, and it was the same with Doom. An hour or two a day was enough to keep his skills sharp.

His playing style diverged from traditional gamers who played Doom and that was his advantage. Most single-player action games could be defeated simply by memorizing patterns. A good player in most games learned when to jump, when to duck, where the treasure was buried, and where the weaknesses lay in various monsters' attacks. It was complicated puzzle-solving at times, often requiring considerable creativity to win, but it was ultimately rote play once you figured it out.

It wasn't completely different playing other people in the Doom world. The game still had rules that were predictable and could serve as the basis of consistent strategies. Different levels had different characteristics that could be learned the same way a general might study the terrain before a battle. Controlling a particular area might provide the best platform for shooting, while giving opponents little chance to fire back, for example. Weapons or extra power might appear at particular times at particular places in the game, and running a set path around the map might be the most efficient way to capitalize on these bonuses.

These were reasonably good tactics. Players who learned the idiosyncrasies of a particular map were formidable opponents, virtually unbeatable on their "home" turf. Dennis did some of this, but he also found himself applying the skills he learned playing tennis and other sports. There it was important to know the physics of the game and have enough skill to make the ball do what you wanted. But it was also important to understand the other player, to be able to learn what he or she was doing and why, and then try to anticipate and counterattack at precisely the right moment. To Dennis, Doom was multidimensional chess. All you had to do was anticipate what the other player would do, and you were almost guaranteed to win, no matter what map you were playing on.

Todd Gehrke, a Microsoft programmer and top-notch Doom player on the Seattle DWANGO servers, later told of playing Thresh and seeing this style in action. Gehrke dialed in to the Bay Area from the north and played with a higher "ping rate" due to the distance, which meant he was playing with a potentially substantial disadvantage. (Ping rate is the common measurement of the time it takes information to travel from one computer to the game servers and back. A high rate means a perceptible lag time between a player's own actions—moving the computer's mouse to fire or dodge, for example—and the moment that the effects show up in the game world. This is measured in milliseconds, but in a "twitch" game like Doom, an eye-blink's duration can easily mean the difference between victory and an ignominious, bloody defeat.) In this case, Thresh compensated for the difference in their ping rates by playing with a lowly pistol as his weapon, while Gehrke played with the full range of vastly more lethal Doom weapons at his disposal. It didn't matter. Thresh won handily, Gehrke remembered.

The worlds of DWANGO and Doom would become entwined in the fortunes of mainstream software giant Microsoft in 1995, and Dennis would prove to be one of the points of contact for this. The software giant was then developing a new multimedia technology called DirectX as part of its new Windows 95 operating system and was trying desperately to persuade game developers that the platform could be used to make good games. Microsoft technology didn't have a good reputation for multimedia applications—those were still the domain of Apple Computer, although that company was losing ground fast—and most PC game companies still wrote directly for DOS instead of for the Microsoft Windows operating system. In hopes of breaking through this skepticism, a talented Microsoft programmer named Alex St. John went to John Carmack and asked if the company could make a version of Doom that ran on DirectX.

Carmack agreed and gave St. John the Doom source code, and a team of programmers was hired by Microsoft specifically to work on the project. It turned out a version called WinDoom, and with that in hand, Microsoft was able to convince other developers that its technology was strong and stable enough for other game platforms. Other programmers started coming on board.

In large part to show off the new Windows 95 operating system's ability to play games, Microsoft decided to host a huge Halloween party that year for its game developers. In conjunction with this, it arranged with DWANGO to sponsor a national Doom tournament, where people on each of the company's regional servers would vie for a spot in a final round tournament on the Microsoft campus, at the party. "Deathmatch '95" would be the first time that the best Doom players around the United States would be able to meet face to face and play—in theory, at least—on a completely level playing field. No long-distance calls would slow any of them down, and no suspicions could arise that a faceless player on the other side of the telephone line was cheating or had a computer so much faster that it might as well have been cheating.

Gerhke signed up and almost immediately lost in an early qualifying round. But the tournament was on his own employer's campus, so he wasn't about to miss any of it. Dennis, of course, was one of the finalists.

Microsoft went all out for the party, spending close to $1 million on props, a giant volcano, food, and other entertainment. The company dedicated one of its parking garages to the event, turning it into a giant haunted house. Each of the initial DirectX developers was invited to create a section, and scores of journalists came for tours. Party organizers and staff didn't keep a tight control on the content, however. Id showed up with a band called GWAR, famous for dressing up in freakishly cartoonish horror costumes and spitting fake blood on its audience. The band brought along its own props: an eight-foot-tall vagina with a few dozen little phallic sculptures, and a giant penis-shaped monster. The id attendees loved it. Microsoft's public relations staffers were horrified, but it was too late to change anything.

Microsoft CEO Bill Gates even got into the Halloween mood. The company created a little video, in which he was projected into a Doom background. He ran around for a few minutes, blasting demons with a shotgun, and then he stepped out of the world to tell the crowd about the advantages of using Windows as a gaming development platform. While he was talking, a live demon—a Microsoft employee dressed up for the event—jumped into the room and started running toward Gates. He pointed the shotgun and fired, snapping, "Don't interrupt me while I'm speaking." Above him, a giant Microsoft logo popped onto the screen, with the company's Internet slogan twisted just a little to read: "Who do you want to execute today?"[1]

For the gamers in attendance, this was public relations fluff, even if it was cool to see the CEO of the biggest software company in the world pay homage to their world. Most of them didn't see much of the show anyway—the Deathmatch competitors were cloistered in a little lounge for most of the day and allowed out to see the trade show and party only under supervision. The matches were littered with equipment complaints despite the efforts to forestall controversy. Some competitors didn't like the Microsoft keyboards, the Windows 95 computers didn't support the mice that some players had brought along with them, and the games were played through a DWANGO server instead of by linking the computers directly together as some players thought should happen.

None of it mattered in the end. The final match happened late at night, when janitors were already vacuuming the auditorium. Dennis won easily. "It was here that I realized that while I was good, there were people that were insanely good," said Gehrke, who'd stuck around to watch. "Obviously, they were aliens."

The gaming wasn't over. When the official tournament had finished, a group of the best players went back to another Microsoft building to keep playing, like jazz players going to an after-hours club to keep jamming after their gig is over. It was late, close to 3 A.M., and most of the rest of the partiers had long since gone home. The Microsoft offices were quiet and deserted—a perfect place to keep playing.

Gerhke was there, along with Dennis and "Mr. Elite," one of the Microsoft contractors who had helped build WinDoom. Mr. Elite was a consummate trash-talker on the Seattle DWANGO servers, and he challenged Dennis to a match here. Out of the public eye, the two matched guns. Maybe it was a fair match, and maybe it wasn't. Mr. Elite was on his own machine, Dennis on a borrowed computer with equipment very different from what he ordinarily used. Mr. Elite won.

Dennis laughed later when reminded about the late-night duel with Mr. Elite, and said he'd been forced to use equipment that was so completely different from what he was used to that the match wasn't fair at all. Later, he would beat Mr. Elite handily.

Already famous inside DWANGO circles, the now-18-year-old Dennis exploded into national notoriety after the Microsoft tournament. He had won a $10,000 computer (for the first time giving him a better computer than either of his brothers), as well as a lifetime supply of id games. Reporters started calling and showing up at his house. A profile of him ran on the front page of the staid *Wall Street Journal*, treating him as emblematic of the new, confusing world of online gaming. He started getting well-paying sponsorship offers from technology companies. Still, he went on with his ordinary school life. Many of his friends at school, the ones who didn't play games themselves, didn't even know he was a budding superstar. He wasn't the type to brag. He just didn't think it mattered that much.

* * *

In 1996, id released Quake. Dennis wasn't excited about it at first. He didn't want to learn a new game. He'd spent enough time getting used to Doom that the prospect of starting at the bottom again and crawling his way through the ranks was distasteful. It was early in the community's tournament play, but he was right—few players would ultimately make their mark in multiple game worlds.

He held out for months. His friends switched over and told him it was a better game. The ability to play over the Internet, instead of using the dedicated dial-up servers, was a powerful new feature, although that type of service signaled the end of the Fong brothers' company. Quake opened up the competition; that would mean he could match guns with people around the world more often, at least in theory. In practice, high lag times meant that games against people too far away would always be less than satisfying, but at least the potential was there. The problem that he and his brother had faced, of playing on separate servers, wouldn't be a problem anymore.

Eventually, Dennis gave in. The Doom II community had dwindled to the point that much of the fun had gone out of it. He got a copy of Quake and found it to be similar in game play to Doom. There was an initial learning curve—adjusting to the new weapons and game motion—and then he launched himself into the Internet Quake servers. He had a decent computer now, thanks to the Microsoft tournament win, but he was still playing with a slow dial-up modem. His brothers were still the computer hardware guys, upgrading to the latest and greatest technology as it came out. He was a player, without much of a head for the gear involved.

He wandered into the new Quake servers looking for a fight. He took a different name, since it was a different game, calling himself "Legacy." As he'd done with Doom II, Dennis began deconstructing the game, looking for shortcuts that he could exploit. One setting, for example, helped players center their guns' crosshairs on an opponent, easing the task of hitting a bouncing, ducking, and weaving opponent running through the game world at the equivalent of a hundred miles an hour or so. A powerful weapon in the game was a rocket launcher, but it was hard to use this in conjunction with the auto-aim—by the time the rocket hit the point the game had determined was accurate, the target had usually moved. Dennis figured out a way around this, using the rocket launcher and aiming away from the player, deliberately missing and hitting the ground nearby. It still caused damage—not as much as a direct hit, but a few blasts in quick succession proved devastating. He was on his way.

Other players picked up on his game play, and it didn't take long for people to cotton to the fact that Legacy was actually Thresh. He reclaimed his name, and joined a clan of old Doom players, called IHOS, or "International House of Spork" ("Don't ask," he said later, queried about the origin of the name). As word got out, his old reputation filtered through a growing community of Quake-playing young guns. The Net really was, and still is, like the Wild West, he said later. "You basically fight and crawl your way up by beating well-known people. Then after you establish your reputation, you have to take on all comers."

That aspect had started in the Doom years, but the size of the DWANGO population had limited the number of challenges. Now he was getting up to 1000 emails a day from other trash-talking kids convinced they could knock the mighty Thresh off his pedestal. He had to play some of them to shut them up, but he couldn't play all of them. As it turned out, he didn't have to. People from his clan, or even just people who had played him before and knew how good he was, stepped in to respond to the taunts of newcomers, challenging them to prove themselves at lower levels first. It wasn't a matter of King Thresh sending his minions out to do his bidding. It was just the community responding in a way that kept its own hierarchies intact. If newcomers could beat people lower on the ladder, then they could certainly take on Thresh. But it was an insult to everyone for newcomers to think they could start unproven at the top.

Almost nobody actually beat Dennis, particularly in tournament matches where money was on the line. But he made close friends out of many of these opponents, particularly those who played in the local San Francisco Bay Area. They would go to LAN parties, bring their computers, be ready to shoot all night, and wind up not even playing—instead, just hanging out and shooting the breeze watching movies, or catching up in ways that it was hard to do in the context of an online chat room. Thresh took some people under his wing and trained them. Others were just friends.

❋ ❋ ❋

The Microsoft Deathmatch made the computer world sit up and take notice in 1995. The first QuakeCon in 1996, as small as it was, helped signal that the game community was growing strong. But the Red Annihilation frag-off held at the 1997 Atlanta Electronics and Entertainment Expo (E3) introduced high-stakes computer gaming to the public eye.

By 1997, DWANGO, the Total Entertainment Network (TEN), Mpath, and other private online gaming services had helped feed the network desires of more than a million and a half people around the United States. Players were mostly boys and men in their 20s—but some women played as well. LAN parties had sprung up across the country, too, and the level of play was improving. Mythologies were developing around Thresh and other standouts, and rivalries developed between regions, particularly between the West Coast and East Coast players.

After reaching a certain level of competitive play, online gamers on each side of the country often tended to develop friendships or at least casual acquaintanceship with each other. If someone in Seattle—Microsoft's Gehrke, for example—wanted to take on Thresh, he could do it on the Internet without either player being put at too much of a disadvantage. The same wasn't true for cross-country rivalries, however. Players would meet online, to be sure, and they would talk up their local champions, but serious matches between players on opposite sides of the country were rare. The matches weren't really fair—by the time a player in California logged into a New York server, he was already at such a disadvantage from the lag time needed to transmit his signals across the country and back that the game was barely worth playing. As a result, the coasts developed their own rivalries and distinctive personalities, even explicitly identifying with some of the ritualized rivalry between West Coast and East Coast rap artists of the time.

The Red Annihilation tournament was meant finally to bring the two regions in direct conflict. Let the champions from each side face each other at last. Put the trash-talkers' time and money where their mouths were. This was to be a real event in the history of gaming—not a corporate-sponsored public relations fest like Microsoft's version. Id and Carmack got involved. Carmack said he'd donate his Ferrari, bought with the proceeds from record sales of Doom and its sequels, as a prize for the winner.

Even more than money, a Ferrari was a symbol of radical success for any teenage boy. These were the unattainable cars that emblazoned millions of high-school bedroom wall posters, cars that you might see one day driving past on the street if you were lucky. Nobody ever had the chance to actually drive one, much less *own* one.

Dennis was one of the representatives of the West Coast, of course. So was his brother Lyle. They both made it easily through early rounds of the elimination tournament there. Lyle made it to the top 16, but finally washed out. Dennis cut a swath through all comers. He wasn't nervous. He never got nervous. It just wasn't in his character. Even when his tennis team had gone to nationals, he had stayed cool. It was why he was good. Cool was part of his style. He didn't trash-talk either. The East Coasters thought he was arrogant, he said later, but it was because other Westerners had bragged on his behalf. It was easy to mistake the boastful words of someone's supporters for the person's own attitude—he was willing to admit that. He had a similar view of the person that he ultimately wound up playing, a frag-artist known in Quake circles as Entropy.

The game stage was set up as an eight-sided group of tables, with computers facing in, and little cubicle walls separating the machines so that the players couldn't see each other's screens. The E3 crowd was kept behind the gamers, but they could circle the stage and watch the players' screens. Before the final match, Dennis met Entropy, a kid about his own age, and they negotiated on which level to play in for their final game. Entropy seemed nervous. He had a reputation for being practically unbeatable on one particular map, and the luck of the draw had let him play on that level almost all the way through the tournament—it was only the final match that was up to the players' choice. But he'd also seen Thresh eviscerate one of his opponents on the same map, and he didn't want to take the risk that Thresh knew the lay of the land even better than he did. They negotiated cagily for a few minutes and finally settled on a map that neither had played many times. They sat down on opposite sides of the octagonal stage to play, Carmack's cherry-red Ferrari glittering on display directly behind Thresh's chair.

For all the lead-up, the match proved anticlimactic. Dennis lived up to his supporters' braggadocio, quickly taking control of the level's key strategic areas. "At that point, you have to make mistakes to lose," he said later. "I didn't generally make mistakes." By the time the game started its countdown to the final seconds, he was ahead 13 kills to –1. Entropy was shaken enough by the beating that he had accidentally blown himself up with his own weapon.

Something about the countdown caught Dennis's attention. For the first time he noticed the reflection of the Ferrari behind him in his own computer monitor. And for the first time in the entire tournament, he got nervous—not at the prospect of losing, because at that point it would have been an impossibility. But something about the reality of winning the car made this surreal experience feel suddenly more real than before. A red Ferrari sat behind him, and in ten seconds, nine, eight, it was going to be *his*.

The awards ceremony was the first time the 20-year-old had really met the boyish Carmack. They chatted for a few minutes after the presentation of the keys.

"How are you going to get the car back to California?" Carmack asked Dennis.

He thought about it. He didn't even know how to drive a stick shift. "I think I'm going to ship it," he told the developer.

Carmack thought about that. "I'll be right back," he said, and disappeared. He came back a little while later and held out a thick stack of bills. "That ought to cover it," he told Dennis.

That hadn't been part of the deal. Dennis counted it a few minutes later. It was $5000, more than he needed to cover the costs of shipping. He took his friends and brothers out that night, treated them at a local steakhouse, and paid for it all with Carmack's generous contribution; still, he had more than enough left over to pay the shipping bills.

The tournament marked another big change in Dennis's life, and in the public's perception of gaming. For years afterward, when journalists wrote about the nascent "professional" gaming world, the story of Dennis winning Carmack's Ferrari was routinely cited. For Dennis, it helped convince his mildly skeptical parents that what he was doing was worth pursuing. "They had been a little concerned," he said. "But I remember the day they became OK with it was the day I brought home a Ferrari."

Dennis would go on to win dozens of other tournaments. Once he hit his stride, few people beat him in individual games, and he never failed to place first in a set of tournament matches. His star power bled over to the industry at large. In 1998, he and a group of lesser-known but still stellar players converged on San Francisco's Candlestick Park, then home of the city's baseball team, the Giants, for the launch of the Professional Gaming League (PGL). The privately owned organization wanted to do for computer gaming what Major League Baseball had done for that sport. Atari founder and video gaming legend Nolan Bushnell took the reins as commissioner of the new league, and attending journalists were given trading cards featuring Thresh and other league superstars.

Dennis and his brothers were already taking their gaming in a different direction. As soon as Quake was released in late 1996, it had been clear that their H2H dial-up gaming business didn't have much of a future. It had done well in the Doom years, but Quake and the Internet had changed the market. Anyone with a modem and an ISP could find a Quake game online. Nobody needed the dedicated services anymore, even if they did provide a better quality of game play.

By 1997, however, the Web business boom was on. Netscape had gone public almost two years earlier, proving that the Net could bring big money. Portals such as Yahoo! and Excite were drawing millions of people a day to their doors. Community was already a buzzword in Silicon Valley. Venture capitalists had the words on their lips, books were being written, and obscene amounts of money were being spent to create "community" in a thousand different places on the Web. It was an elusive concept; people seemed to gather where they wanted to, rather than where the most money was being spent, but companies and investors kept trying.

The brothers talked. There was undeniably a gamers' community by this time, even if it was a fractured one. The old DWANGO servers had definitely been communities. People there knew each other, warmed to each other as friends even outside the arena of video games, and watched out for each other. Bringing the games onto the broader Internet had changed the character of that—the communities that developed weren't as regionally driven, since people could log in from anywhere in the world. However, they were fragmented by game, by region, by style of play, by clan and guild, and by any number of other differences.

The brothers decided to start a new company. It would be called Gamers Extreme and would serve as a gamers' home on the Web—a portal *by* gamers, *for* gamers. Plenty of sites talked about games, but they were mostly sponsored by journalists—not that writers couldn't play and love games, but it wasn't the same thing. It was early enough in the Web's gold rush that the brothers were able to register the domain name *Gamers.com*, and with that bit of nomenclatural luck and Dennis's reputation, the site was launched successfully.

Dennis kept playing for the next few years, but his attention slowly shifted. As the focus of the communities moved away from the games on which he'd won his fame, he dropped out of tournaments to focus on building the site. The business flourished, surviving even when many better-funded web sites had fallen victim to the Internet crash. As years passed, other names succeeded his as the "World's Best Gamer." Younger gamers entered the scene knowing nothing of his reputation for excellence. Memories were short in this world.

✳ ✳ ✳

Dennis's path to the top touched many aspects of the early online gaming circles, but in truth it represented only a small part of what was actually going on. For every Thresh, hundreds of players formed their own clans and competed at a lower level. For every clan member, thousands of people played on their own. The outside world looked on the gaming community with some bemusement. People unfamiliar with the scene found it laughable that kids could win tens of thousands of dollars playing computer games. But the big computer hardware companies understood the value of the competitions—these were the people who would push computer technology to new heights, and sponsoring events like Red Annihilation was simply good marketing.

Those who were closer to the scene saw something else. Many of the kids who gathered together to play hadn't had Dennis's ability to join a stellar athletic team, and now for the first time found the rewards of being part of a team. "The great thing about online play is that there are large groups of kids who would love to play on a hockey team or a football team, but they aren't the right kind of kids," said Tim Willits, the former Doom player who wound up working for id as a lead designer. "It's all virtual, but it's still a team."

Still, as gaming cultures began to expand online in 1996, some of the less savory aspects of traditional sports carried over too. This was a very male society, for one thing. Few were surprised by that—these were shooter games, after all, and the initial point was to frag each other as quickly as possible. On the face of it, that was a far cry from traditional girls' games, which—popular wisdom had it—were supposed to be more about cooperation and social interaction.

Nor was there much racial or class diversity in the online gaming arenas. Although it was theoretically impossible to tell what race, class, or gender any digital warrior actually was, it was pretty clear that the games tended to skew towards Caucasian and, increasingly, Asian males. Certainly that was an artifact of the spread of technology itself. At that point in the explosion of the Internet, policy-makers and public interest groups were already highlighting the so-called digital divide and making efforts to bring Net connections and PCs to low-income and minority populations.

The relative lack of diversity *did* have an effect on the online culture, however. Later, this would become a hotly debated topic, but it seemed clear that the online trash-talking didn't produce the friendliest environment for women. Homophobic language was common. Racial slurs were not unknown. No one expected these ad hoc communities to be utopias, certainly, but their culture quickly proved to be the product as much of who was absent as of who was actually participating.

None of this meant that women, minorities, rural farm kids, or any other group was altogether missing. Indeed, some of those who did log on and start shooting used the communities' tools to build niches of their own, earning a visible role in Quake and broader online gaming cultures. This was particularly true for a scattered group of young women who carved out a visible role for themselves online, showing that they could frag and brag as well or better than most of their male counterparts.

❋ ❋ ❋

In mid-1996, Vangie Beale was a college student in Victoria, British Columbia, a Canadian island city in the cold waters north of Washington state. She was originally from a Nova Scotian town of barely 250 people, where entertainment came in the form of arcade games at the local tourist campgrounds. Along the way, she'd picked up the computer bug, and when she moved out to a bigger city, she had started hanging out on local bulletin board systems, talking with regulars there and increasingly meeting them offline. They had started gathering in a local Internet cafe where a few of them were playing a game called Doom.

She found the game a little boring at first, but several of the men in the little group were almost fanatical about it. They would drag their computers to each other's houses and hook the machines together just so they could dial up the local bulletin board all at once and play each other in the same room. In a way it didn't make sense, but Beale wasn't one to sit by and watch while other people were having fun. She and a few other of the women in the Net cafe started playing the bloody game, and to their surprise it was fun. Soon she was mowing her way through little digital men with rockets and shotguns. And it was a blast.

At that point, there weren't many women players like Beale, or at least their presence wasn't readily apparent in the world of Doom. At Microsoft's 1995 Deathmatch, female faces had been few and far between in the crowd, and even more scarce in front of the clicking keyboards. This was true for other video games, too. Since the late 1970s, developers had known that they were making games largely for teenage boys, and it was almost a happy accident when a significant demographic slice of women found something to like in a game. Centipede and Ms. Pac Man had that appeal. Younger girls liked some of Nintendo's Mario games. But women certainly weren't flocking to Doom deathmatches. By 1994, a "girl games" movement had started in the industry, with a few game companies trying to appeal to younger girls with themes familiar from toy stores—dating, shopping, fashion, and the like. A few titles with built-in appeal such as the

Barbie brand name sold well, but most did not. Critics accused the companies of reinforcing sexist stereotypes, while proponents said they were simply doing their best to expand a market with egregiously lopsided gender dynamics.[2]

Beale wasn't the likeliest candidate for gamer fame. Her tiny Nova Scotian home was a continent away from Silicon Valley, and its cultural distance might as well have been measured in light-years. The community had offered little in the way of nearby diversion; by the time she reached high school age, it was a cold, two-hour ride on the bus every morning just to reach campus. She had played Atari games at home, and the arcade games that had been installed at nearby campgrounds wound up being one of her favorite ways to pass the time.

She'd stumbled onto computers a few years before, when her middle school purchased a handful of Apples. Students were given assignments that required using the machines, and Beale learned her way around quickly without any explicit training. That school experience was enough to hook her on computers. She decided that she would have computers of her own from then on. Her machines were always older and often used, but they were enough to keep her interest piqued.

Shortly after Vangie and her friends started playing Doom, the first versions of Quake were released. That proved even more fun. The group would line up at computers next to each other at the Internet cafe, log onto the same servers, and proceed to shoot each other silly or team up against outsiders, laughing and screaming at each other across the room.

It didn't take long for people to start forming more official groups. The men she knew, many of whom had been playing Doom for years and were already good at Quake, joined other peoples' clans or started their own. The women found themselves suddenly excluded. They'd felt bits of this online; few women were playing, and the chatter on servers was often sexist or downright abusive. Their friends weren't typically like this, but closed doors still existed. "It was like, 'When you get better, you can join our clans,'" Beale said later. "But we *were* getting better."

Fine, she and her friends said. If you can't join them, beat them. And thus PMS—the Psycho Men Slayers—was born, the first all-female clan to hit the Quake server circuit. Beale was later quick to say that the name didn't indicate any special animosity toward men. It was simply drawn from the fact that men tended to be the only people they found online to play.

The response in the Quake community was mixed. Guys weren't always happy about playing women, particularly when the PMS-ers won. "There was verbal harassment and abuse. But to us it was funny," Beale said. "A very sensitive female might have taken it harder." It helped that they were a clan and that their own local friends were on their side. When the harassment from some trash-talking player got to be too much, the PMS-ers would gang up on him. They had numbers on their side and the kind of confidence that came from flying together in the face of expectations. They weren't top-ranking players, but they were good.

It didn't take long for the rest of the world to see what they were doing. Other female players were beginning to make waves, too, and the phenomenon of women carving out a decidedly separate spot in the community—with all the hard-edged, frag-driven determination of their male counterparts—fired imaginations.

Wired magazine sent a photographer to Victoria late in the year, and the four PMS-ers were featured in a subsequent issue of the publication. Almost immediately, email began coming in from other Quake players, writing that they were astonished to see other women players, that they thought they had been the only ones. A few of them joined the clan, and before too many more months passed, PMS was international.

Even better, other all-female clans started up. Women's tournaments started popping up. Women started having more of a presence at the marquis QuakeCon tournament. Famously, one of the top women players, Stevie "Killcreek" Case, beat John Romero in deathmatch play. When the Professional Gaming League started up in 1998, several women's faces were among the player cards handed out to reporters and fans.

As the women's online presence grew, the harassment didn't go away. Women players routinely cited problems online that men didn't face. Cloddish pick-up lines were routine. Players were jokingly asked to star in pornographic movies or assumed to be lesbians. Pornographic photographs with faces altered to look like prominent players were passed around servers.

Beale and others quickly realized that more was needed. Even the myriad of web sites that had sprung up to post news and gossip about the games' community were all very male-centric. For most of the sites, it was as if there were no women playing the game at all. That worried her, particularly given the response from women gamers that her clan had elicited. "Everything I've done since I was a teenager has been male dominated," she said later. "I have tough skin, and it didn't offend me. But I thought that other girls might look at these sites and say, 'That's stupid, that's not something I'd be interested in.'"

She decided to start her own web site. She called it *Gamegirlz.com*, and she designed it as a place where women gamers could come and read their own stories, publish their own thoughts, and understand that there were plenty of other women in the world who liked the same things they liked. It wouldn't be dogmatic, wouldn't be particularly political, but it would provide a place where a more diverse community of gamers could grow. Launched in 1997, it was still going strong in early 2003, long outlasting some of the most popular gaming sites online.

The atmosphere by that time had improved somewhat, both for women and other minority groups, some said. Caryn "Hellchick" Law, a Quake player and columnist for the PlanetQuake web site, had by that time been a consistent critic of the community's seeming blindness to sexism and racism online, but was optimistic. "Racial and sexual slurs are pretty prevalent online," she said. "But I do see a more general movement to eliminate the use of racial and sexual slurs among gamers. I'm not sure if that's because maybe the community is all growing up a bit together and realizing that we don't want that kind of behavior in our community, or if it's because of minorities being a bit more vocal and saying, 'Dude, I'm black and it ticks me off when you throw around those words like that.'"

Over the course of these years, Beale and her clan did find something in the game that was often overlooked. On the surface, Quake was about running around and shooting anything that moved, seemingly channeling the simplest of teenage boy power fantasies. In reality, it had become a social experience. It was a game taking place in the context of a community that rewarded social participation. It certainly was not for every girl—or every boy, for that matter. The quick response, the simple goals mixed with complicated manipulation of the mouse and keyboard, and the subject of the game if taken at face value added up to considerable hurdles for anybody who wasn't already hooked by something in the game's play. But sitting shoulder to shoulder in the cafe, Beale had seen that this was a social game, too. It wasn't all about solitary killing.

"I can have a blast sitting in my room with 30 women from around Canada and the U.S. on the same server. We'll just talk, and someone will complain about her husband, or talk about her kid's new tooth," Beale said. "It's still social whether you have friends in the room with you or you have people with you out on a network somewhere."

The rise of women inside the action game culture continues today. But it would be other online games, among them Richard Garriott's own Ultima series, that would ultimately find themselves reflecting the face of broader society more directly. Massively multiplayer worlds would be built with the explicit idea of creating and sustaining a social environment within the games themselves, more so than were the fast-paced shooters. But importing a culture into new online worlds, no matter how technologically advanced, would prove to bring along many of the headaches and problems of the real world.

7

Losing the Game

Late in 1994, Richard Garriott was not a happy visionary. Sitting in Electronic Arts' CEO Larry Probst's office, listening to the older man's explanations for why online worlds weren't a good investment, he sighed. This was the third time he'd been here making the same pitch. He might as well be an arcade game character—with three lives. This was the last one, at least for this game. He was ready to call it quits. This corporate game was no fun at all.

That Probst didn't fully believe in Richard's idea was hardly surprising. Sitting in that office, the programmer was pitching a relatively new—or at least commercially unproven—idea that would link tens of thousands of gamers together in a virtual world with its own economy, ecology, and political system. It was a massive undertaking that had never been tried on the scale Richard had conceived. He wanted to put Ultima online, something he and his team had been talking about for years and had even tried on a rudimentary level once or twice in their New England offices, but had never gotten terribly serious about.

Until now, the technology simply hadn't been ready, but the emergence of the Internet as a commercial medium was changing that. Suddenly, the idea of an online community that was accessible to everyone—not just university students and intrepid techies—was a reality. Although Ultima had always been a single-player game, its roots were in Dungeons & Dragons, where a dozen or more people would gather in the same room and wander through the same imaginary world together. The idea of

148

Richard Garriott, engaging in some early medieval
role-playing during his high school days

The Garriott children

Astronaut Owen Garriott talks to the nation about his adventures in space

Garriott's first commercial game, Akalabeth, was distributed in Ziploc bags

The staff of Steve Jackson Games in 1984. Jackson is standing, wearing a suit

Role-playing extended beyond video games. The annual Richard Garriott haunted house was filled with monsters and contraptions that took months to build

A typical Renaissance Faire

Doom co-creator John Romero in his early days at Softdisk, and then later, with much longer hair, in his office at Ion Storm

The Cyberathlete Professional League runs lucrative gaming tournaments, drawing thousands of players from around the world

The online digital worlds you see today exist largely in server rooms created to handle hundreds of thousands of players at once. Ultima Online's original home was packed a bit tighter than more modern server farms

Starr Long may be the most trusted non-Garriott at NCSoft. The game designer helped launch Ultima Online and then followed Richard to his new company, where he has a hand in most games

Bill Trost, co-designer of EverQuest

M.I.T. Professor Henry Jenkins, one of the leading academic figures studying games and other popular media

Richard Garriott has gone back to his roots, designing complex new worlds he hopes will combine the strengths of single-player and massively multiplayer games

Robert Garriott continues to run his brother's business operations

The online gaming world continues to grow. Here, an adventurer unfurls the Lineage flag at the South Pole

creating a communal world in which to play a computer game was a natural step. The more he'd thought about it, the more Richard became convinced that this was indeed the logical next step for mainstream gaming. People had been playing networked games almost since the first computers were unleashed on university campuses in the sixties. Persistent virtual worlds like Bartle's MUD were commonplace. Richard wanted to build Britannia, the virtual world of the Ultima series, as a place in cyberspace where gamers could wander through the towns and forests with parties of their friends, and would meet people who were real players, not just stilted computer-generated characters. The world of Lord British had always lacked this ongoing social aspect, and that had always rankled Richard just a bit.

Selling that idea, particularly to a gaming company rapidly building a marketing empire on uncomplicated mega-hit titles, had so far proven difficult. Twice before Probst had said no. Too expensive. Too untested. Too weird, he said. But this time Richard's persistence paid off. Maybe Probst figured the only way to end this discussion would be to let the whiz kid fail.

"How much would you need?" he asked Richard.

Richard thought for a minute. He and his team had kicked around estimates before, but the truth was, he had no idea. Nobody had ever done a project like this before, at least not the way he was imagining it. By this time a regular game—a sophisticated one—could take millions of dollars to create once the talents of all the programmers, artists, and designers had been brought to bear. Development teams no longer consisted of just a handful of programmers. They were counted in dozens now. It had been a long time since it had been just him sitting in front of his Apple II. Sensing the risk, the Origin Systems' teams had opted to start small, just to get their foot in EA's increasingly skeptical corporate door. "A quarter-million dollars," Richard suggested. "We could build a prototype for a quarter million."

Probst mulled that over, and finally said the magic words. "OK. See what you can do," he said, reaching for his yellow legal pad and scribbling a note signaling his permission. "But you can't screw up the next real Ultima for it."

Richard left the office, his mind already turning over possibilities. After months of wrangling, he'd finally gotten the go-ahead, although the note was practically the only recognition he'd receive through the early part of the development process. Few outside the Origin Systems team—and even its members had their doubts—believed online games of this scale would be part of the immediate future of gaming.

There was good reason for the skepticism. The world Richard was imagining was considerably different than what Carmack, Romero, and other multiplayer gamers were doing with their online play. In those games, people could connect their computers, either directly or over a network, and then run through the same virtual game space, but it was only a "world" in the simplest sense of the word. A Doom playing field existed only so long as there were people playing in it. Each multiplayer game effectively spawned a different little bubble-universe that would disappear when the players were done.

Ultima Online would be a persistent world. From the developer's perspective, it would be uncharted territory. The company—Electronic Arts, in this case—would have to maintain computers that kept the world operating around the clock. Those computers would have to support hundreds, thousands, or even tens of thousands of players acting in the same world at the same time. From the player's perspective it would be more complicated than an ordinary game. It wouldn't just be as simple as turning on the computer to play. They'd have to rejoin a world that had gone on without them every time. Every time players logged in, they might spend at least a few minutes trying to figure out what had transpired since they were last online. It would be the digital equivalent of reading the morning paper, checking out what had happened overnight as hundreds or even thousands of people wandered though the world simultaneously.

This wasn't the first time a persistent world had been conceived, but the scale and ambition of Richard's project would set a benchmark by which all later "massively multiplayer online games," or MMOG's as they would be known, would come to be measured. The game would feature pre-designed adventures that players could go on (although one of the obvious problems was that many people in the world would wind up going on the same adventures), but one of the most exciting features for gamers would be that Ultima Online would allow players to create their own stories, essentially bringing the Dungeon Master into a graphic, virtual world. Many of these adventures would be put together by guilds and clans, and would often take the form of wars with other factions within the game. For those who wanted to avoid player-killing adventures, common areas like village pubs would allow them simply to chat with others in the game.

From the outside, the game would be radically different than previous versions of Ultima. It would lack the kind of focused, linear story that had grounded the previous games. With this amount of freedom, it would ultimately be both an experiment in player psychology and in defining the boundaries of what a game really was.

The issues raised by Ultima Online would resonate throughout the game industry and player communities for years, as massively multiplayer gaming grew in popularity. Soon after Ultima Online, other games including Sony's EverQuest, Mythic Entertainment's Dark Age of Camelot, and NCSoft's Korean-based Lineage followed. Millions of players around the world would eventually sign up to play these games, paying monthly access fees to continue playing in large part to retain access to the community of people they played with rather than to find out how the game ended. The traditional model of a game creator as a god-figure who determined the course of the story and the history of a world would vanish. These would be players' worlds.

* * *

For years, game makers and science-fiction writers had toyed with this idea of giving players a kind of existential independence. The all-text Multiple User Dungeons, or MUDs, that Richard Bartle created in Britain in the late 1970s and early 1980s had provided a first look at what persistent online worlds could be, allowing players to wander and act with a high level of freedom. That strain of development had been picked up by game makers around the world throughout the 1980s, and by the early 1990s, thousands of different kinds of text MUDs had emerged. Many had retained Bartle's swords-and-sorcery theme, but plenty were devoted to other themes—from science-fiction worlds to flat-out sexual simulations, all allowing dozens, hundreds, or even thousands of people to interact.

Graphic multiplayer online worlds were newer, but game developers had been experimenting with those for a few years, too. Lucasfilm Games, a division of *Star Wars* creator George Lucas' LucasArts Entertainment company, had aimed at creating a cartoon-like online game world called Habitat beginning as far back as 1985. Released in 1987 as a trial project on the Quantum Link online service—the company that later evolved into America Online—the game let players chat, spend money, go on treasure hunts, and run businesses, among other activities.

As the MUDs had before it, Habitat demonstrated that game psychology was as tricky an issue to manage as was technology. Developers Chip Morningstar and Randy Farmer quickly found that managing an online world with real people as citizens was far more difficult than they had imagined, so much so that they wrote a series of early 1990s papers describing their experience, hoping to guide other developers around the land mines they had faced. Players would consistently cheat or game the system (a trait that persists in game worlds to this day, spawning an entire business sector called "punkbusting" around stopping cheaters), exploiting bugs or inconsistencies to their own advantage. An early economic system in Habitat was nearly shattered when players learned how to take advantage of varying "vending machine" and "pawnshop" prices to buy items, pawn them at a higher price, and become rich in just a few hours of play. In another episode, a game staffer playing the character of "Death" was unexpectedly killed, and his special "kill-at-one-shot" gun fell into the hands of a player, a potential catastrophe that was wholly unplanned for by developers.

"Again and again we found that activities based on often unconscious assumptions about player behavior had completely unexpected outcomes (when they were not simply outright failures)," Farmer and Morningstar wrote in their 1991 paper about the project. "It was clear that we were not in control. The more people we involved in something, the less in control we were. We could influence things, we could set up interesting situations, we could provide opportunities for things to happen, but we could not dictate the outcome."[1]

The Habitat game world went on to mild success in various incarnations. By 1990, about 15,000 people had subscribed to a new version of the game called Club Caribe. The game was successful enough that Fujitsu took over the project and extended it on an online service in Japan. Eventually, the resources it took to maintain the game led to the world's end, but it provided the digital community with the term "avatar," which would become the standard name for virtual representations of players in online worlds. (The fact that Richard had used that same name as the hero of his Ultima tales was little more than a coincidence.)

Writers and academics were discovering virtual communities along with game developers by the early 1990s, in large part because of the success of MUDs, online services such as CompuServe, and bulletin board systems. The goings-on inside these virtual spaces were being dissected and studied by an increasingly large population as they took on both positive and negative features of the real world, often with twists unique to the online realm. In 1993, author Howard Rheingold published *Virtual Communities*, the first popular book about these communities, as a follow-up to an earlier book on virtual reality technologies. That same year, a "virtual rape" inside the LamdaMOO world, a text-based MUD-like system dedicated to social interaction rather than adventuring, was written up in the *Village Voice* newspaper, providing another window into the mysterious online culture for a popular audience.[2]

Networked multiplayer games, played independently or on one of the online services such as America Online, the Total Entertainment Network (TEN), or MPath Interactive, were proliferating. With only a few exceptions, persistent online worlds were still largely the domain of the text MUDs, however.

That would soon change. The World Wide Web was exploding into the national consciousness by 1995, and the itch to create virtual online worlds was palpable in technology circles. Richard wasn't the only developer thinking in terms of creating these online worlds. Dr. Cat, the former Origin programmer, launched his own graphic MUD called DragonSpires in early 1995. In 1996, Sierra's Ken Williams began beta testing The Realm, a cartoony medieval-themed online multiplayer game. A small development house called Archetype Interactive began work on a multiplayer MUD

called Meridian 59. With a few minor tweaks to accommodate the burgeoning popularity of the Web, game giant 3D0 purchased and launched
the graphical world in 1996.

Online gaming was on the minds of developers everywhere. Few others
envisioned the initial scope of Richard's project, however. After a few
years in programming exile, watching Doom take the gaming world by
storm and trying to integrate Origin Systems with Electronic Arts, Richard
wanted his next game to put him back on the playing field.

* * *

It was clear from the beginning of the project that Ultima Online was
something of a bastard stepchild in the Electronic Arts family. This wasn't
Richard's doing—he was squarely behind the project, and he did his best
to dedicate time to it, but another project was drawing his attention as
well. Persistent worlds may have been the future, the next step in the evo-
lution of gaming, but his own past demanded attention. He desperately
wanted to finish the ninth, and final, Ultima. In his mind, this would complete the final chapter in his planned trilogy of trilogies. Ego had a little to
do with that decision. The poor performance of Ultima VIII, which Richard attributed to corporate pressure forcing the release of a buggy, unfinished game, meant that Electronic Arts' dedication to releasing another
single-player Ultima had waned, yet he felt a paternal desire to finish his
long-running series on a high note.

The split between the two games put Richard in an awkward position.
With just $250,000, he didn't have the luxury of finding the industry's top
graphics programmers for the online project. Nor was he allowed, per
Probst's instructions, to raid his own Ultima IX team. Much as id Software
had turned to the mod community to keep Doom fresh with new game
play, Richard and Starr Long, one of his top lieutenants, went to the text
MUD world to find programmers who knew how to create online worlds.
The MUD community had been built almost entirely by hobbyists, students, and companies that never expected to make the kind of money that
Origin had. These programmers were smart, they came cheap, and they
understood how online gaming worked. Richard hired some of the best
for Origin's Ultima Online team.

If the new programmers had any delusions of grandeur regarding their staff positions at Electronic Arts, those were quickly dispelled. The team's office quarters showed clearly where they stood on the corporate totem pole. The Origin Systems' offices off the Capital of Texas Highway in Austin were being renovated throughout much of the development process. The three-story complex was in disarray as builders knocked out the entire inside of sections of the campus, rebuilding them to accommodate a THX sound studio, server farms, and office space. As a result, the ragtag Ultima Online team was constantly shuffled in and out of half-finished rooms. In the middle of development, the team found itself set up in a hallway as the walls were knocked down around them.

Richard, ensconced in Ultima IX, turned much of the UO team's operations over to Starr Long. He gave them the graphics code from Ultima VI, technology that may have been outdated for single-player games but was perfect for the online experiments, and let them go to work. Within a short time, they'd created a prototype that allowed four players to chat and kill each other. It was small and much simpler than their goal of a world that would support tens of thousands of players, but it was a start.

In early 1996, the company posted a message on its web site and sent news through online newsgroups that it would conduct a "pre-alpha" test. Beta tests are used to flesh out early versions of games, using players as guinea pigs who search out bugs and give feedback to developers who then hone the code. The pre-alpha test meant a handful of lucky players would get a firsthand look under the hood of Ultima Online, literally playing the game as it was being made. News of the tests spread quickly through an online fan club known as the Ultima Dragons and other aficionado communities. Three thousand people—roughly twice the size of most large text-based MUDs—were accepted into the trial. "Well done, my friend," read the email successful applicants received. "By applying to test the pre-Alpha version of Ultima Online, you not only get to experience an exciting new world, but also help us make the world more stable and enjoyable for all." Only 250 people would be allowed online at any one time in this initial stage, and the game would be limited to a single city, but the world would expand dramatically later on, the company promised.

The test got off to a clunky start in March 1996. "At that time, they were still just working out how they wanted the world to function," remembered

Robert Gregg, a student and Ultima Dragons club member who joined the pre-alpha test. "Needless to say, there were a lot of basic programming issues to work out, and at first, things didn't work so well. I logged onto the system for the first time, and here's what I saw: 15 people standing naked on top of a table, frozen solid, all saying 'Why can't I move?' over and over again. It was so funny I just about busted a gut laughing."

By the middle of 1996, the team thought they were close to doing a much larger beta test, but there was a problem. Much of their seed money had been spent in creating the first iteration of Ultima Online. On the cusp of launching a real beta test, the little team didn't have enough funds left over to manufacture and ship enough CDs to players, and Probst had made it clear that EA wouldn't be putting up any more money. Out of options, Origin turned to the players themselves for help. Richard posted an advertisement on the Origin Systems web site, asking players who wanted to be involved in the beta to send a $2 check to the company to cover shipping and production of the CD. The developers expected a reasonable response but kept their expectations low. Asking people to pay to be part of a beta test was an imposition.

That made it all the more surprising when responses began pouring in. Within two weeks, Long's team was knee-deep in money. By October, the company had received more than 32,000 checks, and that number would eventually climb to 50,000. "We were stunned. Fifty thousand people signed up and started sending us cash," Richard said. "Our total projection was that 20,000 or 25,000 would ever be playing the game, and all of a sudden we had 50,000 people paying money for testing. That was a huge turning point."

The response shocked Probst as well. He immediately realized that Ultima Online could be an incredible, wholly unexpected success. If 50,000 people agreed to pay to play an unfinished version of the game, who knew how many people would come on board once it was finished? And, with a monthly subscription fee, who knew how much the game could make? Immediately, he ordered resources shifted to the project and approached Richard with an ultimatum: Work on either Ultima IX or Ultima Online, but not both. The choice tore at Richard. He wanted to finish his trilogy of trilogies, as much for himself as for the loyal fan base that had stuck with him over the last two decades, but the new challenges presented by Ultima Online were enticing. Painfully, he choose Ultima IX, fearful that if he left that project so early in its development, Probst would kill the final game. He turned full development of the online project to Starr Long. A lifelong gamer and a former actor, Long slipped easily into his own game persona of "Lord Blackthorn"—a counterpoint to Richard's Lord British—taking on the role of intermediary with the player community. "Role-playing games by their very nature are a kind of theater," Long said later. "Understanding that they are both a form of entertainment, just with a different medium, was important for me."

Outside the company, anticipation built—and built, and built, but there were no signs that a beta test was actually coming. Players were promised an Ultima Online beta in late fall or early winter of 1996. That time passed, with considerable grumbling from the masses online. Spring 1997 came and went as the Origin team feverishly tried to get the world ready for the masses. Garriott, sensing the pressure, pulled much of the development team from Ultima IX and reassigned its members to Ultima Online, leaving the final single-player game with little more than a skeleton crew. Finally, almost a full year after the beta test had been announced, CDs started shipping in June 1997. An initial group of 2000 people was let into the world for a first test that was displayed at the E3 computer trade show that month. Long sent a letter to the anxious community, thanking them and telling them to wait another two to three weeks while issues with the game raised by the first test were fixed.

"On a personal note," Long added, trying to quell rumors of disarray in the development process, "I would like to take this opportunity to remind the loyal citizens of Britannia to pay no heed to idle rumor or malicious gossip, even that which purports to come from the very highest levels of society." The note only helped spur more rumors and speculation online.

The beta testing disks finally began shipping in July 1997, and much of the grumbling quickly disappeared. It had been a tortuous wait, but from the designers' point of view, the time had been well spent, even if they were aware of the massive debugging yet to be done. Ultima Online represented the most ambitious attempt ever to simulate the real world in an online environment. They had built in a market economy, in which the value of goods such as weapons and magical items would fluctuate based on supply and demand. Players could take all kinds of roles, from aggressive warrior to peaceful baker. They had programmed an ecosystem replicating aspects of the real world. Herbivores would gravitate toward plant life. Carnivores would follow them, eating the herbivores. If this balance was disturbed—if, say, too many of the herbivores were killed by players—the ecosystem would respond, sending carnivores into human towns in search of food. The world itself was huge, requiring considerable travel time to reach one side from the other.

As the Habitat developers had discovered a decade before, the reality of letting people into the world proved very different from expectations. This was the largest test of an online gaming world ever mounted, and the players quickly proved that they could almost instantly confound developers' plans.

When the game opened, it was like the first few minutes at an amusement park, when kids pour through the gates to populate a park deserted just moments before. The killing began almost immediately, as players sought to gain instant points, experience, and levels. The ecosystem—plants, herbivores, carnivores, monsters, and anything else that moved—was decimated too quickly for any of the subtle balancing effects to show up at all. Literally thousands of programming hours were wiped clean at the hilts of the beta testers' swords.

Players also tested their blades on each other. A few people had already complained about rampant player-killing in the pre-alpha test. Now the world turned truly murderous. New players were dispensed with almost immediately after logging on, and God forbid a relative amateur track down some valuable magic sword or expensive treasure. That unlucky character wouldn't last two hours in Ultima Online before marauders would murder the unsuspecting victim and take his or her possessions. Even Richard's supposedly invulnerable Lord British was killed as he addressed his subjects near the end of the beta test after neglecting to turn on his invulnerability mechanism.

Ultima Online players did their best to police their world in whatever creative ways were available to them, taking lessons from their days in text MUDs. One early character proved particularly troublesome, showing up at in-game weddings or picnics and killing anyone around. An angry group of players came up with an ingenious solution. They created a female character who befriended the killer and spent several weeks gathering information about him: his ICQ instant messenger chat number, his name, home address, even his sexual predilections. Once they'd garnered enough information, they launched a web site with every piece of dirt they had and posted the link on any Ultima Online fan web site they could find. The player was humiliated, and he eventually left the game.

Guild structures also helped police the game, like Guardian Angels roaming the streets of New York City. Even before the game had launched, during the long period of waiting for the beta test, players had begun collecting into these social structures. Inside the game, some of these became gangs of player-killers, but others acted as stabilizing forces, joining together to battle their more murderous peers. Many others simply established self-help societies, working to buy buildings or land together, and starting businesses.

The guiding principle for game play was creativity, just as it had been during the early years of Dungeons & Dragons. The old-school gamers understood that even negative actions could be forgiven, as long as the actions happened in character and within the parameters of the world. A virtual murder wasn't always a bad thing, it turned out. Some players actually achieved a kind of Billy the Kid–like status this way.

One player, known as the Highwayman, eliminated players with stunning regularity, but few ever complained because the players felt they got their money's worth out of the show. The roadside bandit would chat up his victims, sometimes leaving the scene and returning in disguise, dropping periodic hints that he actually was the Highwayman and that he would soon be dispatching his victims. He gave the wily traveler a chance to leave, to end the interaction before he took their life (and property). Few did, though, because the role he was playing was so interesting.

Beyond the killing, the basic infrastructure of the game was almost immediately taxed to its limits. Richard later likened the game to creating a city a quarter the size of his hometown of Austin, and moving in a population of 100,000 overnight. Of course there would be problems, and quite naturally the citizens of Britannia complained bitterly.

"In the real Austin, there is a mechanism for change," Richard said. "If you don't like the potholes on your street or you think the city is taking too long to fix them, your neighborhood group can lobby the city council. You can call the utility company if you think your bill is too high. There is a government infrastructure that reaches down to the individuals. In our world, there was no structure of any kind, but everyone still had their opinions. We were flooded with personal emails, phone calls, people coming to the buildings."

The players' response to these infrastructure growing pains proved to be a powerful endorsement of the game's sense of internal reality, despite its myriad flaws. Rather than leaving the world in disgust, many sought in-game solutions. Richard told of one particularly illustrative moment, when a group of players angry about lag time (the time it would take for servers to process individual characters' movements in a crowded room) decided to mount a protest.

That Friday afternoon, several hundred gamers logged on and marched together to Lord British's castle, situated just outside of the main town. Aware of the protest, the design team gathered in their newly refurbished digs at Origin, opened the castle gates in the game, and sat back to watch the action unfold on their computer screens. The protesters poured into the Great Hall, bringing game play to a near halt. With so many people in one area, it took several minutes between punching a command on the keyboard and actually having a character move. The players began disrobing. Within 30 minutes, hundreds of naked protesters stood in the room. The protest soon took on a party-like atmosphere, and the virtual drinking started. Just as in real life, when characters drink too much in Ultima Online, they get drunk. Keyboard commands become scrambled, players wobble, and eventually they throw up. Soon, hundreds of naked avatars, puking in slow motion, filled the room. Richard loved it.

"We were all watching and thinking it was a grand statement about the project," he remembered later, laughing. "As unhappy as they were about the game, they voiced their unhappiness in the context of the game."

Role-playing could be a problem for some of the new players, however. This was a world with no entrance requirements other than the willingness to pay a monthly fee, and that meant that the population was drawn from well beyond committed role-playing game devotees. This potentially made for a more diverse society, but the corresponding drop in role-playing skills drove away some early Ultima players. "It just didn't have a strong Ultima feel to it," said Rich De Francesco, a longtime Ultima fan who now operates the "World of Ultima" fan site. "It doesn't take much to wrench you out of the role-playing frame of mind, especially when other real people are involved—people who may not have the same idea of what's fun, or of role-playing. For example, I jump into the game, new to the world, and within one minute, I see folks bopping around saying things like, 'dats SO phat!' or 'look at all the n00bs!' It's hard to suspend reality in an environment like that."

Nevertheless, enough genuine role-players were involved to give the world its own distinct character quite quickly. It was one of these players who ultimately illustrated for Richard just how much independence from him the players had established. He was walking through the streets of his world one evening and he heard a woman screaming. Feeling benevolent, Richard's Lord British decided to go help her. When he asked her what happened, she said that somebody had come running by her and stolen all her possessions, moving so quickly that the thief had barely been perceptible. Bemused, Richard explained that stealing was part of the game, but that he'd help the woman get her property back. The thief had programmed a series of automatic commands into his computer, running and stealing with a single keyboard click that made it almost impossible to guard against, Richard surmised. He transported himself immediately to the thief's side, stuck him with a freeze spell, and told him not to steal from the woman anymore.

"Yes sir," came the reply from the thief, who returned the belongings.

Richard teleported back to the woman, and returned her belongings. While he was wishing her well, a blur came by and took her things a second time. Stunned, Richard froze the thief again.

"Hey, I just told you not to do that," Richard said. "What are you doing?"

"Sorry, I won't do it again," the player said sheepishly, once again returning the belongings.

"If you do that again, I'm going to ban you from the game."

"No problem."

Richard blinked back to where the woman was standing, once again returning her belongings.

"No problem. You won't have any more trouble with—"

Zip. A blur flashed across the screen, and again, the woman's possessions were gone.

"Damn it," Richard thought, leaping to the thief and freezing him. "I said I was going to ban you, and now I have to," he said. "What's wrong with you? I told you not to steal from that woman." He was furious, and ready to throw this player out of the game. He was Lord British, after all, and this guy was breaking the rules.

"Listen," the thief said, breaking character for the first time. "You created this world, and I'm a thief. I steal. That's what I do, and now you are going to ban me from the game for playing the role I'm supposed to play? I lied to you before because I'm a thief. The king caught me and told me not to steal. What am I going to do, tell you that as soon as you turn around I'm going to steal again? No. I'm going to lie."

Richard was taken aback. The thief was right. Ultima wasn't his anymore, and it wasn't right for him to try to control its population. To a large extent, players in earlier games had been puppets playing roles nearly as clearly defined as the computer-generated characters. The hero hunted the villian. There was a right way and wrong way through the games, and Richard had controlled all of it as designer. But not here. Here the players had free will; they had control over their own environment and destiny. The puppets had cut their strings and taken over their world.

So Richard, a deposed god, let the thief go.

* * *

Ultima Online became the fastest selling computer game in Electronic Arts' history. By November 1997, two months after its retail release, it had sold more than 65,000 copies, topping the computer role-playing game charts in the month of its release. By the standards of the wider industry that was good, but not spectacular. Blizzard's Diablo, a simpler role-playing game that allowed four people at once to play online for free, had sold more than half a million copies a few months after its own release in January 1997. By the time of the Ultima Online release in September 1997, more than one million people had signed on to Blizzard's free Battle.net service, largely to play Diablo—far more people than would ever populate Ultima Online at any given time.

The game's impact was felt beyond its sales figures. It was viewed by a fascinated media as a social experiment as much as a profit center, and feature articles on its social dynamics periodically found their way even into the biggest newspapers in the United States. An October 1997 *New York Times* by-the-numbers comparison to Quake, the previous year's gaming standout, gave a snapshot of how the game was operating differently than its predecessors.[3] The comparison looked like this:

	Game Released Online	Cost of Game	Number of Units Sold	Maximum Players in a Game	Average Number of Players in a Game	Average Time Spent Online	Players Who Are Male
ULTIMA	Sept. 24, 1997	$64.95	40,000	15,000 (across six servers)	5,000 (across six servers)	6 hours a day	96%
QUAKE	June 21, 1996	$44.95	700,000	32	10	2 hours a day	98%

Even if the Ultima Online initial player demographic wasn't terribly different from that of Quake, it was clear from the outset that players were creating a new type of online experience. The open-ended, social game started to attract people who normally steered clear of complex PC games, as well as hard-core gamers. Before long, the stories players told about what happened inside the game sounded more like travelers' tales than a game player's accounts of successes and failures.

Christine Gilbreath was one of those early players. A programmer and former elementary school teacher, she had worked long years selling software in the mid-1980s, taking classes on many of the products that came through her store. She'd never developed a serious gaming habit. She'd play the odd game of Solitaire or Blackjack that came packaged on her PC, but more ambitious gaming had never interested her.

When Ultima Online was released in 1997, other programmers in the health insurance office where she then worked began talking about the game incessantly. Four other friends of hers said they needed a player who could cast healing spells so that their team wouldn't be easy prey for the bands of roving marauders. Wanting to join her colleagues, Gilbreath joined the game as a cleric, hooked up with another friend she knew who had also just started the game, and set out to find her co-workers somewhere in the sprawling virtual world. It wasn't easy. Ultima Online was a huge place, and players all began in the main city. Her friends had been traveling for a few days, and were no longer close by. It was as if she'd been dropped in Kansas, but her friends were already in California. To find them, Gilbreath would have to set out across the wilderness of Ultima Online, something she wasn't entirely excited about doing. After all, player-killers salivated over people like her. If she stepped out of the city, she'd likely be dispatched hundreds of times before she ever found her friends. She was on her own until she could gain enough experience to defend herself.

There was a slight problem, though. To get better at certain skills in Ultima Online, players needed to study and then continually practice to keep them sharp. Swordsmen needed to practice against other fighters. Silversmiths needed to go through an apprentice period. If players neglected their practice, instead choosing to spend their time socializing with others, their characters could become easy prey for killers who spent an inordinate amount of time honing their assassination skills. Gilbreath, though, found that socializing was more fun than practicing.

Not wanting to become an immediate target, Gilbreath decided to hang out in the game's port city—a city teeming with mariners, merchants, fisherman, and newbie players like herself. She started chatting with anyone who would talk with her, particularly those folks on the docks, where people sat fishing lazily by the water's edge. Like many players, she found the early days of Ultima Online were simply about dropping a line in the water and seeing what bit. It was the safest activity. Wandering out was a sure way to get killed. Sitting on the docks, talking with people, Gilbreath collected 10 others who decided they were willing to travel with her. After a week, they set out across the open lands to meet her co-workers. Along the way, they picked up stragglers who'd left the confines of the city. The group—by now an official guild called the Platinum Sphere—continued to grow even after they found her co-workers. Within a year, the Platinum Sphere's ranks swelled to 46.

Over time, the players who found their way into Gilbreath's circle would come and go. Real-life issues sometimes forced players to cut back their role-playing, but more often than not, new games would pull players away. EverQuest was launched, taking its toll on the group, and Dark Age of Camelot drew a few more away. But the bonds the group formed stuck despite their changing interests, and the Internet allowed them to maintain their relationships. In the past, when a player left a Dungeon & Dragons game or if somebody moved, players often lost touch with each other. Now, the online gaming communities of players were no longer confined by geographic distance or time. To keep their relationships fresh, the leaders of the Platinum Sphere built a password-protected message board, where members could keep up to date on their latest adventures—both in real life and online.

Like neighbors who'd moved on, guild members could still keep up with each other, even though the group split up across three different games. Gilbreath, for one, hasn't let her friends go, even though she rarely plays the game anymore. Illness has forced her to spend much of her time indoors these days, but still she keeps up with her guildmates. "We're all friends outside the game, and most of us talk about real-life stuff when we get together," she said. "We have our own friendships that have formed because of the guild."

Stories like Gilbreath's grew more common as the game grew older. As it increasingly became a social as well as an adventuring environment, the ranks of atypical gamers swelled.

By late 1997, 27-year-old Heather Pierce had seen her husband work his way through years of PC games. She'd had precious little interest in computer games, but in the interest of domestic harmony, she'd watched him shoot his way through Duke Nuke 'Em and scheme to take over the world playing the strategy game Command & Conquer. All of these were silly, she thought. A waste of time.

Then came Ultima Online. Her husband came home one Friday with the game in hand, and started playing. With growing interest, Heather watched him build a character, choose its clothes and appearance, and select a profession. By the time her husband started roaming around town trying to master the fine art of swordsmanship, she was sitting transfixed, playing with him now instead of watching. She realized that other people just like them were roaming around town trying to figure out the game. With no money, and no way for their character to get food, they decided to take up fishing. They wandered down to the docks, where they encountered a group of players who had the same idea. They ended up chatting with people from around the United States while they passed the time—several days in fact—fishing and selling their bounty to local merchants.

"This was the first game that I thought was cool," she said later. "Here we were, playing this character, and you were trying to help this little guy figure out how to be a swordsman. It was really challenging."

It also caused mild strife in the household, as the couple had made only one character and they both wanted to play. They started fighting over screen time. Eventually, Heather bought herself a computer, her own phone line, and a copy of the game. She created her own character, and once again trudged down to the dock to make money. She got friendly with a group of other players who decided to band together to form a guild, The Anchor of Light. The group gathered every day to fish, chatting about what was going on in their personal lives while passing the time.

Eventually, Heather and her husband made enough money in the game to start their own virtual business. They purchased a house outside of town and began selling weapons. Again, she found friends among other merchants, and before long, she'd put together the Cove Merchants Guild. In its heyday, 100 players attended the guild's monthly meetings. That guild would later expand again, bringing 60 different guilds under the Great Lakes Guild, creating a huge society inside the game.

Players again formed such strong bonds with each other that their meetings began to spill offline. In 1998, Merchants Guild players who lived in Richard's hometown of Austin started meeting every other month for lunch. Quickly, the lunches evolved into social outings. Four times a year, the group would vote on a group outing, typically a lunch or dinner. By 1999, people grew more ambitious, and rented a boat for an evening of revelry. Word of the outings spread through the Ultima Online message boards, and soon, players from around the Southwest were showing up at the Austin events. The next year, when Austin played host to the Texas Renaissance Festival, the very event where Richard first stumbled upon the Society for Creative Anachronism nearly two decades before, more than 100 players registered for the Ultima Online event.

"Word spread through the message boards and the game itself, and before we knew it, there were people from all over the place registering and flying down," Heather said. "At first, I was surprised by the types of people who showed up. I was always expecting this to be a bunch of weirdos who showed up; but you know, these folks that we play with are really pretty normal."

Normal enough that she let some of them into her personal life after her marriage broke up. Now a single mom with two children, she found the game gave her a community of people to share her life with. Her best friend, Gwen, who she'd met in the game, finally made the trip down to Austin in 2001. The two bonded as quickly in real life as they did in the game.

"I hang out with other people who play," Heather said. "The guy who I'm dating is an Ultima Online player. I'm not tied to the new people so much, but I'm bonded to the people who I used to play with. I met a lot of people who had common interests."

Baking, fishing, setting up as a merchant—all these turned out to be viable activities in the game world, even if more people were interested in adventuring. As the game went on, players turned even more creative, setting up lives and activities that Richard and his developers hadn't anticipated at all.

Joshua Rowan, a 34-year-old gamer, had been an Ultima player for nearly two decades when he found Ultima Online. He'd played Dungeons & Dragons briefly in the early 1980s, but when Ultima III came out, he quickly ditched the paper-gaming scene for the world of Britannia. When Ultima Online was announced, he was ecstatic, calling his friends and putting together a guild who would fight under the moniker Golden Knights. The guild was made up of law-abiding characters called Paladins, who would roam the countryside in search of people in trouble. This was childhood hero stuff.

"We joined on day two," Rowan said later. "I'd been really disappointed that I couldn't get into the beta test, but when the real game came along, I was so excited I could barely contain myself."

There were just five Golden Knights in the beginning, and they spent their days doing what they'd imagined—looking for bad guys. It wasn't a difficult search. The game had already degenerated into a massive player-killing war, but the constant fight against evildoers turned out to be less fun than they'd expected. They spent much of their time overwhelmed by player-killers, who took joy in whacking the good guys. More and more, the group stayed indoors, heading to the local tavern. They never had time to hang out when they were getting butchered from every direction. After spending an awful lot of time in the local pub, talking with other locals and having a good time, they decided one night in 1998 to pool their money and buy the tavern.

"We really just wanted to have a place to hang out, because we were all into the social aspect of the game," Rowan remembered. "So the Golden Knights became the Golden Brew."

It proved a successful plan. Safe within the city limits, they didn't have to worry about fighting desperadoes. They could relax and chat with the steady stream of players making their way to the bar, just like real bartenders. Their numbers also began to grow. Many people wanted to kick back and relax instead of wandering into the dangerous hinterlands. The Brew's membership swelled to 48 in the space of months. Like good hosts, they wanted to provide their patrons with something more to do than just sit around and chat. Brainstorming finally led to an idea: Ultima was a role-playing game, and everyone in the game seemed to like pretending to be someone else. So, why shouldn't they form an Ultima acting troupe? The idea met with cheers from the other Brew members, and just before Thanksgiving, they formed the Golden Brew Players, a theatrical troupe that would stage plays in the back of the tavern. The Ultima Online software gave people the opportunity to do just about anything they wanted. They could build a stage, make costumes, and publicize the event—and they did all three.

With Christmas just two months away, the troupe decided to put on Charles Dickens' *A Christmas Carol*. The 15-person company split up their activities. Some worked on building sets and making costumes, others hunted down the script and pared it down to two hours, and others worked on promotions. They scheduled rehearsals and worked on their parts. On opening night, Christmas Eve, 50 gamers crowded into the little bar—its maximum capacity—quietly took their seats, and watched the first-ever theatrical performance in Ultima Online. The play went off without a hitch. Richard, who'd heard about the play through Ultima message boards that were now sprouting by the hundreds on the Internet, attended one of the early performances, amazed at the players' ingenuity.

"The biggest problem we had was timing the dialogue to make sure people weren't talking over each other," Rowan said later. "As you'd paste your dialogue into the box you used to communicate, it would pop up over your character's head, in a little bubble. We had to make sure we weren't talking over each other, and it'd usually take us about a month of rehearsals to get that down."

Over the next two years, the company would stage a half-dozen other plays, packing the house for each performance and gaining quite a bit of notoriety throughout the online world. "All we ever wanted was a social place to hang out," Rowan said, "but it's turned into more than that."

❋ ❋ ❋

Back in the real world, Richard was struggling to complete the final single-player Ultima. He wanted to finish the story that had become as much a part of his real life (Lord British continues to make appearances around Austin for holidays and parties), as it was of his gaming life. The success of Ultima Online and the massive attention from the media had derailed the project almost completely. The code the Ultima IX team had originally written was now completely outdated, and EA executives weren't all that enthusiastic about restarting the project from scratch. Richard was finally given permission, however, and the game came out in late 1999, the most technologically sophisticated iteration of any of the series. But like Richard himself, the Ultima gamers had for the most part been drawn elsewhere. Sales were disappointing for Ultima IX, and it never cracked the top 10 list of best-selling games, even in the few weeks after its release. The market that year was more interested in games like Roller Coaster Tycoon, Who Wants To Be A Millionaire, Quake III: Arena, and Half-Life.

With his relationship with Probst and Electronic Arts deteriorating, Richard decided it was time for him to leave when the company asked him to start work on Ultima Online II, a game he felt was entirely unnecessary considering the adaptability of Ultima Online. Developers could expand the current game by adding new realms. Besides, he'd been working on a new online gaming idea that he called "Project X," and EA wasn't interested. It was time for him to move on. In March 2000, he quit and headed off on his own.

He left behind almost everything he'd worked on for the last twenty years. Electronic Arts would own the Ultima series and would continue to run Ultima Online, a world that was thriving even if its population was dwindling. Around him, the massively multiplayer phenomenon he had helped spark was expanding rapidly. EverQuest, a game created by a Sony subsidiary, was growing quickly. Dark Age of Camelot would soon come out, growing at twice the rate of Ultima Online. Just a few days before he left EA, Sony announced it would create a massively multiplayer world based on the *Star Wars* universe. World-making was on the rise.

The game Richard left behind showed just how diverse the gaming community—and gaming activities—had become. The EA developers continued to release new add-ons that featured new monsters, new adventures, new story lines, and new geographies to explore. But some of the most popular parts of Ultima Online later became nonswashbuckling activities. The game—if that was still the right word—was not being driven by the designers, but by the players, and those players were growing beyond the old gaming rules of level-climbing and killing. Back from bloody travels around the world, many gamers simply wanted to build houses and cultivate their own gardens.

Part III

The Era of Gamers

8

Gamers, Interrupted

On a cold Tuesday morning in April 1999, two students stormed through Columbine High School in Littleton, Colorado, setting off homemade bombs and shooting students, teachers, and finally themselves. When the smoke cleared, 15 were dead, and people across the United States were desperately asking how any of it could have been possible.

Eric Harris and Dylan Klebold's actions sent American society lurching into a period of bitter self-examination—giving particular attention to the nexus of teenagers, violence, and the media. Columbine wasn't the first school shooting of its kind. Harris and Klebold's rampage capped a string of student shootings that had occurred with alarming frequency over the previous years. This was by far the most extreme, however, its impact exacerbated by cable news outlets that broadcast the horrifying events to a rapt nation. Images of scared children streaming out of the school and police officers surrounding the area were beamed into America's living rooms. In one particularly harrowing videotaped sequence, a young student climbed out a second-story window, desperately looking for escape. The vivid images shocked suburbanites and traumatized Columbine students stayed on the nightly news and on the front pages of newspapers for weeks, while investigators, journalists, pundits, legislators, and parents pored over every detail of the two students' lives, searching for clues to what could have triggered the attacks.

Much of the subsequent soul-searching was valuable, prompting discussion about the complex and often overlooked social, familial, and economic pressures faced by modern teens. Some of it was less rigorous, as people looking for solace turned to simple answers and scapegoats. Harris and Klebold hadn't been popular kids. They had been on the fringes of a group referred to in the popular press as the "Trenchcoat Mafia," a group of students who had been picked on with some regularity by the school's athletes. The Trenchcoat Mafia was quickly associated—wrongly, local students later said[1]—with the music of Marilyn Manson and "Goth" groups, a subculture filled with people of all ages who dress in black and are often fascinated with thanatological images. These influences, foreign to many despite their presence in virtually every high school across the country, became an easy target for frightened parents and teachers. In the weeks that followed Columbine, students reported being disciplined or criticized in their own schools for wearing trench coats or other badges of Goth fashion.

Harris and Klebold had another secret, one that would change the nature of the public debate. They had been avid Doom players. As the investigation continued, the Simon Wiesenthal Center—a group that tracked hate groups on the Internet and elsewhere—reported that it had a copy of Harris's web site in its archives, and that it contained a "mod" version of Doom based on the layout of Columbine High School. Harris had set his game in "God mode," which meant that characters couldn't be harmed while they traveled through the bloody levels that came with operating instructions such as "KILL 'EM AAAAALLLL!!!!!" The revelation that these gunmen had played out their rampage using a computer game set off a wave of public discussion about the effects of interactive media.

Journalist Jon Katz responded by opening up his column on the Slashdot web site to students who suddenly felt alienated and harassed by school administrators cracking down on student conduct by implementing dress codes and, in some cases, restricting Internet access at school. "Suddenly," Katz wrote in an essay titled "Voices from the Hellmouth," "in this tyranny of the normal, to be different wasn't just to feel unhappy, it was to be dangerous."[2]

Teenagers from around the country wrote in, expressing their anger and confusion at the hatred being directed at them. Brandy, a New York City student, summed up much of the feeling within the game community:

I'm a Quake freak, I play it day and night. I'm really into it. I play Doom a lot too, though not so much anymore. I'm up til [sic] 3 a.m. every night. I really love it. But, after Colorado, things got horrible. People were actually talking to me like I could come in and kill them. It wasn't like they were really afraid of me—they just seemed to think it was okay to hate me even more.[3]

On a broad level, the adult fear echoed the earlier panics over youth violence and subcultures that had periodically swept through the United States in the latter half of the twentieth century. Like their predecessors, from greasers to gangbangers, Goths and gamers seemed to be a subculture developing in the heart of ordinary society, a subculture in which kids created their own rules uncontrolled by any adult authority. For gamers, this world was virtual, and players—like Harris—apparently had the ability to mold the world explicitly to fit and reinforce disturbing fantasies. Worse, critics said, it was game designers, movie producers, and record labels that were providing the raw materials for these fantasies, essentially subverting parental influence. Some large retailers, including Wal-Mart, took note and stopped carrying Doom and Quake altogether.

Id Software wasn't entirely taken by surprise. The company's games had been associated, fairly or not, with youth violence before. After 14-year-old Michael Carneal opened fire at a school in Paducah, Kentucky, killing three students in 1997, parents of the victims sued id and several other publishers for releasing violent video games. Although those legal claims would eventually be tossed aside by the courts—just as claims that rock music encouraged teenagers to kill themselves had been dismissed over the years—the stigma had stuck with the video and computer game industry.

Few voices blamed Columbine directly on computer games. Gaming culture was nevertheless subjected to a wave of criticism and hostile attention. Critics glossed over the differences between the complex worlds of Ultima Online, fast-paced action games, and even the vastly more popular sports games. It quickly became clear that the legislators and pundits had little understanding of the variety of play or of the variety of players that had evolved over the past few years. In ordinary times, that ignorance would have made little difference. In the wake of such a tragedy, however, this broader societal attention carried the potential to change or even destroy game communities with legislation, market pressure, or other more subtle means of censorship.

The shootings did spark some soul-searching inside the industry. Developers interviewed at the time often conceded that they wouldn't let their young children play their own companies' games—but they said that it was parents who needed to take responsibility for their own children's use of media. Gamers themselves blasted Harris and Klebold on Internet bulletin boards and in private conversations, but most agreed that the games themselves weren't responsible. Games were cartoons, graphic representations existing in a digital world that was only as real as the strength of players' imaginations. Cyberspace wasn't an actual place. It was just a construct, and if people like Harris and Klebold couldn't tell the difference between blasting digital opponents and turning guns on real-life classmates, they clearly were deeply disturbed by something beyond the games. Blaming games and condemning the entire culture was unfair.

"That argument was never taken seriously inside the community," said Dennis "Thresh" Fong later. "I've been to so many LANs, so many tournaments, and I've never seen a fight. How could I believe it? I've spent time with the hardest of the hard-core gamers there are, and I've never seen any sign of violence."

Politicians and pundits stumping against video and computer games weren't sitting down with the game players, however. Instead, a host of intermediaries stepped into the public spotlight to help explain the medium and the culture that had grown around it. The airwaves soon filled with media critics, public interest groups, pundits from the right and from the left, and professors. A whole spectrum of interpretation arose, asking and answering the questions that gamers, immersed in the game and in their own communities, rarely asked themselves: What were the effects of these games on players and on society? How did they change the players? Most important of all, were they dangerous?

Some of the loudest voices believed that games were in fact dangerous, and they called for outright censorship of violent and explicit games. Dogmatic voices on the other side declined to give any credence whatever to the idea that violent games might have an effect on some of their players.

More thoughtful voices ultimately came to the fore, arguing that the effects of the games on players were complicated and not easily reducible to sound bites. Massachusetts Institute of Technology Comparative Media Studies Professor Henry Jenkins, drawn reluctantly into the public forum, argued in Congress and on TV that kids used the imagery in games as modern building blocks of age-old stories, reminding the world that even the bloodiest shoot-'em-up games were little different from the longtime backyard fantasies of adolescent boys. A thoughtful counterpoint was David Walsh, a psychologist and head of the nonprofit National Institute on Media and the Family, who contended that violent media contributed to a subtle but real, and potentially dangerous, coarsening of the culture.

This wasn't the first time that game players and communities had been in the spotlight, but it was the first time that so much had been at stake. People had died, and the popular image of gamers had swung into deeply negative territory. For game communities, whether the players knew it or not, it was a sign—even if an unwelcome one—of their own maturing. It was time for them to face the same public scrutiny that other art forms and underground entertainments had borne for years.

It was time for the communities to start growing up.

* * *

Video and computer games had sent waves of concern rippling through a nervous culture before Columbine. Entertainment activities had long been the focal point for underground youth subcultures, and like others of these—pool halls, pinball parlors, rock 'n' roll, and even Dungeons & Dragons—electronic games were periodically suspect in a wider culture that saw them as unfamiliar. In the medium's early years, computer and online games missed this public scrutiny, protected in large part by their relative obscurity. Arcade and home video games, which caught the public eye much earlier, were easier targets for criticism. Simpler and less community-driven than their online counterparts, video games raised early concerns about possible ill effects on children.

The worries began in the mid-1970s, just a few years after Atari's release of Pong—the simplistic ping pong–like game that kicked off the arcade video game revolution—when a little San Francisco Bay Area video game company named Exidy released Death Race. Aside from the lurid skeleton-headed racers on the side of its cabinet, the 1976 arcade title didn't look like much. It was a driving game in which players would use a big plastic steering wheel and foot pedals to guide little blobs of light around the screen. The game's designer, Howell Ivy, had originally created it with a smash-up-derby theme, but contract issues and hopes of making a splash on the market had persuaded Exidy to modify it. In the new version, players drove their cars around the screen trying to run down little stick figures, which turned into tombstone-like crosses after being hit.

The designers knew they were pushing the boundaries of what was acceptable in the market, but it was a call from a Seattle reporter that showed that they might have stepped farther across the line than they had bargained for. The figures were undead "gremlins," not people, Exidy CEO Pete Kaufmann explained to critics. That didn't matter. The game quickly triggered national attention, garnering write-ups in the *National Enquirer* and other, more serious newspapers. It even prompted a segment on TV's *60 Minutes* probing the psychology of video game players. Exidy ultimately took the game off the market, but the company released a sequel, almost unchanged, not long afterward.

Exidy eventually receded from the spotlight (although its 1986 game Chiller would again push the boundaries of blood and gore to a level several years ahead of its time). It was clear, however, that the industry's honeymoon was over. Concerned parents began paying more attention to this new activity, which seemed to be drawing away so many of their children's spare hours. Many parents weren't initially as worried about the content of the games as the environment they created. By this time video game arcades were popping up by the thousands. Stray arcade machines could be found anywhere from movie theaters to corner stores, and parents worried that kids would skip school and be exposed to bad influences while they were playing.

The dawn of the 1980s saw the rise of a movement calling for regulation of these machines on the local level, in much the same way that localities from New York City on down had once banned pinball machines. A Long Island mother and PTA president named Ronnie Lamm rose to national prominence as a spokeswoman for the cause against video games. Her activism started with petition drives, speeches to community groups, letters to state politicians, and even calls to the local fire department to ask them to check whether crowded local arcades were violating fire safety laws. Her own community of Brookhaven ultimately imposed a moratorium on new permits for arcades.[4] Other towns went further, making it illegal to place video game machines near schools or barring video games from being used during school hours altogether.

While parents' groups fought to stop the spread of arcades, many eyes turned to a legal case originating in Mesquite, Texas—ironically, the same Dallas suburb that would ultimately become the home of id Software. In 1976, in part fearing connections with organized crime, Mesquite had passed several regulations targeting an ambitious arcade builder, one of which would have blocked children under 17 from playing the games. The case went to the U.S. Supreme Court in 1982, drawing close attention from the games' critics; justices declined to rule on the case's constitutional issues, however, diminishing its use as a role model for either side.

This wave of concern wasn't wholly focused on arcade environments. Critics including Lamm bolstered their arguments with the opinions of psychologists who criticized the games for being simplistic, aggressive, and potentially damaging to children. At this point, little medical research had been conducted to study the effects of interactive games, but prominent doctors were nevertheless ready with opinions. In 1982, even Surgeon General C. Everett Koop weighed in with an opinion, saying that, "There is nothing constructive in the games…. Everything is eliminate, kill, destroy."[5]

Other groups found arcade games objectionable for other reasons. Creative readings of Ms. Pac Man and Donkey Kong found rape metaphors hidden in the games' subtext. A few games made sexual violence more explicit, although these were hardly mainstream. The most prominent of them were created by Mystique, a company that designed a series of games with sexual content for Atari's home video game system. Released in late 1982, its Custer's Revenge featured a tumescent, pixilated General Custer fighting his way past a hail of arrows to a woman tied to a pole at the other end of the screen. Success meant that a player had guided Custer successfully through the arrows and raped the smiling American Indian.

A preview of the game at the New York Hilton was picketed by groups that included Women Against Pornography, the National Organization of Women, and the American Indian Community House. A second game by the same company, called Beat 'em and Eat 'em, had similarly obscene content, and Atari sued the distributor's parent company for tarnishing its game system's image by associating it with pornography.[6]

The video game business crash in the mid-1980s drew some attention away from the industry. Critics breathed a sigh of relief, thinking that the gaming fad had been short-lived after all. The respite was temporary, however. By the late 1980s, Nintendo's home game system had wholly revitalized the game market, and sales were stronger than ever. Grounded in the cartoonish world of the Super Mario Bros. titles, Nintendo catered primarily to teens and younger children. Arcade games were getting more violent though, and rival Sega started taking advantage of some of these titles to distinguish its own home-gaming system from its stronger rival.

This trend peaked in 1992, when the arcade mega-hit Mortal Kombat was released. It was bloody, and kids loved it. A fighting game that pitted two martial arts heroes against each other, it featured "finishing moves" that separated it definitively from other similar games—including the ability to set an enemy on fire, punch his head off with a single uppercut, or rip an opponent's heart out of his or her chest. Nintendo and Sega each wanted the game for their home systems, but they didn't agree on how to handle the violence. Nintendo took out the bloodiest parts of the game. Sega didn't, and went on to sell far more copies than its more cautious rival.

Another game released at roughly the same time helped add fuel to the building fire of criticism. One of the first games created with live-action video, the Sega-published Night Trap featured a group of bumbling vampires-in-training raiding a slumber party led by TV show *Diff'rent Strokes* actress Dana Plato. The object of the game was to keep watch over the girls' home via a simulated set of surveillance cameras and trigger traps inside the house to catch the vampires as they stalked the girls. If the bumbling evildoers caught the girls, they would try to extract their blood using a long, drill-like device. It was a campy game, based on barely-B-grade horror films, and it was widely panned for poor game play. Despite this, it became a lightning rod for criticism of violence, and particularly sexual violence, in games.

In late 1993, Senators Joe Lieberman and Herb Kohl called a congressional hearing on violence in video games. Some in the industry muttered that the hearing had been spurred in part by complaints from Nintendo, angry at seeing rival Sega gain ground with the sale of its more violent games. The lawmakers' attention was focused industrywide, however. In the hope of defusing some of the criticism, a large group of leading companies, including Sega and Nintendo, announced early on the first day of the hearing that they had agreed to create a rating system for their games. The peace didn't last long. In the hearing, a Nintendo representative attacked Sega for its release of violent games and said his own company had tried to mitigate the industry's worst excesses. In response, the Sega representative pulled out a prop—a bazooka-style gun accessory used by some Nintendo games—and asked if that was the appropriate means to teach nonviolence to children.

The ultimate outcome was predictable. The game industry joined forces and created a ratings system similar to, but more detailed than, the system the movie industry had evolved decades before when faced with parallel criticism. The move toward self-regulation pacified the industry's critics for several years, and the immediate pressure again declined just as Doom and Quake were released in the computer world, kicking off a whole new genre of bloody games. The console world was no less bloodthirsty, and as computer graphics grew exponentially better and sound quality improved, the gore got gorier. Industry spokespeople countered criticism by saying that violent games, which were rated "mature" under the new system, constituted only a small percentage of the titles released, were not intended for children, and were outsold in any case by rival titles such as sports games. For the most part, the growing game communities ignored the background hum of the outside world's opinion. It had little relevance to their daily lives, unless a rating prevented a young fan from getting a game.

Then came Columbine, and the outside world's vision, skewed or not, came crashing in.

✳ ✳ ✳

Nearly two weeks after the Colorado shootings, MIT's Henry Jenkins got a telephone call from Washington, DC. A Senate committee was holding a hearing on media violence and children in just a few days, and they wanted him to testify. He thought hard about it. He'd never done anything like this before. He looked at the witness list, and it looked stacked against what was apparently supposed to be "his side," the presumed apologist for violence. Was he to become the defender of the crassness of modern culture? His was probably the officially designated "wrongheaded" side. But it would be a chance to defend what he saw as a necessarily complex reading of modern culture, including the video games that the Columbine killers had played. For that defense of his beliefs, it was worth taking a risk.

He agreed to come.

A year earlier, Jenkins had published a book on gender and video games called *From Barbie to Mortal Kombat*, and he had helped trigger some discussion in academic and industry circles on issues of gender in gaming culture. The wider media had focused on the elements of the book that dealt with violence in games, and almost overnight he'd entered media culture as the professor who defended violent games. The complexities of his argument tended to get lost in most newspaper articles, but he kept trying. Now the Senate wanted him to play the same role on a larger stage.

Jenkins isn't an avid computer game player himself, but he looks the part. From a distance, catching a glimpse of him across the campus of the Massachusetts Institute of Technology in Boston, Jenkins might be mistaken for a "grandfather" gamer. He is balding slightly and carries a little extra paunch in the stomach underneath a pair of suspenders. He has a slight shuffle when he walks, and has the soft voice and gentle mannerisms of a therapist. He's an academic, used to teasing complex conclusions out of decidedly inconclusive cultural material and discussing his theories with others who take them seriously. The posturing and simplification of a Washington, DC, hearing room in 1999 was daunting.

He arrived to see posters on the wall, blown-up advertisements for the bloodiest video games on the market. The room was full of reporters, legislative staffers, other witnesses, and supporters of the anti-game group. (He had no one to help him.) One section of the audience was filled with a group of women, mostly mothers, representing a group staunchly opposed to violence in children's media. He was snubbed by some of the fellow witnesses. Leery of being labeled, he stayed away from the representatives of the entertainment media and the heads of the film and video game developers' trade associations. He was on his own.

No specific bills or proposals were on the table. This was an informational hearing, aimed at shining a spotlight on the way that violent images and stories were being sold to children. "We are in the strange intersection between freedom of expression and the damage that can be done when freedom is abused," said Senator John Ashcroft, the conservative Missourian who would become U.S. Attorney General just a few years later, in one of 14 opening statements by the assembled legislators. "And it's a very difficult place to be."[7]

The senators and successive witnesses denounced films, music, and video games for wantonly giving way to, and ultimately encouraging, the most violent impulses of the human psyche. The bloodiest bits of games like Mortal Kombat, Postal, and Resident Evil were shown wholly out of context, as were short clips of a handful of movies. Former Education Secretary and cultural critic William Bennett excoriated films that depicted gratuitous violence, contrasting the violence of Shakespeare's *Macbeth* or Hollywood's *Clear and Present Danger*, which he claimed was there to serve a purpose in the story, with the mere titillation of *Scream* or *The Basketball Diaries* (an autobiographical tale of drug addiction and recovery written by poet and rocker Jim Carroll). Former military psychologist Lt. Col. (Ret.) David Grossman told the legislators that violent video games were literally teaching kids to kill, using precisely the same techniques the military used with its soldiers. Criticizing the dark images of singer Marilyn Manson, one senator joked about whether the musician was actually a "he" or a "she." "Precisely the kind of intolerant and taunting comments that these [Columbine] kids must have gotten in school because they dressed differently or acted oddly in comparison with their more conformist classmates," Jenkins wrote later in an article published in *Harper's* magazine.[8]

Jenkins nervously took the stand late in the day, when most of the reporters had already departed. He pleaded with the senators to understand that young gamers weren't puppets manipulated by media images. Instead, they were constructing their own fantasies out of the raw materials available to them. Disturbed teens like the Columbine killers might create disturbing fantasies—but even the darkest images could wind up being used in positive ways by kids hungry for images that speak to them, he said.

Don't rush to judgment on the basis of 20-second clips of violent power fantasies, Jenkins pleaded. The real issues were complicated, just like kids' lives. "Listen to our children," he told the senators. "Don't fear them."[9]

Jenkins has spent his career listening to children and studying people's lifelong creative uses of stories and popular entertainment. He's not trained as a psychologist, but his studies have taken him into psychological territory. He's not a film, television, or video game critic, but his analyses of all three mediums and the subcultures that exist on their fringes have given him a critic's eye.

Growing up largely before video games came into prominence, Jenkins spent his childhood playing board games like Monopoly and Candyland, simple games that couldn't be played alone. They required at least one other person, and often the fun grew exponentially with the number of players. He and his friends took the same games outside on a grander scale when they tired of sedentary play. Outside of his house in suburban Atlanta, there was a sandlot that they could transform into a giant-sized game board. A tree house doubled as a pirate ship, Tom Sawyer's raft, or a hot-air balloon that could take them anywhere they wanted. It was versatile, malleable, and best of all, it was his. Many years later, Jenkins' eyes focused in recollection while he told the story of his own childhood games. In his years studying video games, that concept of physical playspace—and particularly the loss of physical space in which children can run around, playing, pushing, and fighting—would assume an important role in his thoughts.

Jenkins was exposed to video games when he was young, but he was never a dedicated player himself. His younger brother bought a Pong machine while they were still kids, and in the late 1970s, his future wife's brother owned an Atari gaming system. He occasionally played the games with her brother, but ultimately real life called, Peter Pan grew up, and the games were abandoned in favor of term papers and academic study.

By the mid-1980s, Jenkins was a graduate student in film studies at the University of Wisconsin at Madison. He and his wife had a son, also named Henry. When the boy turned five, he asked for a Nintendo Entertainment System game console, and his father agreed. Having paid little attention to video games' progress in the years since he'd played with his brother-in-law's Atari system, Jenkins assumed that his son would be playing something similar, with blocky graphics, simple game screens, and digital bleeps and bloops playing the twin roles of sound effects and background music. What he saw instead came as a revelation. The machine was packaged with Super Mario Bros., the latest title from Nintendo's wunderkind Shigeru Miyamoto. The lush graphics and the musical score brought the world and its main character, Mario, the very same Mario from Miyamoto's earlier Donkey Kong, to life. "I felt like Rip Van Winkle," Jenkins said. "I thought I had a taken a catnap and slept through a revolution. I felt myself in the presence of a medium that had transformed itself overnight."

Even more than the character, it was the game's world that fascinated him. He remembered Space Invaders, which had barely qualified as a universe. You had a task, defending the world against unyielding hordes of aliens, but as the lone defender, you were given just one dimension to move in. Even in later games like Pac Man and Donkey Kong, you could see the whole world at any given time as you moved around the board. Not so with Super Mario Bros. Miyamoto had created a world to inhabit instead of an icon that you moved from place to place.

Just as interesting was the way that his five-year-old son and his friends began interacting with the game. They played it obsessively, talking about it all the time. On the phone, at school, after school, they brainstormed over the best ways to complete levels and swapped information on strategy, hidden treasures, and stunts. They played the game together; it was very much a social experience, with groups of boys gathered in front of the television set, cheering each other on, swapping the controller around to take advantage of each kid's strengths and skills. A few kids in the neighborhood became temporary celebrities as they learned how to beat particularly difficult "bosses," the chief monsters that guarded the end of each level of play. These kids would do victory tours around the neighborhood, showing off their newfound skill and knowledge on other kids' machines.

The more he watched the kids in front of the TV, the more Jenkins thought he recognized what they were doing. This was similar to what he'd done in his own suburban backyard and out in the forest as a kid. They were exploring, bonding over the territory they conquered in their imagination. "I realized they weren't doing this for points. They were exploring space," Jenkins said. "My original insight was that it wasn't about saving Princess Toadstool. It wasn't about narrative." For Jenkins, that insight was enough to add games into the body of popular media works that he would spend his life studying. It would take time before many others agreed that it was a worthwhile subject for scholarly attention; just as he'd met skepticism from professors when he'd lobbied to have television issues added to the film studies curriculum, many in the academic world weren't sure what to do with his work on games. It fell between niches. Games weren't film, they weren't literature, and it wasn't immediately clear that they were even an expressive art form at all. But as the medium advanced, others joined him, and by the late 1990s, papers and books were streaming out and conferences were being held all over the world. Jenkins, by that time director of MIT's comparative media studies program, had become one of the godfathers of video game studies.

Those initial observations about his son's use of games have remained a cornerstone of the way Jenkins understands computer and video games. He is the first to admit that many games make little attempt to tell stories or to produce the same kind of emotional effect created by earlier, more narrative art forms such as film or novels. If the industry is given a chance to mature, he believes games with these characteristics will likely evolve. He's worked with game companies, including Electronic Arts, to help train developers to build games with character, story, and plot development. He uses classic literature and film as models in these lessons, trying to help developers identify what made Homer's *Odyssey* so compelling and to help them incorporate those lessons into the designs for their game worlds.

But these studies in narrative and character aren't necessarily the fundamental strengths of games, at least today. Many game makers, from Miyamoto onward, have focused on creating environments or worlds to explore rather than trying to tell complicated stories. Watch a game being played and it quickly becomes clear that it's an exercise in dexterity and movement, not the physically passive experience of reading or watching a movie. A more appropriate metaphor than film for gaming might be dance, he argues. Certainly dance productions can tell stories, but the real expressive core of the art is the relationship between motion and space. A dancer moves, and the motion *is* the story. So, too, in a video game; the movement of the digital character through space and the act of exploring the virtual environment can be more important than the more superficial content of the game.

That interpretation helps explain why kids, and particularly boys, have been drawn so wholly to games. He contrasts his own childhood, where he had lawns and whole forests to explore and turn into fantasylands, with his son's world of city apartments, with a tiny stretch of green in front to play. Exploration of the environment has long been a critical part of growing up, particularly for boys, and video games have become that space for urban children without access to forests and fields, he says.

That, in turn, has helped lead to the moral panic over violence, Jenkins believes. From the beginning, games have had to be "hypermasculine" for adolescent boys to feel comfortable staying inside and playing them. No boy wants to be seen as the "mamma's boy" sitting inside when peers are roughhousing outside. As the boys play these macho games, their parents—and particularly mothers—are suddenly exposed to the content of adolescent fantasies that traditionally have been kept well outside parental view. "This means that mothers are for the first time seeing the content of boys' fantasies as they grow up," Jenkins says. "They are shocked by the scatological content and by the competition. But any boy growing up in America wouldn't be shocked."

Jenkins has spent much of his professional career arguing against the analyses of what he calls the "media effects" establishment: the body of doctors, psychologists, parent groups, and others that focus on a one-way line of influence between entertainment media and viewers, particularly children. In these critics' minds, there is a fairly simple cause-effect relationship between, say, a child and a game of Quake. The game affects the child in one of several different ways, such as contributing to violent behaviors, or desensitizing the player to real-world violence.

In reality, audiences' responses to media stories and programming are much more complicated, Jenkins contends. Children and adults alike take the raw materials of media stories and transform them to fit their own purposes. Kids play superheroes, army, or *Buffy, the Vampire Slayer* as a way to exert control over their environment. Jenkins' early studies were of fan groups like Trekkies, the dedicated *Star Trek* base. Just as those people turned the world of the Starship Enterprise into a canvas on which to create their own fantasies and theatrical productions, he saw video game players use the game worlds and characters as tools for their own creativity, either in playing the game or in imagining different variations of the game, as his son had done. Even the most violent games could act as catharsis and near-therapeutic tools. Games like Doom and Quake provided a welcome release of frustration over societal constraints, giving children a playing field with difficult rules. "All play is about liberation from constraints and taking action in an environment with less consequences," Jenkins says.

None of this means that Jenkins is an uncritical defender of bone-crunching, mind-numbingly violent games. He's not a fan of Bennett's moral crusade either, but he's taken the crusader's idea of "meaningful violence" and used it in the service of his own ideas. He encourages game companies which are adamant on making violence a part of their games to prompt people to think of the ramifications of their actions—much as Richard Garriott had been trying to force his players to ask questions of themselves and see their in-game actions in a broader light. "The formulaic nature of violence I don't like. It's a crutch that game designers fall back on," Jenkins says.

His work with companies might actually have some of the same medium-tempering effects that his perceived opponents have had, he adds. "My hope is that I may be more effective in doing some of the things that parents' groups have been trying to do."

* * *

As congressional staffers lined up Jenkins' post-Columbine trip to Washington, the phone in David Walsh's Minnesota office was ringing almost without cease. Walsh was founder of the National Institute on Media and the Family, at that time a three-year-old nonprofit group known for its measured but unstinting criticism of media violence accessible to children, from television to video games. It was bad enough that Harris and Klebold's rampage drew from action-movie imagery; when they were discovered to be computer game fans, reporters around the world immediately turned to Walsh for an explanation.

Walsh didn't give the media its most sensational headlines. Others in the community of video game critics were happy to do that. But his words sounded a warning that continues to resonate with parental groups and in Washington, DC. "A lot of people try to imply that video games were the cause, which is preposterous," Walsh says. "There is no one cause for a situation like that." But that didn't mean there wasn't a connection. "The impact of violence in the media is not violent behavior; the real impact is that it creates and nourishes a culture of disrespect. For every kid that finds a weapon, how many are there putting each other down, calling each other names? That creates an environment where aggressive or violent behavior is more likely to occur."

Harris and Klebold weren't the first to be teased and harassed at school, but something in them responded to the environment with a horribly extreme reaction. The shape of that was not wholly coincidental, Walsh says. "When it came time for them to act out their anger, where did they get their ideas?" Walsh asks. "Ideas come from popular culture, and media defines popular culture."

In the spectrum of media critics, Walsh is far from an extremist. Others point to far more direct links between video games and violent behavior. Former Marine psychologist Grossman, who testified at the congressional hearings after Columbine and who has studied the psychology of soldiers on the front lines of military conflicts, found that training simulating the action of killing essentially makes the actions of combat a muscle memory rather than a conscious decision. The simulation had helped improve the ratio of soldiers who actually fired their weapons in war. Games that teach players how to mow down onscreen enemies—particularly those arcade games where the motion of pointing and firing a weapon is part of the experience—are literally teaching the players to kill, and therefore need to be banned entirely from the retail market, Grossman contends. A resident of Jonesboro, Arkansas, where a 1998 school shooting helped set the stage for the media frenzy that followed Columbine, he has toured the country calling for programs of "education, litigation, and legislation" against violent video games.

Unlike Grossman, Walsh and his group don't support censorship. They don't support legislation that would impose new restrictions on the video game industry. He's even been quietly "disinvited" from congressional hearings at which potential pieces of legislation would be discussed when his reluctance to support specific bills was discovered by congressional staffers. Nevertheless, his group's campaign of research and education has made him one of the most influential voices on Capitol Hill and in the medical establishment on the issue.

Walsh started his career as a high school teacher, for 10 years bouncing between schools in Massachusetts, Washington, and his current home of Minnesota. He made a gradual transition to the role of school counselor, and from there to professional psychologist. In the late 1980s, he wrote a book called *Designer Kids*, which dealt with the effects of consumerism and competition on children. It sold reasonably well, and his publisher asked him several years later to do a follow-up. He chose to study the influence of media on children, focusing in part on the effects of violent media.

This second book wasn't explicitly about video or computer games. At that point, games like Doom, Mortal Kombat, and Duke Nuke 'Em were just arriving on the cultural scene. Decades of research on the effects of television, movies, and other media had been undertaken, however, and *Selling Out America's Children* brought all those studies together. It struck a nerve, particularly with journalists. Bill Moyers featured Walsh and his book on his television show, and other media outlets followed suit. The American Medical Association even called Walsh for information when the organization was putting together a public information campaign on the impact of media violence.

From that point on, there was no turning back. Walsh realized that he was doing something he felt strongly about, and he started looking for corporate sponsorship for a nonprofit organization focused on media issues. In mid-1995 he found funding and the Institute was born. The group's underlying philosophy would be that the various media that kids spent an increasing time of their growing life watching were not necessarily good or bad, but were powerful influences. He realized from talking to kids, talking to educators and parents, and even from watching his own three kids, that video and computer games were an increasingly important and influential part of that media tapestry.

Even then, a few years after Lieberman's first rounds of hearings, few groups in the nonprofit world were talking about video gamers. The medium was still relatively new, and games were evolving so fast that people who hadn't grown up with them still found them difficult to understand. Walsh's group was one of the first to begin talking publicly about their effect. The message was heard on Capitol Hill, and Senator Lieberman's office called Walsh one day. They'd been looking for a nonprofit to work with on the issue. Walsh agreed to work with them to study the effects of games, and together they hatched a first project. They'd create a "report card" on the video game industry, studying how many of the companies were using and following the new post-1993 rating systems and how much violence was still finding its way into games.

Walsh didn't wholly know what to expect when he released his first report. Because of his association with Lieberman, the unveiling was held in the Capitol Building, in one of the legislative hearing rooms. Walsh walked in to see representatives from virtually all the major TV networks and newspapers there. He was stunned. The news was carried by the biggest news organizations in the United States, and the follow-up report cards his group has released every year continue to receive considerable attention.

The group's primary message is not an explicitly research-based one. It focuses on the impact of media on culture. In this regard, Walsh is not wholly out of Jenkins' territory, although they certainly disagree on crucial points.

"Whoever tells the stories defines the culture," Walsh says. "This has been true for thousands of years. We've been telling each other stories forever. What's new is who the storytellers are. For the past 50 years, the dominant storytellers have become the electronic media—movies, television, video, and computer gamers. And their real impact is in shaping norms of behavior."

This is true for any medium, he says. "If we believe *Sesame Street* teaches four-year-olds something, we better believe that Grand Theft Auto: Vice City"—a game that rewards carjacking, murder, and killing prostitutes among other goals—"is teaching 14-year-olds something. The impact is a gradual and subtle desensitization, and a shaping of attitudes and values."

Walsh's group is closely tied to the medical and psychological establishment that has examined the effects of media violence using traditional social psychological techniques. Games have been studied relatively infrequently compared to television and film. Indeed, the medium remains in such a constant state of flux that what studies there are have a doubtful shelf life. The influences of Space Invaders may be very different than those of the latest Doom title.

Walsh starts with research performed with other media. A long line of researchers—the same ones Jenkins calls "media effects" proponents—have found links between watching considerable amounts of violent television and increased levels of aggressiveness. Other research shows that participation is a better learning tool than simply watching. It's not unreasonable, Walsh argues, to conclude that participating in the violent onscreen behavior in the form of video games thus has some deleterious effect on kids. "Theoretically, if television violence impacts kids, it's reasonable to assume that video game violence has at least as great an impact or greater," Walsh says.

Moreover, a small but growing number of studies has shown similar correlations between playing violent games and aggressive behavior, he notes. These have ranged across several types of social psychological study. Some tests have brought players into the labs, had them play various kinds of games, and measured their aggressiveness before and after playing. Some tests have used outside reports, such as letting classmates rate each other's aggressiveness and then comparing these ratings to the time each child had spent playing violent video games.

One of the most influential researchers is Craig Anderson, chairman of Iowa State University's Department of Psychology, who has constructed a broad theory about the interaction between media and aggressive behavior, and has written a series of papers on how video and computer games fit into the model. Along with several other researchers, he has also conducted a set of studies that have formed the backbone of recent research on the issue.

One of his studies interviewed a group of 227 undergraduates and drew correlations between video-game playing habits and factors such as aggressive and destructive behavior, grades, and general attitudes about the world. They found a small correlation between playing violent video games and aggressive behavior as reported by the students—things such as "hit or threatened to hit other students" or "attacked someone with the idea of seriously hurting or killing him/her." In his published version of the study, Anderson and his fellow researchers were careful to note that a correlation didn't necessarily imply causation, however. For example, it could be true that aggressive people were more likely to be drawn to violent games, rather than the games helping to produce the aggressive behavior.[10]

A second study set out to look at the cause-effect link more closely. Students were to play either id Software's Wolfenstein 3D, a fast-paced, first-person shooting game, or Myst, a nonviolent, slow-paced game requiring little in the way of manual dexterity. In a first session, students played one or the other game for 15 minutes, and then responded to survey questions measuring levels of hostility, agreeing or disagreeing with questions such as "I feel angry" or "I feel mean." After a second 15-minute game-play session, they were presented with another task aimed at measuring "cognitive" effects, or changes in their thinking patterns. For this, the computer flashed a series of words on the screen, and the students were required to read them out loud. Some of the words were deemed aggressive, such as "murder." Others were various types of control words, associated with anxiety ("humiliated"), the desire for flight ("leave"), or no particular subject ("report"). At a later session, the same students were brought back to play the same games. Afterwards, they were put into a situation in which they believed they were competing in a game of reflexes against another hidden student, in which the winner would "punish" the other with a sharp burst of sound. Increasing the volume or the length of the sound, each of which was left up to the student, was deemed a measure of aggressiveness.

When the researchers looked at the first set of data, measuring the students' hostility levels, they found no significant difference between the groups of people who had played Myst and Wolfenstein. They found some difference in the groups' aggressive thoughts, however. People who had played the fast-paced shooter games tended to read the "aggressive" words faster than those who had played the mellow Myst, while there was no significant difference between the way they read the nonaggressive words. This could mean that the violent video games helped prime aggressive thought patterns, rather than making people hostile or angry. On the last measure, people who had played the fast-paced, violent video game were more likely to "punish" their fictional opponent with longer bursts of sound, an effect the researchers interpreted as aggressive behavior. In none of these cases was the difference large, but it was statistically significant, the researchers said.[11]

Anderson appeared with Walsh at a congressional hearing specifically on video games a year after the Columbine shootings. He defended his own research and others' against critics there, noting that no study was perfect, but that the body of literature on the effects of violent media taken as a whole was at least as conclusive as the body of literature on smoking and lung cancer. "About 30 years ago, when questioned about the propriety of calling Fidel Castro a communist, Richard Cardinal Cushing replied, 'When I see a bird that walks like a duck and swims like a duck and quacks like a duck, I call that bird a duck,'" Anderson told senators at the hearing in 2000. "The TV and movie violence research community has correctly identified their duck."[12]

Walsh, who testified at the same hearing, has done research of his own more recently in addition to his group's annual report cards. In one study, he had kids rate each other in terms of aggressive behavior, along with surveying them directly to see how angry they were, based on standard psychological measures. He found that kids who played more violent video games tended to be rated by their peers as more aggressive than those who did not, no matter how angry they were on the other measures. Again, that was not necessarily a sign of cause and effect, but another data point to be aware of, he says.

Walsh, along with Anderson, dismisses the idea that the games can actually serve as catharsis or stress relief, at least to the extent of lessening stress over time. Virtually all psychological research shows the opposite—that if people practice a kind of behavior, it intensifies the behavior rather than lessening it, he says. An analogous example might be the "scream" therapy popular in the 1970s, in which people were encouraged to scream at the top of their lungs to release pent-up stress and anger. When researchers studied the effects of that therapy, they found that screamers tended to be angrier than nonscreamers. That's a lesson that proponents of video game catharsis should take to heart, Walsh says. "If you've got someone who is angry, you don't want to make them more angry," he says.

It has nothing do with research or science, but Walsh says the issue itself certainly prompts aggressive behavior. He's never gotten much response from his group's work on violence in film or TV. Not so with video games. Every time the group releases a survey or report card, angry email pours into his box. He quotes one sample email, sent to him a day after the December 2002 report was released:

> I've been playing video games all my life and NEVER ONCE has it affected me. Maybe you were affected cause you've got your head stuck up your ass. By the way, bash Vice City or any other game one more time and I'm gonna come down to your wacko office and shove that biased report card so far down your throat you'll be crapping corrupt soccer moms until next Christmas.[13]

* * *

From inside game culture, this debate among Jenkins, Walsh, and their more radical counterparts seems distant. But even if the initial spotlight on the industry following Columbine has faded somewhat, the possibility of legislation, social pressure, or legal changes that could affect games and gamer culture remains a real one. In 2002, a first court ruling that games were not entitled to the free-speech protections of the U.S. Constitution was released. Federal legislative activity slowed—although by 2003 two senators had introduced a bill that would fund several studies on the effects of media on children. State lawmaking bodies were taking more direct action on issues such as marketing violent video games to teenagers.

The history of other entertainment media could provide some guidance for the future. Jenkins worries that games could be derailed at a critical point in their development, not unlike comic books in the mid-twentieth century. Then, too, a culture worried about corruption of its children found something to fear and criticize in a new entertainment medium, and comic books suffered for it.

In the early 1950s, the comic book industry looked much like the video game industry in the early part of the new millennium. Comic books had started out as an entertainment medium for children decades earlier, but World War II had helped take the industry in a darker direction. Superheroes and shadowy detectives turned their attention to fighting the forces of Hitler, Mussolini, and international communism, and as a generation of children raised on comics grew up and went to fight overseas, they brought comic books with them. War themes became common, and the art grew more violent. When the war was over, many companies kept publishing titles for adults, with war or gory horror themes.

Meanwhile, fan communities were rising up around the comic books, in much the same way that contemporary fan communities have gathered around TV's *X-Files* or Garriott's Ultima series. The publishers helped support many of these. Author Robert Warshow, for example, wrote of his own son's membership in a club called the E.C. Fan-Addict Club, which cost 25 cents to join and entitled its members to such perks as a membership certificate, an ID card, various paraphernalia bearing the Fan-Addict logo, and a newsletter that included gossip, articles, and interviews with authors and artists.[14]

However, a crusader against the comics rose to speak for broader parental concerns. Psychiatrist Fredrik Wertham believed that the bloody titles were a dangerous influence on children. Working as a consultant to ambitious Senator Estes Kefauver, he helped spur high-profile hearings spotlighting the excesses of the comic book industry in 1954. Just a few months before the hearings, he published a book outlining his thoughts on the issue, titled *Seduction of the Innocents*.

At those hearings, the psychiatrist testified that his own research, which was done without any financial support from either side, showed that comic books were certainly a contributor to juvenile delinquency. He went further than most other critics, focusing even on relatively tame Superman comic books as well as the over-the-top horror and crime comics. It made "no difference whether the locale is western, or Superman or space ship or horror, if a girl is raped she is raped whether it is in a space ship or on the prairie," he told legislators.[15]

Just as defenders of video games and filmmakers would later stumble trying to defend their craft, the comic book publishers proved lame in their own defense. Taking the witness stand, publisher William Gaines defended many of his bloody horror comics as having important moral lessons about intolerance and racism, even if told in ways that might make some people in America uncomfortable. He said he drew the line at publishing anything that fell outside the bounds of good taste. Kefauver turned on him, and in an exchange that was widely publicized in the media, held up a comic cover that showed a homicidal man holding a bloody axe and the severed head of his wife. Trapped in his own words, Gaines avowed that the cover was in good taste, and that *bad* taste would have been if the head had been held at a different angle, and showed blood dripping out of the severed neck.[16] It wasn't an argument that went over well, any more than did a video game advertisement shown on the Senate floor in 1999 describing the game to be "As easy as killing babies with axes."

Also testifying at that mid-century hearing were sets of psychiatrists on both sides of the issue. Those who defended comic books, saying that they found the graphic violence "more silly than shocking," were attacked and ultimately discredited in the newspapers as paid consultants for the comic book industry. It was true, although one witness remuneration for serving as an advisor to a comic company had reached no more than the princely sum of $150.[17] Jenkins, who worked for several video game companies, found himself wary of similar treatment following the Columbine hearings.

In the case of comic books, no legislation was proposed or passed, but the intense public criticism ultimately helped push the medium into a kind of publishing ghetto until the artistic resurgence of the mid-1990s. By that time, enough artists were creating complex, psychologically sophisticated stories that graphic novels, as they had come to be called, had begun climbing back to respectability. Those years as culturally despised child's things were not inevitable. In Japan, where no Wertham or Kefauver ever emerged to question the medium's legitimacy so successfully, graphic novels had long been among the best-selling books in the country for adults and children alike.

The financial success of the game industry argues against this kind of ghettoization. Still, after a period of relative quiet following Columbine, late 2002 and early 2003 saw a resurgence of debate over violence in games, clearly showing that the issue remained on the cultural radar screen. Critics drew parallels between violent video games and the weeks-long sniper attack in the Washington, DC area in October 2002. The success of the violent Grand Theft Auto III and its sequel, Grand Theft Auto: Vice City, was bitterly condemned by critics, including Walsh, whose group launched a petition drive against the second game. "Video game violence is now an epidemic, and violence against women has become a black mark on the entire industry," he said in a statement accompanying the release of his group's 2002 report card, which gave the industry a failing grade. "Rewarding players for having sex with, and killing, a prostitute is a frightening example to set."

Lieberman and congressional ally Senator Sam Brownback were inspired by Vice City to call for a new federally funded program of research into the effects of interactive media on children. "We are particularly interested in the impact of interactive media on our kids, now that the Internet has become such a staple and video games sales have surpassed movie box office receipts," Lieberman announced at an April 2003 symposium sponsored by the Children's Digital Media Center. "We should know whether games like Grand Theft Auto that celebrate violence against women, beyond being sick and offensive, are actually leading to more violence against women."

"My own take is that the industry had better be careful," Walsh says. "If developers push the envelope too far, then they make it tempting for politicians to jump on an absolutely no-lose issue."

9

Unleashed

Mike Duarte and Kevin Lamar sat in Mike's blue 1974 VW Beetle on their way to school, talking about games. It was mid-2002 and they were both students at De Anza College, a Silicon Valley–area community college. Their friendship reached back to the eighth grade, when they had discovered a mutual love for computer games. Over the years, they'd put together small parties, hosting other gamers who'd bring computers to one of the pair's homes. The games grew, though, and soon finding themselves out of space, the friends commandeered a local church. The players would daisy-chain their PCs together, creating virtual worlds where gamers could battle. It had been months, though, since that last game party, and the two were getting antsy.

"You know what would be cool?" Duarte asked.

"What?"

"It would be cool if we could get a big LAN party going. Bigger than the ones at the churches."

Just a few years after Columbine, the initial wave of public concern had swept over gaming communities and—at least temporarily—receded, and a new generation of gamers was putting its own mark on the culture. The 19-year-old Duarte, a quintessential gamer, had been 16 when the shootings happened. It had been shocking, and he'd talked with his parents about it at length. They'd been concerned, too, but they had wondered more about the fact that the Columbine killers' parents hadn't seen the kids' troubled sides earlier. None of them had blamed the games.

Where Richard Garriott and John Carmack came out of the culture of Dungeon & Dragons players, Duarte is at the leading edge of a generation of gamers who grew up knowing only the modern, complex digital game worlds, and who have been online at least since reaching adolescence. He's a good but not exceptional player. He has no desire to take the competitive route of Dennis "Thresh" Fong or his successors. But like millions of other people around the world, he's internalized the idea of gaming as a social activity. He takes virtual communities as a matter of course, thriving in them as in a natural environment. It's still a little geeky—gaming has a long way to go before becoming the social equal of football or basketball—but it's a natural home for him.

The culture has shifted subtly since the release of Quake. Nascent changes in the gaming culture had been evident at the first QuakeCon gatherings in Mesquite in 1996 and even more so in the rush of people into Richard Garriott's online world. The center of creativity in gaming culture has moved much farther online.

To the wider world, video gamers are still the kids who play Nintendo or PlayStation by the millions in front of their televisions. By the numbers, part of that stereotype still may be true—the three million copies of the controversial Grand Theft Auto: Vice City PlayStation 2 game that sold in its first month and half of release are rarely matched by any online computer game over the course of the game's entire lifetime. But the snowball that started with the networking of commercial computer games in the early 1990s has today turned into an avalanche.

What's apparent in today's landscape of networks and virtual worlds is that players have taken control of their destinies. Much more than is the case with movies, much more than with television, and much more than with books or music, players have a role in creating and maintaining their medium. Since Doom and Quake, gamers have played an increasingly important role in actually making games, and one of the most popular online games in the world at the close of 2002 was created by a player "modder" (someone who changes a pre-existing game by writing new software code, or by building new game levels).

Today's games are increasingly catering to and reliant on the communities that once were an afterthought. Making friends has become a top reason for playing some popular titles. Players determine an online game's character—not just its sales and profit margin. They determine the health of the communities inside and around a game, and how it will be played.

It's a player's world on the Net now, and the online communities are growing by leaps and bounds. Millions of people around the world, like Duarte, share that gamer's identity—they are teenagers, mothers and grandmothers, students and professionals, men and women. The rising numbers of players are reflected in the widening demographics. By early 2003, the average age of a gamer had reached 28. More than 145 million people in the U.S.—43 percent of whom were women—played some kind of video or computer game at least occasionally. When it came to computer gaming, the most frequent players were older than 35, and nearly two-thirds were older than 18.[1]

The range of players is increasingly reflected in the diversity of the subcultures that have evolved around them. Some of these communities, like LAN players and modders, develop around the games. Some, like the guilds and other groups inside Ultima and Sony's EverQuest, take root inside the games themselves.

✳ ✳ ✳

More people in the gaming community know Duarte by his game name, Exar, than by his given name. He doesn't look much like a killer— he's tall and a little heavy, and he blinks deeply when he talks, almost as if he's wincing at his own words. He still has a teenager's face. He visibly composes himself when he speaks to people who are older. You can almost hear his mother, sometime in the past, admonishing him to be respectful.

Duarte grew up around computers, like many kids in Silicon Valley. His father was the pastor at a tiny Foursquare Church in downtown Sunnyvale, a suburban community in the heart of the technology center. His mother was secretary at the local grade school, and he would often stay after school to do his homework while waiting for her to get off work. But not always. As early as 1989, one of his classmates had a pair of computers networked at home, and the gaming possibilities to be found there proved irresistibly seductive. Duarte had played other computer games before, but playing games at his classmate's house where he could play against his friends over the networked systems drew him in a way that other gaming hadn't. It wasn't long before those afterschool homework sessions were replaced with almost daily gaming sessions.

The two boys discovered games they connected with over the course of the next few years: Masters of Orion, a strategy game aimed at colonizing planets; and Duke Nuke 'Em, the sex-heavy, gory shooter based loosely on Doom's innovations. Duarte loved Duke, although he didn't tell his father he was playing that particular title. One day, he went along with his father to his uncle's house, where the two men were working on a car. When they took a break, his uncle walked the young Duarte over to his computer—the technical interest ranged across the family—and pulled out a copy of Doom. The quick trigger action and demonic imagery didn't do much for him. Later that night, he had nightmares that he blamed on the game's dark, intense setting. The experience, though, didn't turn him off computer gaming. In 1995, when Westwood Studios released Command & Conquer, Duarte became hooked. Based very loosely on the *Dune* novels and video games, it was a real-time strategy game that required players to control the movements of armies on a playing field that was itself perpetually in motion. Command & Conquer set two forces on a future planet against each other for control of territory and a valuable spice-like commodity called "Tiberium." Duarte and his friend squared off against each other regularly, moving armies while attempting to outmaneuver each other. It was intense competition—bragging rights were at stake—and the boys loved it.

No matter how hard he tried, though, Duarte was in a hole. He didn't have a computer, and that meant he couldn't practice. He pestered his father mercilessly. The genesis of the desire might have been a game, but he told his dad he could use the computer for programming and doing school work. His father finally relented, but there was a condition: Duarte would have to build the machine himself.

Duarte's father was a rarity, maybe unique to Silicon Valley: A pastor by vocation, he had taken a second job as technical administrator for the local county Department of Education because his church was too small to pay him a living wage. He could see that computer-related fields were already exploding in the early 1990s. If his son was going to be playing games on computers, he might as well learn how they worked and gain some valuable skills. He bought his son a wholly disassembled computer. The boy, then a sixth-grader, studied the components and instructions. His father helped out in a "hands-off" way, answering questions and pointing him to resources in books; but he pressed the boy to learn the process himself.

His machine built, the youngster quickly ditched the programming and school work ideas for his games. He moved on from Command & Conquer to Star Wars: Jedi Knight, a 1997 shooting game based on the *Star Wars* movies. The real draw for the game was its online capability. Games had been something he and his friends had done, cooped up with each other after school. Now, he was connected to people all over the world doing the same thing.

"Playing on random servers itself wasn't all that interesting, but being able to play with other players that you talked with online every day was a real eye-opener," he said later. "I had friends from quite literally all over the world. It was an awe-inspiring change in my perspective on things. I came to the realization that the world really wasn't so big, if a bunch of kids could come together from all around the world and play a game together."

Before long, he formed his own clan inside the Jedi Knight game community, a group called the Sith Knights, a name taken from *Star Wars* lore. He named himself "Exar," after a character in a *Star Wars* book, and he kept the nickname through the years. This little group proved to be another eye-opener. He was 14 years old and leading a group of players that ranged up to 21 years old. Not many social situations existed where he would have been able to meet youths that much older than himself as equals, much less be respected enough to be a leader. They weren't initially aware of his age, but by the time it came out, it didn't matter much.

His pastor father watched with some concern. Jedi Knight combat wasn't terribly bloody, but he was a little worried about the concept of the Force, the invisible source of power for Jedi Knights. It was a little bit close to magic. He made his concerns known, and then trusted his son enough to let him continue playing.

As the years passed, Duarte's mind raced with the possibilities that would be opened up as he learned how to link computers together. By the time he hit eighth grade, he and Lamar had started meeting at each others' houses after school, connecting their own and others' computers together using whatever bits and pieces of equipment they could dig up. They'd spend hours trying to troubleshoot small networks while players' computers were crashing, electrical circuits in the house were blowing, and people were yelling and laughing. His mother worried a little. He was spending too much time indoors in front of computers, and not enough time outside with friends, she told him repeatedly.

Duarte, at least, had already lost much of his interest in single-player games by this time. He still played them, mainly to practice his online skills, much like a basketball player would shoot free throws in an empty gym. Those solo games grew stale quickly. "They're just missing something," he said later. "You can develop the computer's artificial intelligence and make it act human, but there isn't that same satisfaction. It's like you can be a marathon runner and run by yourself, but it doesn't give you the thrill or excitement of being in a 5000-man marathon, seeing other people running with you and against you."

Ultimately, the pair needed a gaming space bigger than Lamar's house. Duarte asked his father if they could use the church—it was a big space, and it had removable pews where they could put in tables instead. His father, who was by that time teaching computers at a local alternative high school in addition to his church duties, thought it was a good idea. He even suggested more. Every month, he'd help bring over 10 or 15 computers from his school's computer lab, and he'd tell kids in his computer classes what was going on. Many of them were from troubled backgrounds; the games his son loved so much might be a way to help them learn the value of computers. Duarte brought his friends, and they'd spend Friday night shooting each other, all the while taunting each other over the monitor tops. Sometimes they went until midnight and called it quits. Other nights the group played all night.

Just as Richard's D&D games took over his parents' house two decades before, Duarte's LANs soon outgrew the tiny church. The building simply couldn't hold all the people who wanted to try their hands at a little Friday night digital mayhem. With nowhere else to go, Duarte and Lamar stopped the big parties. They hosted gatherings every now and then in Lamar's garage, where they'd take the car out to make room for tables, computers, servers, and cords. It was a little like a garage band practice—haphazard and messy. It was fun, but after the church experience, they wanted more.

* * *

The LAN (Local Access Network) party phenomenon ebbs and flows with every generation of game and gamer. Most LANs start small, the way Duarte and Lamar's did, and stay small. Players come to their friends' homes and string network cables across card tables and makeshift command centers. They are fragile setups—one player who drove two hours to get to one of Duarte's parties told of a gaming night where the power circuits at a friend's house shorted out every time the host's mother turned on her vacuum cleaner.

A few of the parties grow into regional events. Not long after Doom was released, a 25-year-old named Dennis Racine started hosting LAN parties in Silicon Valley. Dennis Fong, who Racine had met on the DWANGO gaming servers, was one of the early attendees. It didn't take long for the gatherings to gain momentum, and pretty soon 20 or 30 people were showing up. They had to turn more away. Finally, Racine and a partner dubbed their event "Fragfest," rented a local hotel conference room, and opened the doors to the public. By the time Quake was released, Racine and his partners were renting the Santa Clara County Convention Center for the parties, and were attracting upwards of 250 people.

QuakeCon itself grew like that. From the 40-plus people in its makeshift ballroom in 1996, the event had grown by 2002 to be one of the biggest LAN parties in the world. Hundreds of people lined up at Mesquite's convention center on the hot opening afternoon that year, most of them carrying heavy computers and monitors, while a three-story banner draped over the attached hotel above them trumpeted the impending arrival of id's next title: "Doom III: The Legacy of Evil Lives On." The new crowd was leavened with more women than attended the early QuakeCon events, but the demographic still skewed towards somewhat geeky men in their late teens or early 20s. One, a thin, pale youngster who held himself in line with the awkward dignity of a nervous adolescent, wore a T-shirt that spoke the hope of many of the attendees: "Chicks dig scrawny pale guys."

QuakeCon's original hotel ballroom had evolved by 2002 to a dimly lit convention center hall filled with nearly 1300 computers, lined up so closely that players barely had room to spread their elbows as they sat in front of their machines. Many of the computers in the BYOC (Bring Your Own Computer) LAN area were homemade, with eerie blue or green lights illuminating translucent panels that served as windows into the interior of the machines. A few were virtuoso displays of technical creativity: one standout tinkerer, who had built the innards of a computer into a green wheelbarrow with a clear plastic plate across its top, had simply wheeled his entire contraption into the hall.

The event attracted teams from as far away as Russia. Their reasoning was simple: to play the best gamers and meet those people they'd chatted with online. Not everyone could afford a room at the main hotel. Those who couldn't would crash on one of the hotel's lobby chairs or under the tables in the huge convention hall. There was good reason to stay. The BYOC area never shut down, and these gamers had come to play. Also, the tournament this year was giving out a prize of $100,000 to be split between the best teams playing id's new Return to Castle Wolfenstein game and single-player competitions using Quake III. At the close of the event, organizers talked of moving to a larger convention center in 2003, where they could support 1700 people or more in the BYOC chambers. The big-money competitions were sexy, but it was the three-day personal fragfests that most of the people came for.

The LAN party phenomenon is particularly compelling for its apparent superfluity in the age of the Internet. After all, as soon as Quake came along, almost anyone with a dial-up modem could find a game on the Internet, often with friends or acquaintances. As high-speed Internet connections began spreading in the late 1990s and early 2000s, physically connecting computers to play became less and less necessary. And yet LAN gaming has continued to grow. Many players routinely hop in a car or on a plane, traveling across town or across the country for a game, lugging their PC hardware with them. Computer gaming might be associated more ordinarily with sitting and staring alone at a computer screen, but the social component has cemented itself as a critical part of players' culture.

* * *

Back in Silicon Valley, Duarte and Lamar had no desire to re-create QuakeCon or even to create something on the scale of the original Fragfest. Their plans, born in Lamar's VW on the way to school, were modest, like those of local LAN planners all over the country. They had initially thought there would be plenty of other groups in Silicon Valley, and they hoped to join efforts with one of them. After a little early research, however, the pair decided to do the work themselves.

Later, as they sat at the local burger joint with a few other interested friends, their vision quickly started to take shape. A friend of Duarte's mother was CEO of a little San Jose company called Nuvation, and he agreed to lend them the company's offices for a weekend. They cold-called dozens of companies they thought might help sponsor the event. A few helped out: an energy drink company, a joystick company, a company that operated servers for game companies, as well as the people who ran a big LAN in Modesto, a city about two hours away. With all that help, they got the equipment, the expertise, and the money they needed to hold a party for 50 people. They were ready to go. They decided to call it the Silicon Valley Frag Fest, build a web site, and start spreading the word using other game sites.

The LAN party fell on a clear and cool Friday night, when most college kids Duarte and Lamar's age were partying somewhere other than a Silicon Valley business park. That thought didn't faze them. By the time the party kicked off, the pair had been at Nuvation's offices for hours, stringing cables and wires, testing circuit breakers, and setting up computers for people who arrived early. They had a pretty good sense of who was coming to the event—mostly locals from Silicon Valley, but a few from Sacramento and elsewhere in the state's agricultural centers. There would even be a celebrity visit—one of the programmers who had worked on America's Army, the shooter game that the military had recently commissioned and published to serve as a training and recruitment tool.

By 10 P.M. a few dozen young men in T-shirts—there were almost no women—milled around the office drinking Sprite and coffee, occasionally sitting down to play a game on one of the computers that filled three rooms, but more often just talking with the others. Few had met many of the others in person before this evening, although some of the nearly 50 attendees had arrived in small groups. They told stories about crazy games they'd played and showed off their computers. One of the organizers, an ebullient, heavyset man named Andy, was particularly proud of his machine and displayed it on a desk with one side open to the air. He'd built it himself, in just two hours, at another party like this one. It didn't look much like an ordinary office computer; on its front were three separate sets of digital readouts, all connected to thermometers inside the machine. If any hot spots developed inside the machine—and this happens quite often with high-performance game machines—the readouts would tell him, and he could activate one of the various cooling fans inside. Andy is a different type of gamer, one who gets off on the hardware side of things. He doesn't play much, but he does make sure the local networks are up and running.

Duarte was busy taking care of minor emergencies. Early in the evening, the host company's CEO had tripped two sets of burglar alarms in his own building, and two different security companies had to be pacified. Power issues were critical. The organizers had carefully calculated how much strain each circuit breaker could take, and they'd loaded each plug very close to the maximum. There wasn't much room for error, and every once in a while something unexpected happened: a computer's fan would kick in, for example, and just that little extra power draw was enough to trigger the circuit breaker and an entire row of monitors would go instantly dark. The orange and yellow extension cords draped across the offices were suffering their own stresses. At one point in the evening, Duarte emerged with a disbelieving smile and a plug in his hand that smelled toxic; the power load had burnt the rubber around its metal prongs, and the plug was useless.

As the evening progressed and the inevitable network issues were solved, the gamers started playing in earnest. The people here came from different gaming circles: some were playing America's Army; some were playing the popular Warcraft real-time strategy game; some played older but still popular games like Quake III. They were enthralled as they played; each stared into the glow of separate monitors, constantly looking for the next kill, breaking out of their hunting modes to fire off quick text messages to other people in the room—a lightning-fast movement, as the player quickly tapped a key that toggled from hunt mode to chat mode then back again. Furious typing followed, the audible evidence of a disparaging note, usually sent to someone the player had just killed. The response was as often verbal—"A**hole!"—one half of a phone conversation that players translated quickly. It took less than five seconds, from kill to chat to holler, before the whole room knew somebody had gotten fragged.

It wasn't all shooting, however. In the back room, a thin, intense boy was making digital maps for the rest of the group. He'd arrived early and paced his way around the office complex. The CEO offered to give him blueprints of the building, but he refused. That would be too easy. For hours he had sat at his computer, playing with the digital equivalent of Lincoln Logs, and over time a 3D model that was recognizably Nuvation's office took shape. It was a mod, his own version of a game that he would unveil early in the morning hours for the rest of the players to run around and shoot each other in. He proudly showed off an early version of the map, running a character through its paces: The screen showed the perspective of someone sprinting up the building's front staircase, jumping through a window, and weaving in and out of rooms where cubicles were ordinarily set. (The experiment showed how context-dependent so much can be inside the gaming community—if this had been Eric Harris or Dylan Kleybold, and the map were Columbine High School, people would be understandably disturbed. In this case, though, the kid was simply being creative, and the other players looked on with a mix of awe and anticipation.)

In the breaks between games, Duarte and Lamar took some time to talk about their own history of gaming and the process of setting up an event of this size. Lamar, known as "Killjoy" in Quake III circles, laughed at the prospect of telling people outside the community of gamers that he was spending the weekend holed up in an office park. There was still a stigma attached to that. "I generally don't tell people that I'm here. It's not cool to let them know I'm getting together with 50 gamers," he said.

Lamar is thin, hovering just under five feet, six inches tall. He's soft-spoken, and red splotches of embarrassment occasionally pop up on his neck when he's talking. When he's uncomfortable, he rolls his eyes a little and taps his foot as nervous punctuation. His passion for the games and the community is evident in just his physical behavior. When he starts talking about the players, he becomes animated, his motions free of the earlier tics. His stick-figure arms swing out in front of him as if he's going to lean in and touch you on the forehead, sync up with you, and download his feelings and emotions directly into your brain because there is no way to talk about games without sounding half-cocked and crazed. Why was he here despite the remaining stigma? Why was he spending his weekend with a bunch of increasingly smelly guys in T-shirts and on perpetual caffeine highs?

It was simple.

"It feels like home."

* * *

An hour north, out in the foggy Richmond district of San Francisco, a different kind of LAN scene was unfolding. In a dark room next door to one of the city's best sushi restaurants, computer monitors were lined up on tables by the dozen. A cafe counter advertised tea with tapioca pearls, a popular drink among this neighborhood's Asian-American population. The arcade sounds of explosions and gunfire poured out the open door onto the busy street, where little groups of teenagers were standing in twos and threes. More kids sat at the computers inside, intent on the worlds unfolding on their screen and underneath their fingers.

This was one of San Francisco's growing number of Internet gaming parlors, or "PC bangs" as they're sometimes called in an Americanization of the Korean word for "room." Thousands like this are scattered across the United States, although at this stage it remains more of a Korean phenomenon than an American one. The Korean market has embraced online gaming, often in these "bangs," with a fervor still unmatched by the U.S. market. In Korea, Blizzard Entertainment's StarCraft real-time space strategy game, largely played in arcades like this one, has become a cultural phenomenon unmatched by any game in the United States, with tournaments routinely broadcast on television and teams sponsored by major corporations. Another Ultima-like game, NCSoft's Lineage, has attracted more than four million players to its online world, almost half of whom play in communal arcades instead of on a home PC.

Tastes in the states are different. In that room in San Francisco, as in thousands of others in the U.S. and Europe at the close of 2002, the game that dominated almost every screen appeared to be vaguely military in nature. It looked a little like Quake or Doom, but the colors were different, and the players were working in teams. The action in the cafe made that clear—shouts and shorthand instructions occasionally broke though the gunfire as teammates barked orders at each other.

The game was called Counter-Strike, and maybe more than anything else in online gaming's short history, it had demonstrated the power that players themselves had over their medium. A Canadian student named Minh Le had written the game in his spare time, modding the freely available code of another popular game called Half-Life—itself based on graphics technology originally created by John Carmack for Quake II. In the three years since its release, Counter-Strike had become one of the most popular multiplayer games in the world. During peak times, 90,000 players from around the world would try to frag each other, making it far and away the most popular mod ever created. Each month, 1.7 million players put in a collective 2.4 billion minutes a month on this game.[2]

At the close of 2002, Counter-Strike dominated gaming cafes in the U.S. and Europe the way Doom once dominated the early LAN parties. Professional gaming tournaments such as those held by the Cyberathlete Professional League, a successor to the Professional Gaming League, hosted it. Teams from around the world had won hundreds of thousands of dollars every year playing it. The quiet Le, meanwhile, had turned his attention to a sequel for Valve, the company that had made Half-Life and ultimately picked up and published Counter-Strike. The fact that he was still working in his parents' suburban basement didn't detract from the fact that he was one of the most successful "mod" makers ever, as well as part of a modding community that by 2002 had become deeply integrated into the broader industry's basic development processes.

Mod making is as old as computer gaming itself. Within a few days of the unveiling of Spacewar! at MIT in 1961, other player-programmers had begun adding to the code, making versions with different features, multiplayer play, or changing enough to make the result another game altogether. Don Woods' rewritten version of Willie Crowther's Colossal Cave was, in a way, a mod of the original game. For years, as games floated freely around the various networks, the line between players and programmers was a thin and often wholly illusory one. From Bill Budge's 1985 Pinball Construction Set to Accolade's 1990 Jack Nicklaus Unlimited

Golf & Course Design, a few companies had even released their own tools for expanding the play fields that came with the original games.

Carmack's release of Doom's level-editing tools and code in 1993 brought the modding of commercial games to a new level. Carmack had dug into the code for Ultima games in his early experiments with game programming, and the early mods of Wolfenstein 3D showed that players didn't need special tools and code—or permission, certainly—before they could start fiddling with the games. The Doom tools nevertheless made it easier to make changes, and mods started proliferating online. Some made simple changes to weapons or characters. Others added entirely new levels to fight in. Still others were full revamps of the game into different themes. An Alien Doom appeared, a James Bond–themed Doom, and even an Ultima Doom hit the Web.

That diversity caught the eyes of executives at independent publisher WizardWorks Group. In 1995, they immediately compiled 900 of the best games, many of them freely available online, and started selling the collection in stores. Within weeks, the mod collection rocketed up the sales charts, briefly surpassing Doom's sales.[3]

Quake, with even more developer tools available, helped accelerate this movement. As more people played the games, and as more people learned the computer skills necessary to manipulate the tools and work with their own 3D modeling programs, creative communities grew quickly. Companies licensed Carmack's underlying game "engine"—the software that controlled everything from computer artificial intelligence to the technology that shaped the 3D graphics and in-game physics—to create their own games with different art and game-play styles. Several of these, including Valve's Half-Life and LucasArt's Jedi Knight II, were very successful titles in their own right. In perhaps the strangest reuse of id's technology, a small religious game company called Wisdom Tree licensed the Wolfenstein 3D game engine, kept most of the levels, but changed the art to make the walls look vaguely wooden instead of stone. They called the game Super 3D Noah's Ark and replaced the machine guns with a slingshot, which players would use to shoot food at animals.

It was the masses of people doing this kind of work for free online that really piqued industry interest. Other companies, seeing the positive effect that the modding community had on id's sales and the life cycle of interest in its titles, started getting into the act. Most of the shooter game companies decided to support modding in some way. Some even held conferences to help teach community members about technology specific to their games. Creating a mod soon became seen as a fast way into the computer game industry, and Quake mods became a standard part of resumes. Tim Willits, a Doom modder, was hired at id; and other companies scooped up other talented mod makers as well.

The community did run into hurdles. Game players and programmers tended to follow their own creative instincts rather than the letter of the law. Just as John Carmack and Tom Hall had borrowed Mario for their early version of Commander Keen, many budding game designers decided to integrate characters from other games or pop culture icons into their own creations, believing that if their games weren't commercial, there were no copyright problems. The owners of the copyrighted characters or original games weren't always so sanguine. In one locally famous instance of backlash, Twentieth Century Fox sent angry lawyers' letters to a team of programmers, led by a Swedish student, that was publicly creating one of the games that mixed Quake with images and ideas from the movie *Alien*. Fox owned the intellectual property rights to the game and movies associated with the *Alien* franchise, and its lawyers told the team in no uncertain terms that it had no right to use their images or code in its own work. The project was stopped, and the term "to be foxed" entered gaming lingo, defined as having a mod project derailed by an intellectual property rights holder's complaint.

Many of the mods built on popular game engines found strong fans inside the online players' communities. "Partial conversions," in which a programmer would change just a few aspects of the game—such as turning Quake into a game of Capture the Flag, or simply adding a few new weapons to the game—were particularly popular. Developers and publishers sought out the best programmers and tweaks, and they even released some of the mods packaged along with their own games. This was the environment that Minh Le entered as he began his ascent in the modding world.

Le grew up near Vancouver, Canada, a fairly typical suburban child. He started playing with computers early on, first with a Commodore Vic-20, and eventually on several other computers in the Commodore series before finding his way to PCs. He took whatever computer classes he could find in school, but he was always a game player at heart. Richard Garriott's Ultima 7 was one of his favorite games, he said later.

Alongside computers, he had a twin pair of interests. He was an artist, and from the time he was young he could often be found with a pencil sketching or sculpting with Playdough. He loved comic books, animated cartoons, and from an early age, he loved war stories and guns. He and his brothers would run around the local park playing war games. As he got older, he was always the first in line to see any new war movie when it came out.

The passions finally merged when Carmack and company released the tools to modify Quake. Le took a look at the technical specs and realized he could start tweaking the game's code himself. He first tried his hand at making a simple gun. He worked for almost three months trying to create an M-16 rifle to add to the game. The results were "horrid," he said later. The hands holding the gun were a weird silver color, and the gun itself was pitch black—hardly the mark of an elegant mod. He hadn't figured out the art of "texturing" a 3D model to give it more realism. It didn't matter, though; by now he was hooked on modding.

"The satisfaction of creating a mod, even in its simplest form, was irresistible to me," he said. "Ever since I started modding, I've been working on them at a feverish pace. I neglected a lot of other things like school and a proper social life."

He decided to keep trying. His next attempt would be a more ambitious reworking of the Quake game. He started working on replacements for all the weapons, making models of real guns. He was almost through with that when he realized it didn't make any sense to be shooting fantastic monsters with real-looking guns. He decided to rework the game's characters, too, and slowly replaced the monsters with soldiers and military-themed objects. He named the whole thing Navy SEALS and released it online. It wasn't a multiplayer game, but it quickly attracted an avid fan base. Others added new levels and its growth continued. The obsessive work on the game had taken its toll on his schoolwork, however, and he wasn't making money from downloads of his work. He decided to take a year off from game-making to get his life back on track.

As a first-year student at Simon Fraser University near Vancouver, studying computer science, he began toying with a sequel to Navy SEALS using the Quake II technology. He tentatively called it Rolling Thunder (no relation to the 1989 Nintendo game released by Tengen), and started making 3D computer models for the game. But his school workload soon got out of hand, and he was forced to stop, donating the models to another team. He worked occasionally on that project for a few months, making additional models, but ultimately he dropped it.

Late in 1998, Valve Software's Half-Life hit the streets. Based on the Quake II game engine licensed from id, it led players through an adrenaline-packed and genuinely frightening story of a scientist trapped in a research facility overrun by dangerous monsters released from another dimension by an experiment gone wrong. Like Carmack, the Valve team who had made the game had a program of actively supporting the mod communities. Le took one look at the game and realized there was real potential for something along the lines he'd already been working on. In its natural state, the game pitted the player against squadrons of Marines trying to close his mouth before he could tell what he'd seen. Take the monsters out, focus just on military teams, and it would be another game altogether. His game would feature a counterterrorism squad tasked with stopping a separate team of terrorists from planting a bomb. It was a simple game, with a simple concept, and it would rely on players to make it fun. He decided to call it Counter-Strike.

Le had already done a lot of research on the subject. He knew what kinds of characters and weapons he'd have to build. He didn't have the resources to make a full single-player game with a story line and artificial intelligence controlling the terrorists, so he decided to make it a multiplayer game, like Quake deathmatches but with the rudimentary terrorist back-story providing guidance for players. The terrorist team leader would be tasked with planting a bomb, and teammates would do what they could to facilitate that operation—usually by shooting anyone who tried to interfere. The antiterror team would have to work together to stop the terrorists.

He worked on the game for seven or eight months, mostly by himself. However, he did have some help from other programmers who created different levels to play and tested the game. People from outside the team offered suggestions, but Le said the core group had a clear idea where they were going from the beginning: slowing down Half-Life's speed of play, changing the accuracy of guns in the original game to mirror the action of real-world weapons, and adding other realistic guns, uniforms, and scenery.

The process taught Le a lot about games and about the criticisms of gamers, he said later. The community support helped, but players often missed the subtleties and tradeoffs inherent in the development process if they hadn't participated themselves. "Before I started making games, I never really understood what exactly it takes to make a game and all the factors that need to be considered when implementing a particular feature," he said. "There were countless times where the Counter-Strike team would be lambasted for doing things a certain way, and when I read the flames on the forums, it just irked me so much because I knew that all of those flames could have been quelled if only people understood what goes on in making a game."

Despite the message board flames, the first release of the game in mid-1999 as a free download met with solid approval from other game players. The game was such a success, in fact, that Valve Software—the company behind Half-Life—took notice. The company was primed to look for good mods. A pair of former Microsoft programmers, Mike Harrington and Gabe Newell, had started Valve a few years earlier. While they'd based Half-Life's technology on id's Quake II engine, they'd tapped a community-built Quake level-editing tool to help build their own game's levels. They hired many of their own programmers from the modding community, and not long after Half-Life's release, they created an annual Half-Life Mod Expo event that would spotlight independent programmers' work. The company offered to release Counter-Strike commercially, and lent Le some programming help to fix the remaining bugs. The game hit retail shelves in November 2000, although anyone could still download it for free from the Counter-Strike web site. In the course of two years, it made history—by the end of 2002, it was among the most popular multiplayer games in the world, with the company claiming on its web site that "more gamers are playing Counter-Strike than the sum total of all other games combined."

The range of modding runs a much larger spectrum than Counter-Strike. Working at least 180 degrees from Le and other military devotees were designers Anne-Marie Schleiner and Melinda Klayman, for example, who were using Quake and Counter-Strike mods as expressions of a very literal "Make Love, Not War" philosophy.

As 2002 closed, Schleiner and Klayman were working on a game they called Anime Noir, based on the Quake technology but transporting players instead to the new world of Tochina. Here, the player's aim would be to collect three keys, which in turn would unlock the door to "Dr. Kitty's" laboratory, where researchers had been working on sexually oriented bio-engineering experiments. But that story was a "McGuffin"—a simple plot device used to push the real agenda: getting people to talk dirty to each other. Tochina was a place where flirting would garner you points, and players' ability to get their peers to allow some heavy petting would raise their skill level.

Anime Noir's game play thus relied on a much different, and certainly much slower, kind of social interaction than did Quake or any other shooter mod. Players would create their own anime avatar and wander through the world. Meeting other characters would be an excuse for heavy chatting. Shooting was replaced by touching; players would choose a body part to touch—a hand, for instance—and an action, such as stroking the palm. The more physical interaction a character engaged in, the more points its player would accumulate. Real people were in the game, so the developers cautioned players to start slowly—but advanced moves included the Pony Ride, French Kiss, Lick, Suck, Bite, Inhale, and the ever-popular Penetration. Rejection, which would take points away from the unlucky suitor, was an option, since the developers' idea was to spark erotic social interactions, not simply (or not solely) wanton digital sex.

In one sense, the Anime Noir mod follows in a long and generally undistinguished line of sexually themed games. Many of those earlier titles, such as Mystique's Custer's Revenge for the Atari, were created by men and sometimes featured explicit or implied sexual violence as their themes. Schleiner and Klayman's game was aimed at subverting that tradition, forcing players interested in sexual content to interact with other real people, instead of acting out their fantasies on an unthinking computer.

The pair of unlikely designers met in college, where they found themselves rooming together at the University of California, Santa Cruz, in 1992. Anime Noir, one of several products of their broader "Playskins" erotic media project, was just their latest attempt to make people question the foundations of computer and video traditions. The path they took to programming was as unconventional in places as the game itself.

Klayman took the erotic as her subject of study as an art history graduate student at the University of Texas in Austin. While investigating fetish art, she stumbled upon a sexual subculture in which people—primarily men—paid women to act out their fantasies of domination and submission. Intrigued by the idea, she decided to take a year off school, move to Dallas, and try her hand at being a dominatrix. The step was art, research, and play all at the same time, she said later.

"It was really fun, and I got to take part and listen to all the fantasies," Klayman said. "It's like being an anthropologist, listening to people who have these fantasies and desires, and you don't have to do anything. I never got naked. I was basically doing our game before I ever got online."

She returned to school the next year, finished her degree, and eventually wound up in Singapore, where she started work on a southeast Asian web site dedicated to cyberart. There, she fell in love with the distinctly Japanese animation style of *anime*, an influence she would later bring to her game design.

Schleiner was the gamer, having discovered Myst and Tomb Raider while she was in graduate school. The gorgeous environment of Myst and the female protagonist Lara Croft in Tomb Raider hooked her, and they changed how she looked at computer programming and how she taught cyberfeminist courses in Vancouver, B.C. Part of her teaching program allowed her to make visits to American game companies. In every case, she saw firsthand how these development houses were wholly dominated by men. That made her think: the maleness of the industry surely contributed to the focus on blood and gore and adolescent power fantasies.

She decided she would make a game that focused on something other than killing and violence, and she called in Klayman to help. Together, the two began sketching out characters for their game, using Quake characters as a template. Eventually, they came up with the Anime Noir world, where touching and flirting took the place of fragging.

Schleiner was not against the first-person shooter world. She was an avid Quake player, and she had certainly been known to grab a virtual AK-47 and go hunting in Counter-Strike. Her tastes mostly ran toward peace and love, though, along with a little bit of subversion inside unthinkingly violent environments. Before starting the Anime Noir project, she created a simpler Counter-Strike protest mod called Velvet Strike, which gave players the opportunity to download icons of peace that could be used instead of guns. Using her software, players could spray-paint antiwar messages and other messages of civil disobedience on the walls of any level in Counter-Strike.

She also put together peace recipes—instructions that showed teams how they could disrupt ordinary games. "Ask the members of your Counter-Strike team, (must be at least 14), Counter-Terrorist or Terrorist, to stand in a large, low, flat open area in the game that can be viewed from above," one set of instructions read. "Arrange everyone to stand in the shape of a heart. Do not move or return fire. On all player chat send out the message repeatedly: 'Love and Peace.'"[4]

The vitriol directed at her efforts was quick and bitter. Just hours after Velvet Strike went live in April 2002, hate mail and even death threats filled her email box. Her web site came under attack. Message boards filled with posts dripping with anger.

"What a stupid initiative," read one posting. "If you don't like the game, just don't buy it, and don't piss off other people with your shit. Just a woman could have thought of making something like Velvet Strike. If you don't realize that a videogame is just a videogame, and that it's a fake world, well then, GO PLAY WITH YOUR BARBIE."

Schleiner's brainchild found some sympathetic ears, however. Several programmers signed on to create new Velvet Strike–like downloads. One online protest organization, called the Graphical User Intervention, adopted her software as part of a concerted drive to sacrifice their characters inside games in service of their message of antiviolence. Their web site drew from the ideals of peace protesters around the world, focusing instead on the acts of virtual characters in a virtual world.

"Our mission is to seek out those who would attempt to propagate the vile seeds of strife and division upon the burgeoning fields of online entertainment," the group's mission statement read. "Why are these gaming environments so savage and ruthless? We all exist within these virtual domains and as members we have a duty to each other to coexist in a Utopian world free of hate and struggle."

* * *

In worlds of Counter-Strike or Quake, the range of digital experience is, in fact, limited. The communities and their social activities thrive outside the game worlds, but inside the games themselves the action tends to be bloody, focused, and fast. It's a pace that fits the young, mostly male demographic of the games.

The persistent environments of massively multiplayer online games have spawned a different kind of community, which exists as much inside the game world as it does outside. By the close of 2002, nearly a dozen of these commercial graphical online worlds existed. Ultima Online, going on its seventh year, still had more than 230,000 virtual denizens. Sony's EverQuest, in its fourth year, had more than 430,000 active players and had become a cultural phenomenon that far outstripped Ultima's public profile. These digital worlds are explicitly about building community, often at the expense of the quests, adventures, and other fantasy or science-fiction world components that ostensibly motivate the world's players.

It was easy to see this on a rainy San Francisco fall night in late 2002, as groups of EverQuest players converged on a staid downtown hotel. They collected in the hotel's lobby, slowly drifting across the street to the city's shiny, high-tech Metreon mall adorned with EverQuest logos. A Sony store here was filled with people playing the latest PlayStation games, and a twenty-first century bar/arcade offered networked games—video games were hardly foreign to this facility. Still, something about the mix was a little strange. *High-tech* was the watchword here, and the attendees played one of the most technologically advanced games on the market, but its medieval swords-and-sorcery theme brought a hint of Renaissance Faire into the slick shopping mall. More people wandered around in game T-shirts than in costume, but the occasional man in a leather jerkin or Maid Marion-esque woman wandered past as well.

This was the Fan Faire, a periodic gathering of EverQuest players sponsored by Sony Online Entertainment, the game's publisher. Like Duarte's LAN parties, Fan Faire showed that players still craved physical contact with the people they met online, no matter how vibrant the digital fellowship. It showed too how critical the players' ongoing, creative participation was to the game's health.

At this 2002 event, close friends who had never met each other face to face gathered in corners and talked as if they'd known each other for years—which in many cases, they actually had. They previewed new versions of the games. They met in the mall's bar and excitedly recounted stories of online heroics. On the second day of the event, they were sent on a "Live Quest," and teams of players bounced across the mall on a scavenger hunt. A skinny, long-haired 30-something man approached a young girl who was dressed in a green and white medieval skirt with a sign labeling her as an "NPC," representing one of the game world's computer-controlled "non-player characters." The man held out a piece of cheesecake in a little plastic dish. "I think I'm supposed to give you whipping cream. Is this right?" he asked.

She looked at him a little sadly. "You're supposed to bring me everything on your list."

Teams of programmers, developers, in-game support staff, and other game-related people fielded questions later in rooms packed with players. It was like watching a local city council meeting; people were incensed about bugs in the game or about policy decisions they thought had made play too difficult or too easy. Many had suggestions for new revisions. A wizard's spell that allowed players to kill other players with a quick personal firestorm was too powerful, someone suggested. Fine, take it away, but wizards were too vulnerable to other players in the long seconds it took them to cast lethal spells, another said. No, wizards were among the most powerful players in the game, and they shouldn't be given any more advantages, a Sony developer said. People wanted room for more spells in their spell books. They wanted to push fewer buttons to aim and shoot arrows.

Most of all, players wanted a voice in the game. This was the grassroots, the community that made the game a surprising and lasting success, and it had something to say. Sony, a giant corporation, was listening.

❋ ❋ ❋

By late 2002, EverQuest was the biggest online gaming phenomenon in the United States. Overseas, the Korean game Lineage had outpaced it in terms of number of players. But EverQuest was the game with buzz. Players had spent so much obsessive time online that it has been dubbed "Evercrack," only half in jest, by its adherents.

Alarmist headlines about gaming addiction, reminiscent of the early concern over the Internet itself, started showing up in newspaper headlines and online as early as 1999. An Internet mailing list dubbed "EverQuest Widows" emerged with more than 3400 members. "We're here to support each other, and to discuss the trials and tribulations of living in Real Life while our partner is immersed in EverQuest," the group's mission statement read. The virtual economy of EverQuest's world of Norrath had even developed trade relations with the real world—players sold high-level characters and hard-won magical items for real money, sometimes for as much as $1500, before Sony and eBay started cracking down on the phenomenon.

Like Ultima Online, EverQuest gives the online gaming world a different model than the shooting communities of Quake and Counter-Strike. While still in large part focused on killing monsters, the game bars players from killing each other. The game is structured around working together, and people are encouraged to band together to accomplish goals. Game play is often criticized—much of it consists of waiting in a spot until a particular monster reappears, and then gathering around it as a team and hacking it to death—but the bonding effect of the team play and online social interaction is undeniable. People form bonds, and they cite those social interactions as the primary reason for spending so many hours online.

A few years younger than Ultima Online, EverQuest is one of the first massively multiplayer games to be sponsored by a major corporation. The genesis of the idea came from a game developer at a small Sony-owned game studio called 989 Studios that primarily made titles for the Sony PlayStation. The game's first proponent, a longtime online game player named John Smedley, pitched a succession of senior executives there in 1996 on the idea of doing a Dungeons & Dragons–like game online. He was initially turned down. The market for PC games was minuscule compared to the PlayStation's potential, and online games at that point had yet to gain any serious commercial traction. He pointed to other games hitting the market, and ultimately he was given permission to try out his idea, along with a small team.

The game took shape in others' hands. Brad McQuaid and Steve Clover were already in-house at Smedley's company. They brought in Bill Trost, an artist who McQuaid had found years before, to work on their Ultima-like game. Trost was given nearly full responsibility for developing the world, and he drew heavily on his long experiences as a D&D Dungeon Master. The world of Norrath would be populated by different races: elves, dwarves, humans, ogres, trolls, and more. As with other role-playing games, players would select their own "classes"—the game equivalent of a career placement service—such as warrior, mage, or monk. As in Ultima Online, they could choose and practice skills such as fishing or pottery making, but this would be a game mostly about combat and exploration. People could certainly play it for other reasons, but its economy and ecology were nowhere near as advanced as Garriott's game. This would be about adventure and about making common cause with other players.

"Our game was based upon player cooperation," Trost said later. "In order to be successful, you need other players. No one player can do everything in the game. The more friends you have, the more fun you will have."

In the early stages of development, Sony was not terribly excited about the game. Development costs rose to nearly $5 million as the team of programmers and artists swelled to dozens of people.[5] That was considerably more than the development costs for the average PlayStation game of the time, and the price tag raised eyebrows. In part to protect their game, Smedley and his team formed a different, independent company called Verant Interactive to release the game in early 1999.

Like Ultima, the proof of its success came quickly. Close to 12,000 people signed up the first day. Norrath's population passed the 50,000 mark after the first week. Within no time Verant Interactive was folded back into the Sony family. Propped up by the marketing power of the international media conglomerate, EverQuest's population continued to grow well into 2002.

"Once we got into public testing, our popularity actually hurt some of our productivity, as well as the productivity of some other development teams around the industry. No one was getting any work done because everyone was playing EverQuest," Trost said. "I remember specifically being in a meeting, four months after launch, where we were being cautioned we should not feel bad when our numbers started to decline. But they never did."

The Fan Faire, like QuakeCon before it, was started by a player. Founder Cindy Bowens had come to EverQuest and Norrath with her full guild not long after the game was released in 1999, uprooted in entirety from their original home in a different game called The Realm. The 30-something Bowens had started playing that game during a period of illness at home in Colorado, alone in the house while her kids were in school. The contact with the outside world, even a virtual world, had been invaluable to her spirits.

She did more than just play. Not long after joining the Sony game, she put together a web site called the Women of EverQuest. A community of players began developing around the message boards there, and someone quickly suggested they should meet face to face. Bowens, who had a background in professional event planning, took on the responsibility. She posted a poll to the site asking where players would most like to gather. St. Louis came back as the number one choice. It wasn't quite the magical kingdom of Norrath, but Bowens set up the meeting. Verant caught wind of the event and agreed to give her official sanction: Fan Faire number one. After that March 2000 St. Louis event, she helped put together a larger Fan Faire in Las Vegas. More than 500 people came to that one. The success pleased Sony immensely, and the company hired her to produce the events more or less full time.

It's difficult to tell inside the EverQuest world who, or what, people really are. An ongoing research project by former Haverford College student Nicolas Yee provided a deeper look into who plays the game and why. A former "Evercrack" junkie himself, Yee solicited survey responses from thousands of players of EverQuest and rival massively multiplayer games, and he kept a running set of studies detailing his findings online.

The demographic results he found carried some surprises. The average age of EverQuest players at the time of his mid-2001 survey was about 25. That was older than the average age of Quake players (23) or Starcraft players (18) discovered by other surveys. Only about 16 percent of players were women, although women were more likely to have a leadership role in a guild. About a third of players were single and not dating, another third were single but dating, and the final third were either married or engaged. A large proportion of women involved—close to 60 percent of those in the survey—said they played the game along with a spouse or romantic partner. Just 16 percent of men were doing so. Nearly 20 percent of players had children.

Another, more recent finding bears directly on why people play. In a survey of nearly 4000 online players from several different games, Yee found that a full third of players cited "making friends" as the most important aspect of the game to them, compared to just 16 percent who named "achieving goals or making progress," the next highest category of interest. The response was even higher for women, 50 percent of whom selected "making friends" as their chief motivation. [6]

The popularity of the game has spawned alarmist headlines trumpeting "EverQuest Addiction" in newspapers around the United States. Many people play four hours or more a day, and stories of people slowly losing touch with reality routinely began to surface in the media as early as 2000. A Florida man's nine-month-old son died in 2000 while his father played the game, and the local media picked up on prosecutors' claims that the man had fatally injured the boy while trying to keep him quiet during a game of EverQuest.[7] A Wisconsin man shot himself in 2002 after quitting his job, ignoring his family, and becoming increasingly obsessed with the game. His mother threatened to sue Sony.[8]

Bowens later said people who lose perspective on their regular lives certainly do exist, inside the game and out. "Occasionally, you'll meet someone who plays an ungodly amount of hours," she said. "But the average person plays about 20 hours a week. They don't watch TV. This has become their main form of entertainment." There are people who develop obsessive habits, she noted, but they're few and far between. "I have not seen that. Of the thousands of people that I've met, most seemed pretty normal."

Her memories and stories are instead drawn from community behaviors that sound much like the way neighbors act toward each other. One guild collected money to buy a new computer for a member whose computer had broken, and who couldn't otherwise afford to buy a new one. Another guild registered and paid the way to a Fan Faire for a member who was ill and had just gotten a divorce. One 18-year-old boy emailed Bowens to tell her that his best friend had died of cancer a few weeks before a Fan Faire. He'd almost canceled his trip, but decided to go at the last minute. There, he met an older man who not only played the game but also lived nearby. The older player became a kind of mentor, helping the boy work through his grief, Bowens said. "That's what it's all about—the human interaction," she said. "I think it's as valid as a face-to-face relationship."

A walk through the Fan Faire in San Francisco showed a very different population than the 2002 QuakeCon that had been held several months previously. Fan Faire participants were much older, and many looked like they had ordinary jobs and ordinary suburban family lives. It's difficult to argue that online gaming, at least beyond the occasional game of Hearts or Bridge, is truly a mainstream phenomenon yet, but conversations with many of the people at the Faire showed that it's increasingly hard to stereotype even the most avid gamers.

Bridget Goldstein, a 45-year-old mom who lived in Pasadena, was one of these stereotype breakers. A thin, energetic brunette, she was as excited to talk about obscure Aldous Huxley books—or the bagel business she ran with her ex-stockbroker husband—as she was about the game. Her experiences provided a good example of how unexpected people can come to hold dual citizenship in Norrath and an otherwise ordinary life.

Goldstein had grown up around the first generation of home computers; her younger brother built a Sinclair while she was in high school, and they used it for games. She contributed her own strength to the pair's gaming needs: she got a driver's license first and was able to drive them to the local arcade to play Galaxian and the rest of the quarter-fed machines. When she went to college, computers were punch-card beasts, and she lost touch with electronic games until her husband brought home a discarded PC. She rediscovered gaming then with a few simple text-and-graphic adventure games. It wasn't until the mid-90s, when her children were old enough to be left alone for short periods of time and she had a few hours to herself every day, that she started playing again in earnest. She found her way to the most nontraditional of the solo games: Will Wright's SimCity, as well as to the atmospheric Myst and Riven. Then a clerk in the shop where she bought games recommended EverQuest to her. "Prepare to forget your kids' names," he'd warned her.

Goldstein didn't go that far. But she fell into the world with a passion. By the time of the San Francisco Fan Faire in 2002, she'd been playing three years, without breaking for any other game. She'd tried another Myst sequel, but hadn't gotten far. It had seemed lonely. Why wander around even a beautiful world if it was empty?

In EverQuest's Norrath world, Goldstein is a short, busty bard named Nin. The character is a hyper-exaggerated version of Goldstein, much more flirty and more of an entertainer. She sings songs for people at the drop of a hat; Goldstein has programmed shortcuts on her computer to print the lyrics from a few popular songs with references slightly tweaked to fit the environment. The song "American Woman" becomes "Norrath Woman," for example.

Like any real person, Nin's personality evolved over the years, in this case skewing more and more toward Goldstein's own personality. In the early days, she fell naturally into the flirty persona, but as she grew to know her guild members more closely, Goldstein did less role-playing, and acted more like herself inside the game. When the guild encountered new players, Nin's playful nature came back out, but the online persona she'd developed now took a back seat to her ability to interact with friends in a more ordinary way. That didn't mean that the game world and the real world were the same thing. Goldstein said she hadn't introduced any of her Pasadena friends to the game. Norrath was her world. It was where she went at night and became a wood elf who could fly and fight dragons. Bringing her real-world friends into this experience would have somehow tainted it.

Her online questmates did make the transition offscreen. She said she had met all her close guildmates, and considered them a permanent part of her life, no matter what happened to the game itself. It had taken her about a year to get to the point of wanting to meet them, or feeling comfortable about meeting them. Some of the players said they were meeting at a Renaissance Faire in Houston, which was holding a meeting of EverQuest players as a sidelight. "Why not go?" she had asked herself then. She took a few precautions. She looked up her guild leader, a college professor in Texas, on his school's web site to make sure he actually existed. She refused her guildmates' offers to stay with them, and she got a hotel room instead.

She went in with a little trepidation, but they all turned out to be ordinary people, professionals, and just as interesting offline as on. She said she meets them regularly now, at Fan Faires and in less game-related environments. It just isn't weird anymore.

"My kids now take for granted that mommy has these friends that appear as magical things on the computer, but that I'll fly to visit, and they might show up at our house," she said.

The experiences of Bowens and Goldstein were far beyond what any game developer could have realistically hoped to create. But this is what happens, over and over again, when the players take charge.

10

Herding Gamers

It was a few weeks before Christmas 2002, and 1100 of the most skilled gamers in the world converged on the five-star Hyatt Hotel in Dallas, Texas. More than $140,000 in prize money was up for grabs, along with several coveted "world champion" titles, at the Winter Cyberathlete Professional League (CPL) Tournament. Teams flew in from all over the world. Big companies, from Intel to CompUSA, sponsored the event. An MTV crew was in town, filming the progress of the odds-on favorite in the single-player event for an upcoming documentary. This was shaping up to be the biggest event in a league devoted to turning computer gaming into a mainstream sports phenomenon like Major League Baseball or the National Football League. It was serious business, and the fact that the organizers had made sports leagues their guiding stars was one signal of a radical shift in gaming. There was little hint of the old Dungeons & Dragons culture here. Computer gaming, particularly network gaming, was getting a new vernacular.

Other games that broke with the vernacular of fantasy and science fiction were almost simultaneously being launched elsewhere, making their own attempts to broaden online gaming to include new audiences. Electronic Arts opened the doors on its Sims Online world, hoping that women and nontraditional gamers who were attracted to its earlier Sims game—a simulation of ordinary people's everyday lives—would also be attracted to this new online community. The home game consoles made by Sony and Microsoft were adding network play, and video game football players, surely the most mainstream of gamers, began huddling into online teams that were oddly reminiscent of the guilds and clans found in EverQuest or Quake.

Each of these ambitious new drives toward new audiences was a sign of the same phenomenon: The networked gaming world, the talk of the industry for a decade, had finally reached the industry's version of prime time. With their appetites whetted by the expansion of games like Ultima Online, EverQuest, and others into nontraditional game demographics, game companies were launching efforts aimed explicitly at expanding the universe of online gamers deeply into the mainstream.

Some 136 online worlds were under development at the start of the millennium, and even if only a small fraction of those were launched, those that succeeded grabbed headlines, dollars, and more imitators. Every major game company, and a myriad of small ones, was creating its own online game world, it seemed. Electronic Arts, the very company that originally doubted the viability of Ultima Online, spent millions developing and promoting The Sims Online. Sony Online Entertainment built Star Wars Galaxies, a massively multiplayer world with 5000 hours of game play along with the ability for players to create an unlimited number of their own adventures. Myst, the game that introduced millions of nontraditional gamers to computer gaming, got its own online world. By mid-2002, according to the industry's trade association, one in three computer and video game players had reported in a survey that they preferred to play games online.[1] In response, large gaming companies committed well over $1 billion through 2004 to create online play spaces for the next generation of gamers.[2]

Despite all the excitement over these communities and their power to sell, create, and perpetuate games, there was a disconnect between industry excitement and actual players playing. True, more than 136 million people around the world were playing video or computer games either online or off, according to the industry's figures. But of the people playing online, the vast majority were casual gamers dabbling in games like bridge, checkers, hearts, and other card games—not the types who were likely to spend $10 a month or more subscribing to worlds like EverQuest or Ultima Online, or the types who would pay $50 to purchase a game at retail. The goal for companies now was to expand the audience of serious gamers, convincing people who had little interest in computer games that logging on to interact with other people was as worthy of their entertainment dollar as the latest big-budget Hollywood film.

The NFL-like gaming leagues, the Sims Online title, and the addition of network playing capacity to home consoles all represented the gaming industry's attempts to expand the gaming universe beyond their earlier audiences. All of them held considerable promise based on their predecessors, but the online versions showed flaws even as they were launched. Their task was a difficult one—healthy communities had nearly always been created organically by their members, and efforts to seed communities artificially had almost universally failed. Nevertheless, the drive to bring mainstream gamers into the online world was under way.

* * *

Walking through the Hyatt lobby, a massive room with smooth pearl tile floors and pristine columns, it was clear that big money was behind this manifestation of professional computer game players. There was no dust, no dirt—nothing but a soft glow on the floor, a reflection of the soft overhead lighting. The escalator in the middle of the room ran to the second floor bar and restaurant area. The gamers—many scattered through the lobby and first floor, quietly huddled over their laptops, working out strategy with their teammates—were swallowed up by the enormity of the room.

This was the opening day of the Cyberathlete's Winter 2002 world championships, the sixth such event in the young league's history. The CPL was for now the most successful of several attempts to create high-stakes professional gaming leagues. About 80,000 teams were registered in the CPL's 25 leagues, and they had competed for more than $225 million in prizes and money donated by exhibitors and television networks. Created by former investment banker Angel Munoz, there was more than a hint of financial motivation underlying the competition here—but Munoz's plan was working. ESPN had televised some of the league's events. The league's stars had been profiled in major mainstream publications around the world. At this event, an MTV documentary crew was following around Johnathan "Fatal1ty" Wendel, the quiet 21-year-old deemed by many to be the best gamer in the world today.

Finding the main ballroom proved difficult. No rowdy teenagers were running through the halls, no pulse-pounding noise was heard, and there was no sign pointing participants downstairs. Nothing suggested that computer games were being played here. The implicit message was "If you don't know where you're going, you probably don't need to be here." Once inside, the "Bring Your Own Computer" participants lined the far wall in long rows. As at QuakeCon and other LAN parties, home-built machines stood out here with bright translucent cases, decked with neon lights that glowed as bright advertisements for their owners' creativity. A few gamers were here, chatting with each other or staring into fast-moving digital landscapes on their screens. The tournament computers, rows of identical beige machines separated from the rest of the floor by a red velvet rope, stood in stark contrast to those carried by this independent-minded bunch. The roaring explosions from computer speakers punctuated a lower buzz of conversation.

The exhibition area, smack in the center of the room, was a who's who of gaming technology. Intel showed off its latest Pentium chipsets, which came with increased graphics capabilities. NVIDIA and PNY unveiled a new GeForce FX GPU graphics card that helped create more fluid computer animations. CompUSA displayed refurbished arcade classics like Pac-Man and Donkey Kong, and it hosted a small Unreal Tournament competition on Microsoft's Xbox home console. Telex introduced its latest surround sound capabilities, and NetFire showed off its new high-speed Digital Subscriber Line (DSL) service. Few gamers spent much time wandering through this section, but Munoz and his staff knew this was where the money was. The players here, a third of whom came from households making more than $90,000 a year, were the ones who helped drive new purchases of super-fast processors, 3D video cards, home networking equipment, and all the other high-end gear that kept Silicon Valley cash registers ringing.

By 1997, Munoz had used much of his free time during the previous 11 years scanning online message boards. An investment banker through the late '80s and '90s, his job required him to keep up on the latest technological advances, so he spent considerable time dialing into local bulletin board systems, reading the latest posts from hackers around the world. He wasn't participating in the discussions; he was just watching. By day he sifted through business plans, looking for opportunities and researching ideas entrepreneurs brought to his office—particularly ideas that used multimedia technology. In 1993, boards started buzzing with activity around a new game, Doom; and after it was released, Munoz started making plans to leave his investment company and strike out on his own.

"This really crystallized in my head when Doom came out," Munoz said. "There was really just something about that game that seemed different to me. There was an instinctual, basic environment created in the game, and that really appealed to me."

The deathmatches, in particular, caught his eye. A longtime sports fan, he recognized the inherent excitement in one player's challenge of another in a battle of wits and skill. These might be computer games, but they had all the dramatic potential of major league sports. What they didn't have was a venue where good players could meet. He started mapping out ideas for a professional gaming league, one that would draw from the best elements of existing sports leagues, while tapping into the clan system gamers had built up over the years. It took him several years, but by 1997 he was ready to take it to the public.

In many respects, Munoz's CPL resembled the early days of Major League Baseball. Until 1845, baseball, too, was wholly recreational, played by rich men who made their games the centerpiece of all-day social activities. Invitations were sent. Food and drink were served. Most importantly, there were no official ground rules for the game. Instead, the players used an honor code, agreeing upon rules the day of the game, and then refereeing themselves. That changed with the introduction of 20 rules, the framework for today's national pastime, which allowed teams from the New York area to begin competing against each other in loosely organized leagues. The standardization, meant to foster games between the upper class, opened the doors for blue-collar teams. Anyone who could gather eight players—this was before the shortstop was added—could now play, and 10 years after the introduction of the "Knickerbocker Rules," teams with players from all social castes were going head to head.

Corporations watched as baseball spread from New York City across the country, captivating crowds and players alike. In 1857, the first amateur league formed. By 1868, 100 teams were playing in the National Association of Baseball. Other leagues would sprout up, and companies began pumping money into the game. Eventually, the leagues all came to an agreement: they pooled their resources, created one professional league, standardized a strict code of conduct, and fostered adoption of baseball's new rules.[3] Their gamble proved quite profitable, with Major League Baseball today bringing in $4 billion annually through ticket sales, television revenues, and merchandizing.

Munoz hoped computer games could make a transition similar to that of baseball. A few things were already working in his favor. Unlike professional baseball, which started with no budget and few organizers, the video and computer game world was awash in cash—game companies pulled in $4.4 billion in 1997, according to the industry's main trade organization[4]—and was populated by millions of gamers around the world, many already connected through online communities. Starting the league would simply be a matter of bridging the two sides of the business.

Others had the same idea. In 1997, an organization called the Professional Gaming League, a joint project launched by the Total Entertainment Network (TEN) online gaming service and chipmaker AMD, created its own series of tournaments. The founders hired Atari founder Nolan Bushnell as league commissioner and invited Dennis "Thresh" Fong to be one of the star competitors. The league launched with a party at San Francisco's Candlestick Park, still then the home of the San Francisco Giants and 49ers teams, underlining the organizers' hopes to tap into the professional sports model. That league foundered in 2000 when a cash-strapped TEN changed its business model to focus on casual gamers looking for online card games and board games, rather than hard-core Quake players.

Munoz started smaller, with plans to expand slowly as the sponsorship money increased. The foundation was simple. Top players would be automatically accepted to tournaments, ensuring the best gamers would show up, and unseeded players qualified for tournaments at sanctioned events across the country, in the same way tennis players must win qualifiers to receive at-large bids to tournaments. The CPL certified tournament computers, making sure that every player competed with the same technology. Munoz may have been a relative newcomer to the gaming world, but he spent a considerable amount of time following other events and had heard losers' complaints about equipment that wasn't standardized. Different processing speeds, video cards, and connections could easily change the outcome of a game. His league was based on absolute uniformity, to minimize controversy. The computers, outfitted with the latest AMD chip sets, were identical, and the rules absolute.

With the basic structure in place, Munoz needed a face—somebody he could use to sell the league. The PGL already had Thresh, and Munoz realized he couldn't launch a new league without his own high-profile gamer. He turned to Stevie "Killcreek" Case, the woman who had trounced Doom and Quake creator John Romero at his own game of Quake and one of the few high-profile women gamers in the community. The gamble worked— the gaming press wrote about her involvement, and the free publicity helped launch the league.

By the end of 1997, Munoz organized the group's first tournament at the giant Infomart high-tech office complex in Dallas. The event, with $3500 in cash and prizes, drew 400 people. Munoz deemed it a success. Nevertheless, the league took time to find its footing. Case left tournament play in early 1998 to focus on game design. In interviews later, she said the organization had initially been too focused on money; and she said the players felt like they were being taken advantage of to promote the league's welfare rather than their own.[5]

Ultimately, it took Counter-Strike's explosive popularity to make the CPL soar.

In 1999, not long after Vancouver modder Minh Le had released his Counter-Strike mod online, a former hockey coach turned gamer named Frank Nuccio started volunteering at CPL events. Nuccio had taken a liking to Counter-Strike when it came out. He'd run a few unofficial tournaments in the CPL's BYOC section. The game appealed to his old hockey instincts: teams had to work together, and groups that learned collective strategy instead of playing as a collection of solo stars wound up winning. Soon, he was spending his free evenings in front of his PC, searching for servers where people were playing Counter-Strike. It proved a painstaking search, as the best players were often lost amidst the cacophony of the game's exploding population.

"I got fed up going to game servers with people saying stupid racist things," he said. "I couldn't throw them out of the game because it wasn't my server, and that upset me. They were ruining the games, saying stupid things, and getting killed on purpose. There were just too many people not playing the games."

He ultimately decided to launch his own gaming league, dubbing it the Domain of Pain. He wanted to give good players a place where they could compete with people on their own level, and like Munoz he believed that collecting these stars in one place was good for the game as a whole.

"I wanted to attract the elite teams, because I knew from my hockey days that kids want to be like the best players," he said. "They want to emulate the stars. They want to wear the same equipment, use the same techniques. They want to be just like them." Word spread, and before long, his Counter-Strike servers were drawing as many as 20,000 people a day. Sensing a community that was growing more quickly than the aging Quake circles, Munoz bought out Nuccio's league and combined it with the CPL. By the close of 1999, the CPL Counter-Strike tournaments were being held in earnest.

Counter-Strike turned out to be a genuinely international phenomenon. Teams from Germany, Sweden, the Netherlands, and throughout Europe proved to be extremely competitive. The best teams overseas found sponsors who paid for them to come to the United States and play. One team, the Schroet Kommando (loosely translated as "shrapnel commandos"), founded by employees of a Swedish digital media company called Spray, did well enough in European tournaments that they decided to turn professional. Twenty-year-old Andreas Thorstensson, one of the team's founders, called companies he thought might sponsor them, and he found willing takers in Intel, German Internet service provider QSC, and other technology firms. The sponsorship helped the team become one of Europe's best since they now concentrated entirely on game play. It even allowed two of the players to quit their full-time jobs.

This would have been little more than a hobby had it not been for the influence of the money involved. While giving game players their own stars to look up to helped motivate players, it was less immediately apparent that it helped expand the gaming community. Few people had the time needed to compete at a professional level, and those who weren't already hard-core gamers could hardly follow the lightning-fast play in a game of Quake or Counter-Strike. The money added a new layer of tension to play that the amateur games rarely saw.

The pressure proved too much for some teams, with some fracturing at critical moments. During the Summer 2001 CPL tournament, superstar clan 3D rolled into Dallas expecting a big win. They'd roared though preliminaries, beating opponents with ease. They faltered in the finals, however, and their three best players—Kyle Miller, Shawn Morgan, and Donald Kim—staged a revolt that played out on the CPL message boards. Accusations flew. "Kyle didn't like the captain," Nuccio said, recounting the team's public breakup. "He didn't like being told they needed to practice all the time, and he was the star player on the team, so he got his way." By the end of the weekend, the team captain and one other player had been replaced by two of Miller's friends.

Indeed, with money on the line, the broader sense of community within the professional gaming ranks had begun to erode. The atmosphere at the Winter 2002 games was quiet and business-like, something that Nuccio was worried about. "It's turning more competitive than we thought here, and we have to be careful that we don't drive away the casual gamer," he said. "This is supposed to be fun."

❋ ❋ ❋

Far from these tense circles of competitive Counter-Strike play, Mother Teresa was fighting Britney Spears. The only money on the line here was Simoleans, the currency of the new online world in which these two characters lived, but it was clearly a serious fight. Angry arms and legs flailed from inside a cloud of dust that rolled cartoon-like across the digital room, obscuring the combatants' actual bodies.

Will Wright, the 42-year-old game designer behind SimCity, The Sims, and this new world of The Sims Online, was playing as Mother Teresa. These were the final stages of an in-house play test of the upcoming game in 2002. Nobody in the office knew who was playing which character. The idea was to gain popularity, and both characters were close to winning.

Britney was nice to her fellow Sims; Mother Teresa largely bribed her way to the top.

Wright is a lanky man with a thoughtful, oval face, thin brown hair combed to one side of his head, and glasses. A co-worker walked in his door, wanting to talk tech, and he hastily brought up the screensaver, his heart beating quickly. He didn't want to be outed as the Machiavellian Mother Teresa yet. When the colleague left, he brought the game back up and resumed the fight.

The game he tested was one of the most ambitious attempts yet to build an online world that would appeal to the broad mass of nontraditional computer game players. The Sims Online, released nearly two weeks before Christmas 2002, was based loosely on The Sims single-player game, and its expansion packs have sold more copies than any other computer game in history. Unlike the epic settings or adrenaline-soaked action of other online worlds, these games were based on reenacting the ordinary lives of ordinary people. Wright believed that more traditional computer games, whether they were dressed up in the trappings of professional sports or not, simply would not appeal to a mass audience.

"You look at the games that are out there, and most of them are military titles, or sports, or fantasy, or science fiction," he said. "But that's not what fills 95 percent of the shelves at a bookstore, or what dominates prime time slots on television. There is so much more interesting possibility for interaction and drama reflected in ordinary reality."

Wright is one of the game industry's true intellectuals, a designer who draws ideas and continuing inspiration from social theory, urban planners, and architects as much as from fiction and engineering work. But there's a playful side to him, too: his early love affair with robot-building has never ended, for example, and he was one of the early participants in the Robot Wars and Battlebots robot-fighting events that later rose to television fame. His teenaged daughter inherited the passion, and for years they built fighting robots together. He maintains a kind of free-ranging, robot-themed creative think tank in Berkeley, California, called The Stupid Fun Club, that makes films, digital games, and—of course—robots.

The Sims Online is the networked manifestation of Wright's original drive to build a game simulating the needs, desires, and actions of an actual ordinary human being. Before the online version, however, came the single-player success story of The Sims. The genesis of that idea came in the early 1990s, as Wright was reading the work of Christopher Alexander, a University of California, Berkeley, professor who wrote about the influence of environmental and architectural design on people's behavior. Wright's initial inspiration followed Alexander's ideas: Essentially the game designer wanted to build a digital dollhouse that would have an influence on the people who lived in it. But as the project evolved, Wright and his small team of developers began taking more interest in the people themselves and in modeling the way they reacted to their environment in fairly complicated and semirealistic ways. If a character was hungry, it would have to eat. If a character was sleepy, it would have to sleep. If a character was horny, it would try to seduce the neighbor's wife.

The team struggled to come up with a way to model human behavior in a way that would be realistic enough to be fun without veering too deeply into the quicksand of artificial intelligence. Alexander's work on how environments influenced people's behavior ultimately showed the way out of this problem. Wright decided to program the game so that the dollhouse's objects—food, drinks, and so on—would tell the humans what they were good for, and let the "Sim" humans react accordingly. A sandwich would broadcast what were essentially advertisements for the ability to make people happy by eating. Individual Sims would have different happiness preferences, so they wouldn't respond to the objects' advertisements in the same way; and their behavior would always be different as their states changed and they walked through different objects' advertisement zones. Thus, the single-player Sims game was born—a digital version of the robots that Wright had been building for years.

"We wanted something that seemed plausible at any given time, so you could look at a character and say 'yes, I understand why she did that.' But the behavior wouldn't be predictable," Wright said. "Of course, compared to humans, they're still very stupid little robots."

Like the original SimCity, the Sims project languished at first. Wright had the idea and a small team to work on it with him, but his company, Maxis, had gone public, and he had no control over the purse strings. Maxis' managers didn't particularly understand the draw of a dollhouse game, where the characters would simply be eating, shopping, working, and enduring the rest of the mundane activities that people ordinarily played games to escape. They wanted him to work on the next SimCity. But in 1997, struggling under losses and the increasingly difficult prospect of supporting the entire company on the SimCity franchise, Maxis sold itself to Electronic Arts, much as Richard Garriott had done with Origin almost a decade before. Unlike Garriott, though, Wright almost immediately found champions for his project in the new company.

Wright's project took several years to come to fruition, but The Sims was released in 2000 to an eager public. The mundane quality of The Sims characters' digital lives proved no deterrent to sales. The game sold more quickly than had any Wright title before it. But the initial round of sales was just the beginning. As the developers watched and listened to their fans, they started hearing a consistent story: Gamers, still mostly male, were buying the game, but it was their spouses or girlfriends who were finding it and falling in love. It was those players, disproportionately women, who started driving sales through the roof. The game proved to be one of those rare titles that expanded the audience well beyond the market of traditional computer gamers.

"Everyone has that first game that got them fired up, and that they remember playing nonstop. Well, for a lot of people, this was the first game they ever played, and they were extremely effective at spreading their excitement by word of mouth," Wright said. "It was like a lot of fuel had piled up, and then we threw a match on it."

The game quickly became the best-selling computer game ever, ultimately selling close to eight million copies. The company released expansion packs that gave the little suburban families the ability to date, go to the beach, own pets, and more. By February 2003, when Electronic Arts released The Sims for the PlayStation 2, more than 24 million copies of the game and its sequels had been sold.

Players quickly took a strong hand in creating and customizing aspects of the single-player game. Even before The Sims was released, Wright released tools for creating objects and "skins." Sure enough, players had created their own objects for the game world before the title hit store shelves.

When the game was released, fan sites proliferated across the Net. They varied wildly—people built historical Sims, sex-themed Sims, Western Sims, and they wrote thousands of stories about their Sims and shared them online.

Almost as soon as the company released the game, Maxis had planned to make some kind of multiplayer version. Wright watched the way the community developed around The Sims and took note. He changed his ideas about what the online version should be like based on players' behavior. A pyramid social structure was evolving in the community even without the online game, and it seemed to be one that might be useful in developing the online version. Some people made Sims customization tools and distributed them freely to the community. Others used the tools to create Sim skins, or new looks for their characters. Others made and operated the fan web pages through which the skins were distributed. Far more people visited web pages and downloaded the customized graphics.

Those were useful insights in thinking about how an online social model should work. Creating an online world that was based on everyday existence would be tough, but Wright could take advantage of this varying community participation level. The world would have goals like the real world—get money to survive, make friends, and so on—but the stability of the community would have to rest on this same pyramid social structure. He'd have to assume that a small number of gamers would entertain, inspire, or otherwise attract the larger number of people. That small number of leaders would essentially provide the social draw for the game, instead of the programmers and developers creating plots or story lines—a little like the cool kids in high school serving as social magnets for other students.

The team set about building an online world where people would act the part of their Sim inside a neighborhood world instead of playing god to the family. The idea of the game would be open-ended, with players role-playing a character inside the Sims world without any specific goals. Without official quests or missions, the game's whole idea would be summed up in its advertising slogan: "Be Somebody. Else." In that flexibility, it mirrored open-ended text MUDs such as LamdaMOO (MOO, in that context, stood for MUD, Object Oriented) that had developed in the late

1980s and early 1990s and were dedicated solely to social interaction. It also felt very much like an update of the Habitat game that Lucasfilm had tested on QuantumLink in 1988.

Even with the community models in mind, there were tricky elements in figuring out how to structure short-term rewards and goals. Wright's play tests illustrated exactly how ready most players would be to push that social network just to get ahead. One early test, in which affection was strongly rewarded, found most of the play testers spending times in massive orgies, kissing and hugging each other. That didn't seem very plausible as a game, so Wright and his team changed the rules.

Released well behind schedule, too close to Christmas to have even a chance at the original lofty sales goals that EA had held, The Sims Online proved initially to be a deep disappointment. Official reviews were lukewarm. Many promised features hadn't been implemented yet, a point Wright readily acknowledged, and some reviewers said it simply didn't feel finished. Electronic Arts' President John Riccitiello said that only 40,000 people had started paying the monthly fee by February 2003.[6] Those numbers didn't appear to be getting much better. By the end of April 2003, the company had sold just south of 100,000 games. That was frustrating, acknowledged EA executives, who had originally projected that 200,000 paying subscribers would be signed up by the end of March 2003. Instead, they projected 125,000 active users by mid-2004.

The Sims Online team also faced another hurdle. Electronic Arts, which relies on huge-selling titles, had issued a companywide warning early in the year that studios unable to reach certain financial goals risked being shut down. The mandate put even stronger pressure on The Sims team to fix the flaws before their corporate support ran out.

Richard Garriott, looking at the game, recognized the symptoms of a game pushed out of EA's corporate doors before it was ready—a phenomenon he said had badly harmed the launch of his own Ultima VIII and Ultima Online titles. "The Sims should have been, could have been, great," he said. "My own uneducated assumption is that it received a little too much help."

Wright, although busily working on the components that hadn't yet been released, seemed unfazed by all the criticism. The game was supposed to evolve—that was part of the idea. SimCity had been the simulation of the rise of a city. The Sims had let a family grow. In The Sims Online, the social structures of a neighborhood were intended to evolve. But it would take time, just as real social structures did.

Online game creators had been striving to create virtual reality worlds for years. Wright's vision is less game and more world than most. The Sims Online is still a long way away from a full simulation of reality, and it ultimately may not measure up to its creator's hopes of reaching the broad mass of casual gamers. But it is another step forward towards letting game players create their own universes.

"I think we're really at the tip of the iceberg here," Wright said. "We have an opportunity to make fans co-designers and co-creators now."

* * *

For all the industry's grand plans for world-building and storytelling, the most immediate breakthrough in mainstreaming computer gaming communities may actually come from home consoles, which now arrive with the power of a PC.

Rewind a few months, to the March 2002 E3 digital entertainment trade show in Los Angeles. The buzz leading up to this glittery, glitzy conference surrounded attempts by Sony's PlayStation 2 and Microsoft's Xbox to add network capacities to their popular home gaming consoles. Particularly in the case of the PlayStation, this would open up avenues for gaming communities that vastly outstripped even the immediate potential of The Sims. Wright's basic Sims game had sold 8 million copies. Sony's PlayStation 2 had sold more than 50 million machines worldwide.

In Los Angeles, crowds started lining up for Sony's PlayStation event well before the 8:30 time slated for the doors to open, eager for the first glimpse of the new machine. Valet attendants stood in pairs, just outside the iron gates protecting the covered stage. The scene looked more like the opening of a rock show than a product release. The crowd of more than 800 people inched forward every few minutes, trying to push closer to the gates. Mounted police officers trotted around the crowd's edges, and beat cops stood off to the side, leaning up against the arches on the sidewalk. Local and national news crews set up cameras out front and filmed the crowd.

When the gates finally swung open, a tsunami of people surged forward en masse before splintering off. Fans went straight ahead. Print media to the right. Online media to the left. Impromptu lines streamed through the check-in, a hint of coffee-fueled madness driving the group. Badges in hand, people rushed into the covered auditorium, built specially for this two-hour event. It was amphitheater seating, although there were few bad seats in the house. Twenty-three flat-panel screens ranging from 4 feet to 15 feet across hung from the rafters. Two stationary cameras, set up to broadcast the unveiling, sat several yards in front of the stage. Off to either side of the stage, five gaming centers complete with game consoles and voice-activated headsets sat with cameras pointed at them. Along the back wall, two racks of colored lights hung from the ceiling. Melodic drum and bass sounds thumped from the rock arena sound system, complete with human-sized speakers.

Twenty minutes passed, and the crowd settled in, while the thumping music jarred the early morning sleep from everyone's eyes. Then silence. On the main screen, seven simple words ushered in a new age of online gaming—the home console version: "Live in Your World. Play in Ours."

The crowd burst into applause. Sony Computer Entertainment of America President Kazuo "Kaz" Hirai jogged out on stage looking relaxed, complete with unbuttoned shirt collar. "Gaming has been a part of the entertainment culture for everybody," he boomed. "Not just boys and not just hard-core gamers. Everybody."

More applause, but this was the same message Sony and other home console builders had been delivering since Atari. The crowd wanted more, something new.

Electronic Arts' President Riccitiello stepped up to the microphone. He was the man in charge of John Madden NFL Football, one of the longest running and most successful video game franchises in the business, and the title with which Sony had decided to launch its online system. He introduced Dante Culpepper, the Minnesota Vikings quarterback, and one of the most recognizable stars in the NFL. Culpepper strolled on stage, a bit awkwardly, and grabbed a PlayStation 2 controller. Riccitiello turned his back on the crowd, directing their attention to the largest hanging screen.

"Now, I'd like to introduce Jevon Kearse. You there, Jevon?"

"Hey, I'm here," came the reply as the massive Tennessee Titan defensive end appeared on the screen. Dressed in sweats and Tennessee Titan jersey, Kearse waved to the crowd from Orlando, Florida. He held a PlayStation 2 controller in one hand.

Next, John Madden himself appeared, popping up on the smaller screens around the room, his image beamed into the amphitheater from Pleasanton, California. He'd be serving as live sportscaster for this first public game of networked football on a game console.

A buzz shot through the room as Kearse, taking his controller, kicked off to Culpepper. "The one player you take, the player with eight years' experience, you just have to like him," Madden chortled, as Culpepper's Minnesota team returned the opening kickoff back 92 yards for a touchdown. The crowd exploded into applause. Catcalls, hollers, and clapping ensued as Madden summed up the general feeling of the event.

"You just can't beat this," the genial sportscaster beamed. "Football in May."

Madden, of course, was a little biased. It was his game they were playing, and he had a financial interest in every copy sold. That didn't obscure the underlying promise of the event. Far more Americans were football fans than role-players. Earlier versions of Madden's PlayStation game annually sold 10 times what the most popular Ultima ever did. As far as hard-core gaming went, this was as mainstream as it got.

Sony, Nintendo, and Microsoft have a hold on casual gaming culture that computer game companies will likely never have. The newest generation of home console differs little from the processing and graphics power of home computers, but they are far cheaper and simpler to use. Sony had sold more than 50 million game machines worldwide by the beginning of 2003. Microsoft expected to sell 9 million Xboxes by June 2003 and Nintendo's GameCube was struggling to stay abreast of Microsoft in the United States, while far outselling it in Japan. In 2001, more than $4.6 billion was spent on video games titles, compared to $1.75 billion on computer games. The two systems helped propel the $6.6 billion industry in 2000 to $9.4 billion the very next year.[7]

Part of the draw of the console systems had long been their stability as compared to computer hardware. Even on a $2000 machine, hard-core computer gamers need to upgrade their systems on a regular basis, adding video cards, processors, sound cards, and peripherals. Console gamers, on the other hand, merely invest in a $300 piece of hardware every five years.

Network play had been a long time coming. Nintendo had included a phone port in its popular game system of the mid-1980s, with ambitions to allow networked games, stock trading, and other online services, but the online vision never materialized. The Sega Saturn and even the Atari 2600 could be upgraded to use a modem. Sega's Dreamcast allowed online play, but a limited number of titles and slow home connections kept the number of people using any of these machines to go online relatively small. Microsoft released its Xbox in 2002 with network connections already in place, but the console required an additional "starter kit" to allow people to log onto its "Xbox Live" gaming service. PlayStation required its fans to buy a separate network adapter.

Even hard-core computer gamers and game developers looked at the development with interest. Playing online versions of the kind of quick, arcade-like games that consoles specialized in had considerable appeal.

"I would love to play Dungeons & Dragons games online with a small, intimate group," said Warren Spector, the former Origin Systems developer, who later went on to make such high-profile games as Thief and Deus-Ex. "But what I'd really like to do is play five-on-five basketball with my friends. I don't want to play with strangers. Online role-playing games will always be around, but it will peak out because people don't want to spend their lives online. With casual gamers, it's so hard to get everyone together at the same time. Competitive games are really much better suited for this kind of play."

Certainly considerable hurdles remain for networked consoles. Critics note that most people don't have Internet connections in their living rooms, next to their televisions. Doing the networking to connect the machines to a phone or cable modem line is still beyond many mainstream casual computer users. "I'm bearish on this generation of consoles," Richard Garriott said. "It's just that until the console can be plugged directly into a hot Net jack, I don't see it working well."

The early excitement over games like Madden's online football nevertheless grew quickly. Less than three months after Kearse and Culpepper knocked heads, pockets of football aficionados were making preparations for the first nationwide, online football leagues, forming teams just as happily as any role-playing gamer might look for guilds to go adventuring with.

Brad Shoemaker was one of these game players, a radio producer who never saw himself as part of the online gaming world before. As the release date for the new Madden football approached, he surfed through message boards on his computer, sitting in his tiny office at WNDE, an Indianapolis station that was part of the Fox Sports Network. Anxious to get his hands on the new Madden game as soon as possible, he trolled the Internet checking for any news he could find. He was new to this, though, and he wasn't sure quite where to look. As he clicked through message boards and web sites, his pulse quickened.

"I laughed at people who'd chat online or post messages, but I really needed to find out more information about this, so I just hopped online," Shoemaker said. "I didn't think I would find out that I could play somebody who lived on the other side of the country. I found out what I needed to get for my PS2, and found whole pockets of people who were waiting to play online as well."

Although 6-feet, 4-inches tall, Shoemaker had been more of a sports fan than a player growing up, playing games like NBA Jam for the Sega Genesis and Super Mario Bros. for the Nintendo Entertainment System. Paper games like Dungeons & Dragons were definitely out—way too nerdy, and frankly, a bit strange. Computer games Quake and EverQuest were just arcade games, where the fastest trigger finger won. He didn't want to be sitting at a desk playing games, anyway. Lounging on the couch with his friends playing the 1993 version of Madden's football game, all the while screaming and yelling at big plays and lost opportunities to score—now that was his idea of fun. "That game, and sports games in general, can really be addicting," he said, recalling the magic of those first encounters. "You were playing with your friends, and you never, ever knew what they were going to do, or how the game was going to turn out. It was amazing, and the game was just so real."

Ten years later, saddled with his radio production job and classes at the Purdue University at Indianapolis, he found it much more difficult to get friends together for games. Finding people online who had the same schedule would certainly make playing those games much easier. Thousands of other people were already looking for the same thing, even before the game was released, he learned.

He zeroed in on the Madden 2003 League and clicked the link. There weren't many posts yet, but the people who came wanted to play—and they wanted to keep score. They filled out the league—32 players—and started a waiting list for the scores of others who wanted in. They drafted teams, choosing from any of the real 32 NFL teams, and got ready to play out the 16-week season. The official PlayStation 2 message boards filled with rants and pleadings from those not lucky enough to snag a spot in the official league. The rules were simple: Once a week, you logged on with your opponent and played your game. Statistics were compiled in the league office. Now they just had to wait for the game itself to come out.

Players would exchange instant messenger addresses so they could coordinate where they'd play the games. Then they'd dial in at the predetermined time, and much like using AOL Instant Messenger, they would make a private room in cyberspace simply by clicking on the Create Room tab at the Welcome screen. The room opened a connection, the name of the virtual room where they'd meet was typed in, and then they could dial into the Madden network. It was more like the Doom battlegrounds, which came and went with players, than the persistent worlds. To a new generation of online gamers, though, it was exactly what they were looking for—quick games that didn't require weeks just to master one skill.

Other sites dedicated to gaming leagues sprang up. By early 2003, a quick Internet search for online console sports games brought up hundreds of results, with leagues forming around different kinds of rules. Some allowed players to do anything they could to win. Others required people to adhere to a football etiquette, eliminating unrealistic strategies like going for fourth-and-long plays or running fake punts. *Crushem.com* ranked players, and much like the CPL, provided a secure location with strict rules to ensure that games were fair. Console gaming had learned much from the early days of Ultima Online, where bugs and outright player cheating nearly brought play to a halt.

"Crush'em provides an independent site for all sports video game players to find opponents, have fun, make friends, win prizes and compete online," advertised the web site. "Our goal is to keep our community filled with only the best players who are dedicated to competing and having fun. One of the largest factors in competition is good sportsmanship."

All of that was just for the Madden title. Microsoft would join the fray, too, announcing that it intended to spend $2 billion developing and promoting its console and the Xbox Live network, which allowed players to connect to a central gaming network through the company's servers. Like Sony, the Xbox console would cater to two game types: sports and shooting titles. However, Microsoft's football game—NFL Fever 2003—also caught the fancy of early adopters who logged on in massive numbers to hit the gridiron. By the end of 2002, the company decided to host its own single-elimination tournament, drawing from a pool of 1500 of the best players.

Hundreds of thousands of players would join the online console gaming mix by year's end. Some 700,000 people bought Madden, SOCOM: U.S. Navy SEALs, NFL GameDay 2003, NFL 2K3, or Twisted Metal: Black ONLINE—nearly three times the number who had signed up for Ultima Online after five years. In one flurry, 200,000 eager gamers fired up their PlayStation 2s, snapped their network adapters to the back of the system, clicked on their DSL modem, and ran up one million hours of playtime from Christmas Day to New Year's Eve.

What these gamers were discovering was the same thing Gary Gygax discovered in Lake Geneva, what Richard Garriott discovered in 1977, what John Romero and John Carmack discovered when they released Doom, and what millions of other gamers came to realize over the years: sitting down and playing with other people was a whole lot of fun. The people—the culture of gamers—made the fun. The game itself hardly mattered. Technology allowed them to expand their pool of players beyond the artificial borders of neighborhoods, dormitories, and offices. The only limitations were the spread of phone lines, cable connections, and soon wireless networks.

And, in a very real sense, those die-hard sports fanatics who fire up Madden on their televisions finally have much more in common with Dungeons & Dragons players than they might ever have realized.

"All of us sports gamers, man, we couldn't ever figure out what those guys who were playing role-playing games were doing, whether they were playing in a little group or playing online," Shoemaker laughed. "But, I'll tell you what. Now that our games are online, we figured it out."

Epilogue

Beginning Again

It's early 2003, and Richard Garriott is sitting in a cluttered little office in Austin, Texas, paging through a Korean dictionary. He's working for NCSoft, a Korean company that operates one of the biggest online games in the world, but that's not why he's got the book. He's doing research for a little project he's working on: creating his own language.

His office is a wreck. Books are strewn everywhere, piled along a desk on the back wall, scattered on a table in the middle of the room, stacked in a bookshelf, and toppled over at the base of his workstation. His wall-length white board looks like a five-year-old got hold of a Sharpie marker and started his art career. It's covered with strange doodles, pictures of stick people, faces with open mouths, and arrows. They don't mean much yet, but he hopes they soon will.

"We need to invent a universal language for humankind," he explains, with only the barest glint of mischief in his eye showing that he understands the enormity of the task.

Twenty-six years after the beginning of his own entry into computer games, Richard is still something of the Peter Pan of the industry. He lives in a castle, complete with moat, on Austin's outskirts. He is driving a float shaped like a ship—the "HMS Britannia"—to New Orleans for Mardi Gras. His profile as innovator and visionary has declined rapidly in the years since the release of Ultima Online, but that hasn't shaken him. He's as playful as ever at 41, and he looks much like he did a decade ago. The homemade silver snake he's worn since high school still hangs around his neck, and the long, thin blonde ponytail strand he started wearing in New Hampshire still trails down his back. Most compelling are his eyes, which light up immediately when he starts talking about his new project, flickering back and forth between his notes and his books and his listeners, making sure his audience is still with him. For all his time spent in front of a computer over the years, he's still an entertainer and storyteller at heart.

Richard is free of the Ultima legacy now. He worked on it for 20 years, and that was enough. Now he's going back to his own beginnings in search of inspiration for his new company and project.

He's working on a new game, tentatively called Tabula Rasa, in which he's trying to combine the most vivid excitement of single-player games with the social experiences of online worlds. His goals for it are ambitious. He wants to create a brand-new language that can be understood by anyone, anywhere in the world, with almost no learning curve. He wants to merge the heroic potential of single-player games, in which every player can equally feel like an epic hero, with the community aspects of massively multiplayer games like Ultima Online.

He's not the only one looking for another leap forward in the creation of online worlds. The big titles, EverQuest, Dark Age of Camelot, and Ultima Online, were the first generation of massively multiplayer games. They included basic social environments, places to hunt and kill, and worlds to explore. But, there wasn't much else. Designers and developers were too busy trying to work out the kinks in the games to really push the boundaries of the medium. Six years after Ultima Online, the next generation of games is coming, and Richard wants to be ahead of the curve again. This time he's starting fresh, without the history and constraints from his Ultima adventures. He wants his own creative ideas, and his players' expectations, to start as a blank slate.

"We didn't want to do anything that looked like any piece of Earth history, and we didn't want to do futurism or anything else people could look at and recognize," Richard says. "We wanted to allow people to come in and understand this world on its own terms, instead of relying on what they'd learned for years by playing other people's games."

Since leaving Electronic Arts in 2000, Richard has essentially re-created Origin Systems in this new office. His brother and a few other members of the original team came with him when he left EA, including Starr Long, his right-hand man in game development. Many of the other original Origin employees were laid off in 2001 when EA shuttered its Ultima Online II project, and Richard quickly snapped them up for his own new company, called Destination Games. Barely weeks afterward, NCSoft, the publishers of the runaway hit Lineage: The Blood Pledge, a massively multiplayer game with more than four million subscribers in Asia, contacted him. Within 24 hours, the two companies decided that they were a perfect fit for each other, and their merger was announced at the E3 trade show in June 2001. Since that time, he's been working on translating Lineage to the American market, a project that isn't going terribly well. It's an old game, and cultural differences make it less attractive to Americans than to Asian audiences. But that's a lesson he's taking to heart as he works on his real labor of love, Tabula Rasa.

❋ ❋ ❋

As he digs though his desk drawers for little slips of paper that look like the flash cards tourists use to learn a new language, Richard explains his idea. For his new game, he's creating a near-future, science-fiction world with a history he hopes will be as detailed and rich as any novel. He uses Tolkien, who was a linguist before he was a novelist, as inspiration. Tolkien's *Lord of the Rings* world was compelling in large part because it was so detailed, right down to the languages spoken by the old races of elves and dwarves. In a game, creating a world that holds up to examination at an incredibly detailed level is part of the magic that drives the player's desire to stay, and that helps to sustain an environment where people can create community. One of the most fundamental building blocks of community is some kind of shared language or history.

After 26 years in the industry, Richard recognizes that this mode of creation is his strength. In a way, he's hearkening back to the days when he was creating the much simpler rune-like script that would help him cheat on his high school tests. "There are other people out there who are better programmers and artists than me," he says, waving vaguely at the rest of the office. "What I'm good at is creating a believable world history. Creating a system of virtues and the history of a people—that's my purview."

He finds the flash cards and brings them to the table. They're full of pictures, many echoing the scrawls on the white board above. The language of his world has to be recognizable across cultures, like international road signs, but expressing concepts that are far more complex. He's been studying the origins of languages, as well as modern symbolic systems, for inspiration. His language will be pictorial, emblazoned on buildings and signs in his new world. Looking for models, he studied Egyptian hieroglyphics, but found the symbols were primarily tied to the sound of the language, not directly to meaning. No good for his purpose. He'd had better luck with Chinese pictographs, particularly the most ancient versions. He rummages through a stack of books and comes up with another illustration of how Chinese characters have evolved. "You see how this one really looks like a man? And this one like a house?" he says. "We had to work out the basics of language, go back to the most basic concepts."

The Chinese language model became his base. He's spent months trying to figure out basic pictographic symbols for the limited number of ideas that he wants to express. A little hourglass stands in for "time." A stick figure stands in for "person." An arrow underneath the stick figure means "running" or "go that way," depending on its context. Two lines leaning inward, converging on a horizontal line above them, illustrate the concept of perspective and distance. A little square between the legs of the lines means "here." The same square above the horizontal line, or the horizon, means "there." When he reaches a landmark point like developing a system to describe people—man, woman, child, family, group—he grabs someone in the office, shows them his work, and waits to see if they can decipher what he is trying to communicate. If it takes more than a minute, he chucks the idea and heads back to the drawing board.

The Chinese model, though, has limitations. Hence, the Korean dictionary on his desk. He wants his language to be pronounceable—something the Chinese pictographs don't convey—so he's working on a phonetic alphabet. He's toying with little symbols that mimic the shape of the mouth as it forms phonemes. For example, when you pronounce the letter "o," your mouth makes a circular shape. By equating sounds and mouth shapes, Richard is hoping to create a very basic language that can be spoken as well as read. A colleague had told him that the Korean written language was based on roughly the same idea, so he is studying its characters. With that aspect taken care of, he hopes to create the illusion of a culture with a live language, with hints of its history and culture embedded in the way it is used. "All the buildings in this world will be covered with these runes, which many people will probably ignore at first," he says. "But the players who discover this will quickly find its meaning and relevance. Now, I'm working on sentence structure that sounds no worse than Yoda, so we can actually place clues throughout the game."

Is a universal language enough to create a universal gaming community, one that crosses geographic and linguistic barriers? Probably not by itself. But it could allow communities based on the same game to spring up on different sides of the world, and maybe help break the barriers down over time. "The goal for the game is to communicate the reality of the world without regard to the gamer's country," he says. "It's about re-creating those nationalities that everyone feels at home in. It's considerably a bigger challenge than Ultima IV [where his ideas about virtues were first introduced], which was very English."

The broader game itself will draw from the strengths of both single-player and massively multiplayer worlds. Here, more than anywhere else, he is reaching back to the beginning of his gaming experiences to guide him.

Online worlds sparked the rise of game communities in ways few could have imagined. However, the first generation of games focused almost too much on re-creating reality in a digital space. At Origin Systems, the programmers spent hundreds of hours creating a complex ecology and economy that proved to be utterly useless for players. Developers lost sight of what had been one of the most attractive elements of games: the ability to make the player feel unique, powerful, or heroic.

Thousands of players have gathered online in massively multiplayer worlds, but that meant that thousands of people might be vying for the status of hero. Too many heroes mean that nobody, or only a few, can be special. Fighting even the most dangerous of monsters gives less of an epic thrill when it is clear that it will simply regenerate after you have killed it, and when 13 parties of adventurers are waiting behind you in line for their turn. There is only one Frodo in the *Lord of the Rings*, one Avatar in the land of Britannia.

Richard is still a storyteller, and he misses single-player games' ability to make each player the center of his epic stories.

"Single-player games are great, and I love them," he says. "They have a great feature. Your life is very special. You are *the* hero and you get to save the *whole* world. You live a truly charmed existence, and around every corner you are finding new things. You're blissfully unaware of your neighbor who is also playing the game."

Richard's answer to this problem requires breaking away from the attempts to mimic reality, at least in virtual worlds' most recent sense. Maybe people can fight the same monsters, or go on the same quests, but each player or party must be allowed to do it in his or her own unique version of the world, without running into other bands of would-be adventurers. All of this can be done technologically. There will be a hub for his new game world, a city where the kind of community activities seen in Ultima Online and EverQuest can thrive. People will be able to do all the things they crave here, living out virtual, social lives without ever leaving the common area, if they so desire.

But, for the adventurous, there will also be quests and missions to pursue. Some of these will allow many parties at once to wander though the story, but many others will be closed bubble-worlds, existing only for the player's party. Everyone will be able to go on the same quests, but each group of players will find themselves in a separate game, as if each party had walked into a single-player game. In these separate worlds, the players can complete their quests as singular, epic characters—Frodos and Lord Britishes instead of faceless soldiers in a crowd of adventurers.

"This is like Disney World, which has a hub," Richard says of his new game. "You can go to shops and get food, but when you get on the boat for the pirate ride, you're in your own version of reality. Once the ride starts, you are blissfully unaware of the boats in front of you and behind you. Then when you finish, you are in the hub, and you can navigate over to the next place."

The world he describes is close to a digital version of his own parents' home so many years ago, where dozens of people could chat and eat his mother's snacks together, and then split into separate rooms and their separate games of Dungeons & Dragons. The model that developed so naturally there is one that still resonates with Richard. Gaming is social, and the community is a critical part of what keeps people coming back. But people come to that community for different reasons and to play different roles, and the strongest games will be those that allow heroes and tavern-keepers to exist together and play out their separate roles to the fullest.

There is no guarantee that any of this will ultimately resonate with the gamers of the future, with so many more of them weaned on the action of Grand Theft Auto or John Madden Football than on the old ideas of Dungeons & Dragons. But Richard has already shown his ability to drive the industry forward. If it's not him, someone else may take these online worlds to the next mainstream level; and he doesn't think it's far away. But nobody, including Richard, can plan for it.

"You can't design a mass-market game," he says. "You have to make a great game that happens to also appeal to the mass market."

The decision of what new virtual worlds to colonize and build will ultimately lie with gamers themselves.

Notes

Chapter Two: Machines at Play

1. Edward K. Yasaki, "Computing at Stanford," in *Datamation*, November 1963, 43–45.

2. Stewart Brand, "SPACEWAR: Fanatic Life and Symbolic Death Among the Computer Bums," in *Rolling Stone*, December 7, 1972.

3. Gregory Yob, "Hunt the Wumpus," in *The Best of Creative Computing*, volume 1, 1976, 247–50.

4. Rick Adams, "The Colossal Cave Adventure Page," at *http://www .rickadams.org/adventure/a_history.html*; and Graham Nelson, "The Craft of Adventure: Five Articles on the Design of Adventure Games," 2d ed., 1995–96, at *ftp://ftp.gmd.de/if-archive/info/Craft.Of.Adventure.txt*.

5. Tim Anderson, "The History of Zork," in *The New Zork Times*, Winter 1985, Spring 1985 and Summer 1985; and Hector Briceno, Wesley Chao, Andrew Glenn, Stanley Hu, Ashwin Krishnamurthy, and Bruce Tsuchida, "Down from the Top of Its Game: The Story of Infocom, Inc." December 13, 2000, unpublished MIT article.

6. Steven Levy, *Hackers: Heroes of the Computer Revolution* (Delta, 1994).

Chapter Three: Building Community, Building Business

1. *Author unknown*, "Super Invader Is Reader's Choice," in *Softalk*, April 1981, as republished at *www.Apple2history.org*.

2. John Anderson, "Dave Tells Ahl—the History of Creative Computing," in *Creative Computing*, November 1984, 66.

3. James Hague, ed., *Halcyon Days: Interviews with Classic Video and Computer Game Programmers*, 2002, at *http://www.dadgum.com/halcyon/*.

4. Steven Levy, *Hackers: Heroes of the Computer Revolution* (Delta, 1994).

Chapter Five: Log On, Shoot Down

1. David Kirkpatrick, "Hot New PC Services," in *Fortune*, November 2, 1992, 108.

2. Ken Siegmann, "New On-Line Network For Computer Games: System Subscribers Can Dial for a Duel," in *The San Francisco Chronicle*, March 23, 1992.

3. Kirkpatrick, "Hot New PC Services."

4. Scott Cover and Gaston Lahaut, "Five Years of Doom," interview with John Romero, in *Doomworld.com*, December 9, 1998.

5. Todd Copilevitz, "Software Firm Creates a Monster Hit via the 'Information Superhighway,'" in *The Dallas Morning News*, May 17, 1994.

6. Kessler, Andrew, "Profits from the Underground," in *Forbes*, May 9, 1994.

7. Ed Dille, ed., "Interview with John Romero," in the *Official Strategy Guide Doom 2*, as quoted in *QuakeTalk*, August 10, 1995.

8. DR Bone, "A Conversation with id Software's John Carmack," *Blue's News*, January 8, 1997.

9. John Romero's plan file, July 30, 1996.

Chapter Six: Homebrewed Gamers

1. Kenn Hwang and Bob Colayco, "Alex St. John Interview," at *http://firingsquad.gamers.com/features/alexstjohn/default.asp*, March 7, 2000.

2. J. Cassell and H. Jenkins, eds., *From Barbie to Mortal Kombat: Gender and Computer Games* (MIT Press, 1998); and Dr. Kathryn Wright, "Girl Games: Help or Hindrance?," at *http://www.womengamers.com/ articles/girlgames.html*.

Chapter Seven: Losing the Game

1. Chip Morningstar and F. Randall Farmer, "The Lessons of Lucasfilm's Habitat," Electric Communities. This paper was presented at The First Annual International Conference on Cyberspace in 1990. It was published in *Cyberspace: First Steps*, Michael Benedikt, ed. (MIT Press, 1991).

2. Julian Dibbell, "A Rape in Cyberspace," in *The Village Voice*, December 21, 1993.

3. John Markoff, "The Ultimate Obsession; What Will People Pay to Enter His World?," in *The New York Times*, October 20, 1997.

Chapter Eight: Gamers, Interrupted

1. Mike Anton and Lisa Ryckman, "In hindsight, signs to killings obvious," in *Rocky Mountain News*, May 2, 1999, and at *http://denver.rockymountainnews.com/shooting/0502why10.shtml*.

2. Jon Katz, "Voices from the Hellmouth," *Geeks: How Two Lost Boys Rode the Internet Out of Idaho* (Broadway Books, 2000), 147.

3. Katz, "Voices from the Hellmouth," 148–49.

4. Ellen Mitchell, "Video Game Rooms Targeted by Towns," in *The New York Times*, December 13, 1981.

5. Peter Mattiace, "Surgeon General Says Video Games May Harm Children," Associated Press, November 9, 1982.

6. Tim Moriarty, "Uncensored Videogames: Are Adults Ruining It for the Rest of Us?" in *Videogaming and Computergaming Illustrated*, October 1983.

7. "U.S. Senator John McCain (R-AZ) Receives Testimony on Marketing Violence to Children; Senate Commerce Committee," from the Federal Document Clearing House, Inc., FDCH Political Transcripts, May 4, 1999.

8. Henry Jenkins, "Professor Jenkins Goes to Washington," in *Harper's* magazine, July 1999.

9. "U.S. Senator John McCain (R-AZ) Receives Testimony on Marketing Violence to Children."

10. Craig Anderson and Karen Dill, "Video Games and Aggressive Thoughts, Feelings, and Behavior in the Laboratory and in Life," in *Journal of Personality and Social Psychology*, American Psychological Association, April 2000, 772–90.

11. Anderson and Dill, "Video Games and Aggressive Thoughts, Feelings, and Behavior in the Laboratory and in Life."

12. Craig Anderson, "Violent Video Games Increase Aggression and Violence," Testimony before U.S. Senate Commerce Committee hearing on "The Impact of Interactive Violence on Children," March 21, 2000.

13. Email sent to David Walsh, December 2002.

14. Robert Warshow, "Paul, The Horror Comics, and Dr. Wertham," in *The Immediate Experience: Movies, Comics, Theatre, & Other Aspects of Popular Culture* (Atheneum, 1975).

15. Amy Kiste Nyberg, "The Senate Investigation," in *Seal of Approval: The History of the Comics Code* (University Press of Mississippi, 1997).

16. Nyberg, "The Senate Investigation."

17. Nyberg, "The Senate Investigation."

Chapter Nine: Unleashed

1. *Author unknown*, "Top Ten Industry Facts," from the Interactive Game Developers Association, 2003 fact sheet.

2. Geoff Keighly, "Game Development a la Mod," in *Business 2.0*, October 2002.

3. David Kushner, "It's a Mod, Mod World," in *IEEE Spectrum*, April 4, 2003.

4. Brad King, "Make Love, Not War Games," in *Wired News*, June 8, 2002.

5. Geoff Keighley, "The Sorcerer of Sony," in *Business 2.0*, August 2002.

6. Nicholas Yee, "Most Important Aspect of Game," from "The Daedalus Project," at *http://www.nickyee.com/daedalus/archives/000192php*.

7. David Karp, "Father Guilty in Death of Son," in *St. Petersburg Times*, January 3, 2001.

8. Stanley Miller, "Death of a Game Addict," in *Milwaukee Journal Sentinel*, March 30, 2002.

Chapter Ten: Herding Gamers

1. Remarks of Douglas Lowenstein, CEO Interactive Digital Software Association, from a speech, May 22, 2002.

2. DFC Intelligence, "Online Game Market Review," June 2002.

3. Information from *www.thebaseballpage.com*.

4. Interactive Digital Software Association, "Essential Facts About the Industry," 2002.

5. David Laprad, "Gaming on the Edge: A Killcreek Q & A," in *The Adrenaline Vault*, September 4, 1999.

6. Alex Pham, "'Sims Online' Gives Creators a Painful Reality Check," from the *Los Angeles Times*, February 4, 2003.

7. 2001 U.S. Interactive Entertainment Sales report, NPD Group, Inc.

INDEX

Dr. Cat, 28–29, 62
  DragonSpires, 153
DragonSpires, 153
Duarte, Mike, 199–204
  Local Access Network
    (LAN) parties, 206–209
Duke Nuke 'Em, 202
Dungeon, 34
  See also Zork
Dungeon Masters, 20
Dungeons & Dragons, 27, 53, 257
DWANGO, 127, 128–129
Dykes, Greg, 49–50

E

Electronic Arts, 109
  buying Maxis, 240
  selling Origin Systems to, 80
Elson, Jim, 118–119
Escape, 35
ethics and morals in games,
  73–74
EverQuest, 151, 220, 221–228
Exar. *See* Duarte, Mike
Exidy, 178

F

Fan Faire, 220–221, 224
Farmer, Randy, 152
feedback of groups, 22
Fenton, Mary, 61
  move to Massachusetts, 68
Flight Simulator, 83
Fong, Dennis "Thresh", 125–131,
  133–134
  Gamers Extreme, 140–141
  Quake, 134–135

Red Annihilation frag-off,
  137–139
  violence and games, 176
Forge of Virtue, 80
Forrester, Jay, 83
Fragfests, 128
frags, 114
free-speech protections, 195
Froebel, Elizabeth, 18, 37

G

Gaines, William, 197
GameCube, 245
Gamegirlz.com, 146
Gamers Extreme, 140–141
gaming culture, 141–142, 181
  and violence, 174–177
Garriott, Helen, 15, 17
Garriott, Linda, 15, 18
Garriott, Owen, 11–12, 15–17,
  24, 60
Garriott, Randy, 15
Garriott, Richard, 4, 6
  brother (Robert), 15, 16,
    60, 91
  computer camp (Summer
    1977), 11–15
  on consoles, 246
  current life and work,
    251–257
  development of his first
    computer game, 23–25
  early family life, 15–17
  father (Owen Garriott),
    11–12, 15–17, 24, 60
  getting his first Apple II, 35
  haunted house, 70–72

INTERNATIONAL CONTACT INFORMATION

AUSTRALIA
McGraw-Hill Book Company Australia Pty. Ltd.
TEL +61-2-9900-1800
FAX +61-2-9878-8881
http://www.mcgraw-hill.com.au
books-it_sydney@mcgraw-hill.com

CANADA
McGraw-Hill Ryerson Ltd.
TEL +905-430-5000
FAX +905-430-5020
http://www.mcgraw-hill.ca

GREECE, MIDDLE EAST, & AFRICA
(Excluding South Africa)
McGraw-Hill Hellas
TEL +30-210-6560-990
TEL +30-210-6560-993
TEL +30-210-6560-994
FAX +30-210-6545-525

MEXICO (Also serving Latin America)
McGraw-Hill Interamericana Editores S.A. de C.V.
TEL +525-117-1583
FAX +525-117-1589
http://www.mcgraw-hill.com.mx
fernando_castellanos@mcgraw-hill.com

SINGAPORE (Serving Asia)
McGraw-Hill Book Company
TEL +65-6863-1580
FAX +65-6862-3354
http://www.mcgraw-hill.com.sg
mghasia@mcgraw-hill.com

SOUTH AFRICA
McGraw-Hill South Africa
TEL +27-11-622-7512
FAX +27-11-622-9045
robyn_swanepoel@mcgraw-hill.com

SPAIN
McGraw-Hill/Interamericana de España, S.A.U.
TEL +34-91-180-3000
FAX +34-91-372-8513
http://www.mcgraw-hill.es
professional@mcgraw-hill.es

UNITED KINGDOM, NORTHERN,
EASTERN, & CENTRAL EUROPE
McGraw-Hill Education Europe
TEL +44-1-628-502500
FAX +44-1-628-770224
http://www.mcgraw-hill.co.uk
computing_europe@mcgraw-hill.com

ALL OTHER INQUIRIES Contact:
McGraw-Hill/Osborne
TEL +1-510-420-7700
FAX +1-510-420-7703
http://www.osborne.com
omg_international@mcgraw-hill.com

Sound Off!

Visit us at **www.osborne.com/bookregistration** and let us know what you thought of this book. While you're online you'll have the opportunity to register for newsletters and special offers from McGraw-Hill/Osborne.

We want to hear from you!

Sneak Peek

Visit us today at **www.betabooks.com** and see what's coming from McGraw-Hill/Osborne tomorrow!

Based on the successful software paradigm, Bet@Books™ allows computing professionals to view partial and sometimes complete text versions of selected titles online. Bet@Books™ viewing is free, invites comments and feedback, and allows you to "test drive" books in progress on the subjects that interest you the most.